The Coasts of Down and Derry From A to Z

Book 5 in a continuing series

C000078304

Book 1: The Yorkshire Coast From A to Z

Book 2: The Lincolnshire Coast From A to Z

Book 3: Bolsover and District From A to Z

Book 4: The Antrim Coast From A to Z

The World Wide Web is constantly changing. As a result, hyperlinks to tend to break over time. All have been tested at time of publication, using a Windows 10 PC with McAfee LiveSafe installed. By following any of the links in this guide you are accepting full personal responsibility for the consequences.

Contents

Location Guide

Where to find major centres – to find smaller places, you'll generally find it best to look for the nearest town/city.

Annalong Chapter Z

Ardglass Chapter K

Ballyhalbert Chapter P

Bangor Chapter I

Cloughey Chapter P

Coleraine Chapters C and N

Comber Chapter O

Derry/Londonderry Chapters B, F and W

Donaghadee Chapters J and Z

Downhill Chapter D

Downpatrick Chapter S

Holywood Chapter U

Kilclief Chapter A

Kilkeel Chapters G and T

Killyleagh Chapters A and I

Kircubbin Chapter P

Limavady Chapter L

Magilligan Chapters B and M

Mourne Mountains Chapters G and H

Newcastle Chapters H and R

Newtownards Chapters E and U

Newry Chapters B and Y

Portaferry Chapters A and Q

Portstewart Chapter V

Strangford Chapters A and X

Arrivals

Fáilte! Welcome!

Welcome! Fáilte!

Deciding which greeting to write first rather sums up a thorny problem that's best tackled immediately.

You see, I'm an Englishman, living in Yorkshire and, for entirely understandable reasons that go back over many generations for more than 400 years, the English aren't always highly thought of in Northern Ireland.

I've never lived in Northern Ireland, but my wife has relatives born in County Down, who continue to live there to this day, and we visit Northern Ireland as often as our circumstances permit.

We've generally found the counties of Derry and Down to be full of pleasant, benevolent people and felt very much at home, whether we found ourselves to be in Castlerock or Castleward, Portstewart or Portaferry, Coleraine or Comber, Magilligan Point or Warrenpoint.

We put this down to the kind easy-going disposition that seems to be prevalent amongst most of the Northern Irish folk we've met over the years and, in our experience, it doesn't do any harm to mirror this temperament at all times.

You're likely aware that several things can and often do provoke reactions from people depending on their leanings. So, if I were you, I'd leave my England/Republic of Ireland football shirt at home, refrain from adding my own opinion to a hotly-debated political or religious topic and avoid provocative (if seemingly innocent) acts such as laying on a beach beneath a Union Jack or Irish Tricolour towel[1].

However well-intended your interventions might be, you might make things worse for yourself and cause unnecessary angst for your hosts or neighbours so

---

1   Just in case you were wondering, I do not own either any nationalistic football shirts, or for that matter anything adorned with a Union Jack or tricolour.

spend a bit of time trying to understand the history behind the feelings that are held by so many. Show empathy and be considerate to people, who often diametrically oppose one another, yet often live and work together. If they can do it – and they do, then you can – and should.

It is inevitable that writing about a region with such a troubled past, the *troubles* themselves will come up from time to time. I've tried to keep such stories to a minimum and to present cases from a strictly neutral perspective. I'll repeat this message a few times throughout the book, and said it before in my *Antrim Coast* guide – I don't do politics – I have no opinion on who is to blame for this or for that, and am on the side of no man. So, I'll just sit quietly on the fence, and from time to time describe the view as fairly as possible.

And what views!

On this tour you'll meet mountains and glens, rivers and waterfalls, loughs and bays, cities and villages, a road built for a Bishop and another for smugglers. You'll find the lost settlement of Watertown and the golden treasure of Limavady and read tales of brave aviators, bold architects and belligerent aristocrats.

This book covers the entire coastline of Northern Ireland within the two counties of Derry and Down (County Antrim having its own book published in 2017). As to how far inland we can include, the general rule I've applied consistently through my *A to Z* guides, is that if you can see the sea or take a short drive to reach it, then it counts.

I referred to Derry as a county just now. The Republic of Ireland recognises it by that name, as do most nationalist supporters (who tend to be Catholic), whereas the official British name of Londonderry is favoured by most unionists (who, in turn, are usually Protestant). In practise, the shortened form of Derry is used commonly in conversation. Maintaining a neutral stance, I will tend to alternate between both the two, but please don't count them up (I haven't) – I'm an imperfect human being so if I've written one more than the other, please accept this is down purely to my own fallibility and not due to bias.

As for language, if you are visiting Northern Ireland, you'll find that most people tend to speak English, most of the time, but it won't do you any harm, and will likely be well-received by many, if you learn a little Irish. It may also help you appreciate why elements of spoken Northern Irish English are the way they are.

For example, the Irish language has no words for *"yes"* or *"no"*. So, if someone asked in Irish *"did they go to the rugby match?"*. The response in the Irish language would be *"they did"* or *"they did not"*. In turn, you'll find phrases such as *"so it is"*, *"so they weren't"* being used all the time as affirmative and negative phrases. Another example is the Irish word for that popular drink tea – *tae*. You'll find it pronounced *tae* in Northern Irish English too, whereas if someone offers you *tea*, they're likely inviting you to dinner.

One final point before we get under way. Irish history is full of legends. Every storyteller puts their own twist on a tale, so getting a definitive angle on a particular event is nigh on impossible. For example, the story of *Half-hung MacNaghten* in the final chapter is described by some writers as a tragic accident and others as a cruel case of cold-blooded murder. The only thing they agree on is the outcome – but you'll have to read on to find out what that was.

I've strived to check everything contained within this book using multiple sources, and the most reputable ones too such as museums, published texts and historical/scientific journals. However, some errors are inevitable. Where contradictions occur in the literature, I've tried to describe the alternative possibilities fairly and let you make your own mind up on what/who to believe.

Let's get going!

A is for Awesome!

Amazing! Fantastic! Awesome!

The over-use of superlatives such as these has unfortunately diluted their impact in recent years. Over-playing the importance/significance or impact of a location, person or event can and does inevitably lead to disappointment. Take another example – *outstanding*.

One dictionary defines *outstanding* as something that is *"extremely good or impressive"* while another equates it with the word *exceptional*. Therefore, to be genuinely outstanding a place would need to possess qualities that make it stand out as being very much the exception rather than the norm. For example, to be truly outstanding an area of countryside would need to have features that distinguish it from neighbouring countryside for very positive reasons.

Now, anyone can freely use the word outstanding to describe a personal favourite spot, but the problem is that each person's qualifying rules are different – so a place that you might reasonably call outstanding might be little more than mediocre to the next person. Thankfully, a standard does exist, and the coast of Northern Ireland is particularly blessed with outstanding locations.

Immediately after the end of the Second World War, work began to protect several *"extensive area(s) of beautiful and relatively wild country[2]"*, leading to the creation of thirteen National Parks for England and Wales and, later, 46 Areas of Outstanding National Beauty (AONB).

Northern Ireland has no National Parks (largely due to its size rather than anything else) but has eight Areas of Outstanding National Beauty[3]. All but one of them are either on or near enough to the coast to warrant inclusion in these guides. Two were covered in *The Antrim Coast From A to Z*, leaving *three* to

---

2   John Gordon Dower, Secretary of the Standing Committee on National Parks, writing in a White Paper (1945). He died from tuberculosis in 1947 before his long-held vision became a reality.

3   There are several different designations that can be given to *"special interest"* sites in order to protect them. These include Nature Reserves, Sites of Special Scientific Interest, World Heritage Sites and Marine Ramsar Sites amongst others.

explore in this guide [4].

Mourne AONB will be examined in Chapters G and H and *Binevenagh AONB* is given extended coverage in Chapter M.

Some might say that the coastlines of Counties Derry and Down have a *fourth* AONB.

This is due to Lecale being formerly designated in its own right before being merged with Strangford into a larger single area in 2010. There cannot be many AONB-designated territories where more than half of the surface area is covered by water, but this is certainly true of *Strangford & Lecale*, where the Lough dominates the interior of the protected space.

Strangford & Lecale AONB is an incredibly diverse landscape. Where else can a single days leisurely hike encompass sandy beaches, rock-pools, cliff-tops, mudflats, rolling hills and sweeping river valleys?

At 525 square kilometres, it is not the largest of Northern Ireland's AONBs, but is almost as large as the Isle of Man, which can be seen offshore from several locations including the imposing Scrabo Hill at the northern end of the territory.

The Strangford Lough & Lecale Partnership (SLLP) has the responsibility to protect the *"diverse natural, cultural and historic heritage"* of this *outstanding* area. Perhaps we should investigate what makes this AONB diverse in terms of nature, culture and history?

The geology of the area is certainly old – at least 450 million years old, but much of the landscape we see today is the legacy of the most recent ice age that ended just 12,000 years ago.

Sandstone and shale reminds us this part of Ireland is well travelled – having once been almost half a world away in the time before land masses ended up where we find them on today's maps. The northern half of the AONB is dominated by distinctive round hills, or drumlins, many of which stand partly submerged within Strangford Lough itself and punctuate the water as a series of seemingly random islands.

Numbering around seventy in all, these drumlin-islands are varied in size and form, ranging from appearing to be little more than a tiny pebbly-covered

---

4   Lagan Valley AONB & Sperrin AONB are too far from the coast to be included in this guide. The Ring of Gullion AONB is very near to Newry but is in County Armagh.

sandbank to the 100 metre long, D-shaped Dunnyneill Island[5] a mile and a half north-east of Killyleagh. The Lough also features several *pladdies* – smaller outcrops of rock and clay that are invariably submerged at all times bar low tide. These boulders, deposited by the retreating glacier are well-travelled and varied in form, leading to them attracting different types of marine species, birds and insects within a matter of a few hundred yards.

Whatever you do, please avoid describing Strangford Lough as a *fjord*. This is actually a *fjard*. What's the difference and does it matter? Fjords are generally distinguished from fjards in that the former usually have steep-sided cliff edges and may have one or several distinct branching channels whereas fjards, as is the case at Strangford Lough, are much lower and have a flatter profile. This, in turn, leads to fjards often *"fill"* with eroded materials. This silting up creates very fertile mud flats, flood plains and salt marshes – all of which are present in and around Strangford Lough. Fjords are often cited as natural examples of fractal patterns. Strangford Lough is anything but regular in structure. Sea water enters the Lough through a narrow inlet which rapidly broadens into a shallow basin, never more than 200 feet deep, and often as little as less than 10 feet, even at high tide.

Within these waters can be found large (but declining) beds of horse mussels, as well as brittlestars, prawns and scallops. The Lough's islands provide a sanctuary for ground-nesting birds such as gulls, skylarks and terns, while the waters provide ample food to persuade at least 70 pairs of herons to make home in the nearby wood at Kinnegar. To see these magnificent birds in their somewhat scruffy homes, follow the marked path within Delamont Country Park[6] until you come to a purpose-built bird hide. Please do not try to get any closer as you are likely to distress the birds and their young. If you are a patient person, waiting at the shoreline, watching a seemingly statuesque heron peering silently into the water, will be well worth your diligence when the bird strikes downwards, instantly piercing its prey.

---

5 Erosion is having a dramatic effect on this island formed largely from glacial boulder clay. Current estimates give the island less than fifty years before it disappears completely.

6 Find it off the Downpatrick Road, just over a mile to the south of Killyleagh. The park is also home to the Strangford Stone – a 1000cm tall granite megalith erected to commemorate the millennium.

On and around the Lough, look out (and listen!) for pipits, dunlin, oystercatchers and redshank, all of which are here in large numbers.

Common Seals are a regular feature in Strangford Lough. The summer months offer the best time to see these popular mammals, also known as Harbour Seals as they bask freely in the open air. The Lough has been home to a large colony of common seals since at least 1856, and although seal numbers have varied considerably in the past 100 years or so[7], the outlook for the present population of several hundred is good. Disease is an ever-present worry, though. Twice in the last forty years, seal populations throughout northern Europe have been decimated by Phocine Distemper Virus[8] and other rapidly-spreading infections.

A man-made hazard for the resident seal population was set in place during the spring of 2008. Strangford Lough Tidal Turbine was better known as SeaGen and provided up to 5GWh of electricity by its fourth year of operations. At the time of writing the installation is in the process of being decommissioned, so if you haven't seen it yet, you may have missed it. Environmentalists have always been in two minds about the project. Some argued that the spinning blades of the underwater turbines present a very real danger to the seal and dolphin population, whilst others acknowledged that the installation had a minimal visual impact on the environment, compared to say, offshore wind turbines. The world's first commercial tidal stream generator was only ever intended to operate for around five years, exploiting the tidal energy involved in moving over 400 million gallons of water in and out of Strangford Lough twice every day.

SeaGen was a long way from being the first technological device to harness the power in the tidal waters of Strangford Lough. The monastery of Nendrum was established in the fifth century on Mahee Island just to the north of Whiterock. Scientific analysis of wooden remains[9] from an ancient tide mill on the island date the water-driven mill to the early part of the seventh century, making it the oldest excavated mill in the world. The monastery was excavated in the 1920's with several key artefacts being removed, restored and now displayed in the

---

7   Complete historical data is not available, but censuses conducted between 1956 and 1990 suggest a resident population of around 100 common seals to be typical.

8   New Scientist 18th February 1989 has a very good article on the spread of PDV. It is available to read freely online.

9   Dendrochronology is the dating of timber objects through the analysis of the rings.

Ulster Museum. Mahee Island, the monastery remains and a neighbouring castle are popular with visitors throughout the summer season. Should you time your visit for the winter season and wish to see pale-bellied brent geese, then you shouldn't face too much difficulty as 75% of the entire world population reside on the Lough at this time.

There is a potential successor to SeaGen – trials of which have attracted considerable interest from the local porpoise population and a few bottle-nosed dolphins. This is the *Minesto Sea Kite*, which on the surface of the Lough near Portaferry appears to be little more than a pontoon holding a Portakabin and steel container. Beneath the water is the latest version of the Minesto company's Deep Green kite turbines. The principle is simple – in the same way that a kite flying in the air harnesses energy through its holders string, an underwater kite can *"fly"* in the tidal currents and draw energy through a cable[10].

The entrance to Strangford Lough has attracted interested human visitors for many centuries. As far back as the ninth century, two groups of Vikings even fought a pitched battle with one another over the right to control these precious waters[11] and the fertile land surrounding what was then known as Loch Cuan. In fact, the modern name we use today is derived from the title given in the Old Norse language – *Strangr-fjörðr,* which broadly means the strong sea-inlet. Loch *Cuan* is the older name for the inland tidal Lough, whereas the Norse name was originally given to the narrow waterway connecting the Lough to the open sea. It is only in the past two centuries that a single name has become accepted to mean the entire volume of water from the channel inwards.

People have earned a living from fishing here for at least 1,000 years, with shipping and shipbuilding being major industries in places such as Portaferry since the seventeenth century. If you want to see the oldest surviving evidence of fishing and boatbuilding, though, you will need to talk a walk along the shoreline at Greyabbey Bay. It was here in 2000 that an enormous log-boat was discovered buried in the sand and partially submerged. It was in too fragile a

---

10 If that's a bit much to imagine, take a look here for a lengthier explanation and video: https://minesto.com/projects/strangford-Lough

11 The Annals of Ulster, compiled in the late fifteenth century describe a battle in 877 ce between *"the fair heathens and the dark heathens, in which Albann, king of the dark heathens, fell"*.

condition to remove – and so, it remains there to this day. Analysis including radiocarbon dating of the hollowed-out oak boat have led to the best estimate of its age being around 3,000 years before Jesus Christ. You may not see this amazing specimen as it tends to be swallowed up by the elements fairly regularly, but you shouldn't be able to miss the lengthy stone fish traps set by the monks of Grey Abbey some 900 years ago.

Should you be in the Greyabbey area, keep an eye open for signs of otters, who have been known to live and feed near here for many years. Spotting otters in the wild is a wonderful experience, but should you prefer to take the easier option, then the *Exploris* Aquarium at Portaferry should be the place to head for. Here you will be able to get a close-up view of the Asian Small-Claw variety, and, depending on when you visit, you may seen a new arrival – the most recent being born at the centre in October 2017.

Out on the waters of Strangford narrows you may spot an occasional summer visitor. A lone humpback whale[12] has been sighted here four times in recent years. Whales may not visit too often and are pretty easy to identify. If you want to learn how to name some of the more commonly occurring examples of sea and shore life in the Strangford and Lecale AONB then the official website is the place to go. There you will find a series of really useful poster guides including full-colour photographs[13].

Strangford Lough is captivating and could easily fill the entire book – don't worry, though, we'll return several times as we visit some of the communities and notable sites around its shore, but for now, lets turn our attention to the other half of the partnership – Lecale.

South of the Strangford narrows is the Lecale Coast. This is a wilder and more remote landscape, despite extensive areas of cultivation. To travel between the northern end of this AONB and the Lecale Coast provides an opportunity not to be missed.

The Narrows are fierce waters with powerful currents, back-eddies and whirlpools. At just under half-a-mile to cross, the eight-minute ferry journey

---

12 Observers cannot be sure if the annual visitor is the same whale, but it seems likely to be so.

13 Several can be downloaded from here: http://www.strangfordLough.org/maps-guides/

between Strangford and Portaferry operates every half an hour throughout the year. With return fares for a car and family of four at under £15, this is a trip not to be missed. From a purely practical perspective, for those touring the coastline, the ferry cuts out a drive of over 40 miles in each direction! Don't forget your camera – from the ferry you are likely to get photo opportunities unavailable elsewhere.

From the narrows looking south, Kilclief Bay and its tower-house castle dominate the view. In the foreground, however, don't overlook Cloghy Rocks, especially in the summer months where the seal colony haul themselves out of the water and give birth to pups every year.

The castle at Kilclief is open to the public, but access is limited so check online first. In the past, notices have been left posted to the door telling prospective visitors where to go for a key, but things may well have moved on somewhat nowadays. Kilclief castle is the oldest of the tower-houses dotted along the coast here, and from the look of the others, this one is a well-copied design. The four-storey tower was built for John Sely[14] the local Bishop, between 1412 and 1433. Sely left in disgrace in 1443 when it was revealed that he was cohabiting with a married woman by the name of Lettice Thombe in his newly-built castle. Pope Eugene IV removed him from office and Sely died shortly afterwards. The Dublin Penny Journal noted in 1833 that Sely had been given more than ample opportunity to repent and change his course, reporting that as early as 1434, Archbishop Swain had served him with a notice *"requiring him to turn off his mistress"*. Sely declined, and the rest is history.

The Lecale Coast is one of the most beautiful and unspoilt stretches of shore to be found anywhere in Europe and is easily accessible for walkers by following the Lecale Way stretch of the Ulster Way. The latter is a 625-mile circular route requiring major commitments in terms of time and energy, whereas the former at just 34 miles along quiet roads, beaches and coastal footpaths is realistically achievable for most, including children, over a few days.

The Lecale Way begins at Strangford and broadly follows the coastline as far south as Newcastle, taking in the sights of Cloghy Rocks, Kilclief Castle, Ballyhornan, Ardglass, Killough, St John's Point, Tyrella, Ballykinler, Clough and Dundrum along the way.

---

14 Often recorded as *Cely.*

The route encompasses dunes, wetlands, cliff-tops, tidal loughs, meadows and at least one stretch that is quite justifiably described as a swamp – so not a walk to be attempted in beachwear!

Many parts of the walk are designated as Areas of Special Scientific Interest so do your research beforehand – there are, for example, several rare orchids here that you might miss otherwise[15].

Don't be fooled by this apparently unspoilt wilderness – it has seen invasion, warfare, plague and pestilence over many centuries. Lord Deputy Leonard Grey, under direct orders from Henry VIII, marched into Lecale in 1539, and, whilst ransacking and plundering wherever he could, Grey found time to write *"yet did I never see for so much a pleasanter plott of land"*. Lord Chancellor, Sir Thomas Cusake wrote in 1552 informing the Duke of Northumberland that *Lecaill* (sic) *"is a handsome plain, and champion country of 10 miles long and 5 miles breadth"*. He cautioned on the subject of the tidal waters there *"the sea doth ebb and flow … so as in full waters no man may enter therein upon dry land"*. Yes, the waters of the Lecale Coast are treacherous with countless shipwrecks littering the shore.

Between Ballyhornan and Ardglass, the Ballyhornan Coastal Path is a very pleasant four-mile walk taking in Sheepland and the curiously-named *Steersman's Pad*. Many come here to visit the remnants of a well reputedly to have been *"blessed"* by Saint Patrick and to view Saint Patrick's Road – a formation visible at low tide which legend has it was a bridge built by the man himself to connect Ireland with the Isle of Man.

As for the Steersman's Pad, this is named after the sole survivor of the French brigantine *L'Amitie* which was wrecked here as it attempted to bring in a large supply of weapons for the United Irishmen in April 1797. More than 100 crewman lost their lives. The story goes that a helmsman was the only one to pull himself ashore in deadly seas. He was so consumed with grief and what we

---

15 The Killard Peninsula is particularly interesting due to it being unspoilt over centuries. Cattle graze here in the winter months, naturally keeping the meadowland grass short encouraging flowers and orchids to grow profusely in the spring and summer months. In June and July, the area around Killard Point is a riot of colour. Children will love it here – observing butterflies, grasshoppers and skylarks in a beautiful natural environment. Download a full guide here: https://www.discoveringbritain.org/activities/northern-ireland/walks/killard.html

now term survivor guilt that for the rest of his life he could be seen regularly pacing along the coast, wearing a path that is now known in his name to pay homage to his lost friends and shipmates.

The dangers of these coastal waters was already well-documented. More than forty years earlier Irish historian Walter Harris wrote *"beware of the South Rock on which many brave ships have perished; for it overflowed every tide, and no crew can save their lives … if the winds blow high"*. In 1783 funding was granted to erect a lighthouse on the rock[16]. Work started in 1793 and the first light was seen from the new Kilwarlin Light[17] just three weeks prior to *L'Amitie's* disastrous end.

The Down County Museum in Downpatrick has a restored cannon salvaged from the wreck on display as well as more information about the ship and the supply of weapons during the period.

More recently, the American warship SS *Georgetown Victory* came to grief off Killard Point in April 1946, less than a year after launch. The ship was carrying 1,400 Royal Marine and Royal Navy personnel as well as a regular crew of 90, returning to Scotland from Sydney, Australia. Why was an American ship bringing British personnel home from Australia? The authorities had agreed an exchange – the *Queen Mary* was ferrying American troops across the Atlantic in return.

The *Georgetown Victory* ran aground at high speed, causing an immediate oil spill but there were no fatalities[18]. Some managed to wade ashore with the assistance of many local people, while others were rescued by the Newcastle and Cloughey lifeboats. With many neighbouring residents aware of the stranded ship just off shore, looting of its contents was widespread until it broke in half a few days later. Much was subsequently salvaged, but large sections of the ship are still submerged and have become a popular attraction for divers.

---

16 According to the Belfast Chamber of Commerce's petition, more than 60 ships had been wrecked in 25 years with the loss of over 250 lives.

17 This was only the third *"wave-washed"* lighthouse to be successfully completed in the British Isles.

18 The only recorded injuries from the grounding were a broken shoulder and fractured arm. One man suffered minor injuries when he fell from the scramble net whilst evacuating the vessel.

Many possible reasons have been offered for the grounding. The most popular "excuse" was foggy weather but eyewitness reports from some of those on board confirm that skies were clear. The most likely conclusion is that a navigation error led to those commanding on the bridge to steer towards Strangford Lough believing it to be the mouth of the Clyde!

Before we leave the Lecale Peninsula for now, we have one final and unlikely destination – a pigsty! Beside the main road near the beautiful bay of Rossglass is a fine example of an eighteenth century pig crew to use the local name. The Lecale area is the only place where these stone corbelled buildings are found. Most of them are square or rectangular with a conical roof and an entrance doorway near to one of the corners. Dry stone walls are commonplace, but what makes these animal shelters unique is the construction of the roofs. Large flat stones are neatly overlapped before smaller inclined facing stones are carefully positioned to provide a neat run-off for rainwater, leaving the interiors bone dry. This one at Rossglass is now protected as a scheduled monument. Others exist, but mostly on private ground. Times have changed in Lecale and none of them are occupied by pigs any more.

There is plenty more to see in this beautiful area, as we will find out throughout the book, but for now our time is up as we must turn our attention to another change affecting the coast of Northern Ireland.

Further Reading:

R. Brown, Strangford Lough: Wildlife of an Irish Sea Lough, Queen's University (1992)

R. Brown, C. Nolan & others, Strangford Lough & Lecale, SLLP (2010)

B is for Brexit and Borders

By the time you read this the UK and Northern Ireland may or may not be a member of the European Union and Northern Ireland's borders with its neighbour the Republic of Ireland may or may not be *"hardened"*. So why do we need to discuss this in our book on the coast?

Let me be absolutely clear – I have no political opinion on the subject whatsoever. *"Remain"* or *"Leave"* made no difference to me, and the question of *"hard"* or *"soft"* borders is one for others to consider. Having said that, the issues do matter to many and may or may not affect the dynamics of the border coastal communities in our region so it would be remiss of me to ignore what may turn out to be the biggest change in a generation.

My experience of the borders near to both Derry and Newry is quite simple. Until the road signs turned yellow and speed limits started to appear in kilometres per hour I was not aware that I had crossed a border and entered a foreign land. No passport checks, no *"Welcome to Ireland"*, no customs declarations. Nothing!

So here's the practical stuff. As soon as you enter the Irish Republic on four wheels (or two, or on foot for that matter) the terms of your insurance policies change. For example, standard UK car insurance most likely does not include driving on roads in the Irish Republic and your car breakdown policy probably won't cover you either.

Speed limits are different too – here's a quick (but incomplete) summary:

Built-up areas: 50kph

National roads: 100kph

Motorways: 120kph

Elsewhere: 80kph

There are local variations – so pay attention to the signs, stay within the limits and remember that ignorance of the law is never an acceptable excuse. Drink-driving, failure to wear seat-belts (including ALL passengers) and using mobile phones whilst driving all incur hefty penalties. On the subject of road signs, be aware that in the Gaeltacht areas, where the primary language is Irish, most of the signage is solely in Irish.

Carry your driving licence, MOT certificate and proof of insurance with you at all times[19].

There are several toll-roads in the Irish Republic, but none near to the borders.

Parking rules vary from place to place. In many locations pay-and-display parking is now being replaced with pay-by-text which in turn raises the issue of mobile phone networks – check with your service provider for the possibility of incurring international roaming charges.

It is a good idea to carry some Euros with you if you intend crossing the border. Some retailers will accept UK currency, but most will not.

As for health care, the good news is that you do not need to have a Health Insurance Card to access services (since they are free and take up no more space than a store card, you may as well carry one), but you will probably need to show some form of photo-ID such as your driving licence or passport. Don't expect services to be completely free either. If you need an overnight stay in hospital or emergency dental treatment you will have to pay out. As always, do your research before you travel and investigate health insurance options before you have a problem. One tip, though. Look carefully at your existing policies before taking out new ones – you may already have suitable cover, or be able to upgrade for a small fee.

Where are the borders? Lets start with County Londonderry. The City of Derry[20] itself is entirely within Northern Ireland. To the south of the city, the River Foyle serves as the boundary before it cuts its way northwards overland to the west of the city itself. The B193 Letterkenny Road suddenly becomes the R237 in the village of Killea, part of which is in Northern Ireland with the majority in the Irish Republic, the only markers being road signs showing the speed limit in kph and a helpful yellow sign in English, French and German informing you to "*Drive on Left*" which, hopefully you'd already been doing for some time! To the north of Londonderry, the border skirts the edge of the city and then follows the western

---

19 Take copies of all important documents before travelling. This will be useful in the event that you are required to surrender an original to the authorities.

20 Derry or Londonderry? Both names apply to the same city/county and I will generally alternate between the two.

edge of Lough Foyle beyond the village of Muff.

This expanding village in County Donegal (just!) helps to illustrate some of the issues to be confronted post-BREXIT. Recently, the village has seen an increase in its population, fed in part by an influx of UK migrants. In turn, many of the 1,200 who live in Muff, commute across the border into Derry to work every day. A hard border and tighter crossing regulations are likely to have a major impact on this lovely village.

Many cross the border (and fill up with cheaper petrol) at Muff to take a ride on the *Inis Eoghain 100* aka the *Inishowen 100*. This 100-mile scenic drive encompasses many of the sights of the Inishowen Peninsula. Although it is not within the territory covered by this book, I mention it here so as to include the ferry crossing between Greencastle at the northern end of the drive, and Magilligan Point. The ferry offers a relatively speedy and cheap connection between the Causeway Coastal Route in Northern Ireland and the Wild Atlantic Way in County Donegal, as well as outstanding views southwards into Lough Foyle and Derry City. Where else can you take a 20-minute ferry crossing between two nations, without having to show your passport (for now)?

Actually, there is another one. Between Northern Ireland's own Greencastle in County Down and Greenore in County Louth, the Carlingford Ferry crosses Carlingford Lough and takes passengers and their vehicles on a 15-20 minute trip for less than a tenner. This *"gateway to Ireland's ancient east"* as the ferry owners like to call it, is a popular crossing, so book ahead in the summer months, and consider buying season tickets if you plan to make more than one return trip.

The border between County Down and County Louth is the southern edge of Carlingford Lough until at narrows at the mouth of the Newry River opposite Warrenpoint. From there the border wriggles clumsily inland west and south. The whole of Newry is in County Down, but cross the bridge in Newry by the Albert Basin and travel west or south and you'll soon find yourself in a different land. As before, the only indication is a change in the road signs.

Both Lough Foyle and Carlingford Lough present as yet unresolved post-BREXIT issues of a different kind. Their waters are filled with marine life and many folk on both sides of the borders earn a living dredging for mussels, farming oysters or just plain fishing. With both Northern Ireland and the Irish Republic as EU members, fishing rights hasn't been much of a problem – until now.

C is for Castlerock and a Chronicler

The seaside village of Castlerock lies five miles west of Coleraine and is one of the most attractive beaches in the whole of Northern Ireland. No surprise, therefore, that it is very popular with caravanners these days. If you are looking for a traditional family holiday near to an excellent beach, without too much noise and night-life, this could be the place for you.

One family that took their young children to Castlerock at the start of the twentieth century was the Lewises of East Belfast. Albert and Florence took their sons Warren and Jack to stay in Castlerock many times.

I should explain at this point that "*Jack*" wasn't the younger son's real name. He was born Clive Staples Lewis in Belfast on 29th November 1898, but insisted on being called by this alternative name following the death of the family pet dog *Jacksie* when he was four years old. Family and friends knew him as Jack or Jacksie for the rest of his life. You probably now him better as C.S. Lewis, author of the Chronicles of Narnia.

Downhill House is now just a roofless ruin, but enough of a ruin to allow the imagination to picture is as it stood in the late eighteenth century when it was erected as a mansion for Dr Frederick Hervey, the 4th Earl of Bristol. We will learn more of this building and the famous library nearby in a later chapter, but it is said by many that it was here where the young Lewis allowed his imagination to wander and then be replayed as the house with a rather peculiar gateway into an alternative reality in The Lion, The Witch and The Wardrobe. The actual reality is that Clive and his brother Warren were only known to have visited Downhill House on one occasion, when he was just three years old. How much truth is behind the legend, we will probably never know, but its a nice story and a very good reason to take a look at a once-grand home.

There is no doubt that Jacksie and Warnie, as his older brother was affectionately known, loved their times at Castlerock. They were growing up at a time when the politics of Ireland were particularly unstable, plots were being hatched, rumours spread. It was a fertile time for young imaginative minds. Later in life C.S. Lewis described this as a period when he was "*training myself to be a novelist*".

The pillared-entrance to Downhill House is topped with two giant stone *lions*[23] facing one another – could this be where Aslan the lion was born? Beside the mansion was a large walled garden and a dark mausoleum as well as the cylindrical temple perched on the cliff – all excellent fodder for an inquisitive and imaginative mind. But what of Castlerock itself, could this quiet seaside resort have fuelled the apprentice writer's mind?

Lewis is known to have loved steam trains. Who could blame him when he travelled so frequently on what Michael Palin called *"one of the most beautiful rail journeys in the world"*[24]. The railway station at Castlerock opened in 1853 and was well used by the family – not just for arriving and departing at the end of each year's holiday of up to six weeks , but for outings to the Giant's Causeway, Dunluce, Londonderry and Ballycastle. The Lewis family must have used the station to board and exit trains on dozens of occasions. The station signal box with its bells, levers and mechanical frames would have attracted the attention of thousands of children, most likely including the Lewis boys. Besides it the footbridge was a magnet for the imaginative child to stare along the railway line into the distance and dream of far-away places that exist solely in the mind. From the beaches of the coastline at and near Castlerock sailing vessels of varying shapes and sizes would come into the view of the young boy on a regular basis. Were these fishing for salmon, travelling to and from the oyster beds of Lough Foyle or carrying some intrepid adventurers on a magical voyage – only Clive himself knows what he saw and thought.

Castlerock gets its name from the Castle Rock where the Greenock Brigantine *Trader* ran aground carrying 100 tons of grain from Limerick to the Clyde in November 1826 with the loss of seven[25] lives. A memorial stone in the nearby village of Articlave commemorates their deaths. Just a year later and a folk tune describing the tragic events from the perspective of a sailor onboard was being sung in the surrounding villages and ports. This song stills survives in a slightly different form with the chilling line *"death did appear as we drew near the*

---

23 Actually snow leopards, but the entrance became known as the Lion's Gate and the name stuck.

24 Palin was describing the line between Londonderry and Coleraine which passes through Castlerock.

25 Possibly eight.

lovely shores of sweet Downhill"[26]. It is likely Clive heard songs such as these at one of the many *cèilidhean* he attended with his family over the years, further fodder for his imagination – did this inspire *The Voyage of the Dawn Treader* with its perilous oceanic adventures to find the seven lost lords of Narnia? Perhaps.

So, is Narnia based on the Castlerock area? As we have seen, elements certainly contributed but Lewis himself confided in a letter to his brother that an area bounding Carlingford Lough near Rostrevor was *"my idea of Narnia"*. Having said that, his fondness for Castlerock is undisputed. As a teenage schoolboy charged with producing a poem on the theme of the most beautiful place in the world, the young Lewis chose Castlerock, but unable to fit the polysyllabic word into poetry, he chose to substitute the name of Moville[27].

Castlerock's wide sandy beach comes to an abrupt end at the mouth of the River Bann (known locally as the Barmouth). To the south and east are mighty dune systems, parts of which are reached from Castlerock by travelling towards Coleraine and then crossing the river at one of the bridges in the town before travelling north again. On the westward side of the estuary a mile inland are some of the oldest dunes in Ireland. The Grangemore system rarely reaches 10 metres in height, nearer the sea the dunes are twice as tall, but these have revealed a wedge of muddy soil between the sands containing approximately 5,000 year old fruits, leaves, pollen and mosses indicating a period of flooding[28]. The Grangemore dune system is protected and part of it is managed by the National Trust as the Barmouth Bird Sanctuary which has an excellent hide overlooking the Bann estuary. Access is from the Barmouth Road, but be aware that car parking space is very limited – its probably best if you can get there on foot or on two wheels. If you are into birding, you probably know of this spot already. If you don't, if I reveal that over 220 different bird species have been recorded here, you'll probably want to find out more. Many users of the bird hide, however, aren't looking to the skies. Here is also a great spot to observe harbour porpoises and seals at play in the waters of the estuary.

---

26 The entire song is at: https://www.itma.ie/digital-library/sound/trader_eddie_butcher

27 A small coastal village in County Donegal on the western shore of Lough Foyle. I have found no evidence that Lewis ever visited Moville.

28 Around the time of Noah!

As well as dunes, the inland area behind Castlerock is a mixture of woodland, reed-beds and open fields – remember, the doorway into Narnia led immediately into a dense woodland. The faun *Tumnus* appeared to Lucy by a gas lamp in the forest. Castlerock was not lit by similar lamps, at the time when the Lewis family holidayed there, but nearby Coleraine and Portstewart both were.

Thanks to the *Belfast and Ulster Towns Directory* of 1910,we can picture the Castlerock scene when the twelve-year-old Clive and his family stayed there. Described as being 67 and a half miles from Belfast, the *"pretty little seaside village"* had a population of 145. Postmistress Miss M. Nixon received four separate train loads of mail every day. Refreshments were available at the railway station, Mrs. Mullen's cafe or the Windsor restaurant.

The sole indicator that Castlerock was a potential tourist destination in 1910 was the listing of a *"public baths"*. This was, in fact, a bathing lodge run by J. B. Warke. The building is now listed and serves as a four-bedroomed private house with the title of *"Rock Ryan House"* or just Number 2, The Promenade. Built from basalt quarried to make room for the railway in the 1850's, it was completed in 1862, but was very different then, being partitioned into a series of small bathing cubicles. The Church of Ireland briefly held the property before it was converted into residential accommodation. Records indicate this was the summer holiday home for the Lewis family in the years following 1906. Overlooking the sea and the Barmouth, and with direct access onto the beach, this must have been about as good as the budding author could have hoped for in a summer holiday home.

Amongst the many farmers listed in the 1910 entry was a H. *Hazlett* residing at Liffock. This was actually newly-wed 38-year old dairy farmer Hugh *Hezlett*[29] and his Liffock home was the seventeenth-century thatched cottage which, since 1976 has been managed by the National Trust and known as Hezlett House. This building predates everything in the locality, and, with the exception of three fishermen's huts at the Barmouth, is the sole building on the first Ordnance Survey map to cover the Castlerock area. The railway station came before the village, which by all accounts took its name from the rock offshore that stood out of the sea like a small castle. Where is it now? Rising sea and sand levels over the last century have completely covered the Castle Rock. By the time of the 1862 map revision, the railway line is clearly evident, as is the train station,

---

29 The farm also yielded oats, barley, potatoes and turnips as well as raising pigs and chickens.

clearly marked as Castlerock Station, with a handful of buildings nearby, but still no village. It seems the train came first – perhaps the station was merely built initially to serve those at the nearby Downhill Demesne, of whom more in the next chapter.

By 1918, and without its public baths, the village had grown in both size and stature and was now being described as *"a pleasant and rapidly rising watering place"*, *"advancing in popularity year after year"*. The new golf course was a big draw, as was the availability of angling, both on and off the water. The village at that time also operated no less than three hotels – the Castlerock Hotel, the Temperance Hotel and the Golf Hotel. By the end of the Second World War, only one remained – the Golf Hotel. The village was no less popular by then, it was just that holiday habits had changed. The wealthy were now more likely to holiday abroad, and the rest chose more affordable boarding house or self-catering accommodation. The Golf Hotel managed to struggle on until the early part of the twenty-first century, when, after a brief resurgence, the 15-room beach-facing building ended up being demolished.

The golf club came to Castlerock in 1901, although plans for the first nine hole course began the year before. By 1906 steps were being taken to secure more land to extend the course into a full 18-hole championship venue. In the early years, the public turned up and played alongside members, with prize money of up to £3 available. Nowadays, visitor rates start at £25, and members have to pay a joining fee of £1,500 followed by just over £600 every year for the privilege of playing on one of Ireland's premier links courses.

Castlerock village was expanding before the golf course was begun. The primary reason was the availability of "golden tickets" for anyone purchasing one of the new homes erected from 1866 onwards. The financier was Sir Hervey Bruce, landowner and occupier of Downhill Demesne, the tickets were offered by the railway company and gave new homeowners 10 years free rail travel between Castlerock and Londonderry (or Coleraine)[30]. And so, the fledgling village gradually adopted the name originally given to the railway station born without a village to serve.

The village today is still popular with holidaymakers during the summer season, but remains tranquil for much of the year – many say the same is true in the

---

30 Whitehead in County Antrim had a similar scheme available. See *The Antrim Coast From A to Z* for more details.

summer, and do so quietly in the hope that it stays that way. That's not to say Castlerock doesn't get plenty of visitors. It does. The two holiday parks (don't call them caravan sites whatever you do!) attract a few hundred families every summer, as well as many more staying in the village itself. With overnight pitches available from £15 even in high season, a holiday in Castlerock isn't likely to break the bank.

Clive Staples Lewis didn't have too many bank balance worries. Admittedly many of his book sales have come after his death which went virtually unnoticed bar family and friends on 22nd November 1963. The reason? Lewis passed away an hour before the assassination of John F. Kennedy in Dallas[31]. To date, the Narnia novels alone have sold well over 100 million copies all around the world.

Lewis once wrote:

"One of the dangers of having a lot of money is that you may be quite satisfied with the kinds of happiness money can give, and so fail to realize your need for God".

And with that thought in mind, we should take a short journey west from Castlerock where one of Ireland's most iconic buildings stands (for now at least).

Further Reading:

A. McGrath, C.S. Lewis: A life, Tyndale House (2013)

C. Winchester, Railways of Ireland, Amberley Publishing (2014)

---

31 *Brave New World* writer Aldous Huxley died the same day as well.

D is for Downhill (Demesne and Strand)

A *demesne* in its widest sense is defined by one dictionary as *"a piece of land attached to a manor and retained by the owner for their own use"*. In Ireland, the same word has a subtly different meaning. An Irish demesne is usually an enclosed, usually walled, part of an estate. Like the *"standard"* definition, in Ireland the demesne is kept under the exclusive control of the landowner, unlike the remainder of the estate which was often sublet to tenant farmers and the like. The word *domain*, even used in its modern computing sense, is derived from the same Latin root *dominus* meaning the master of a household.

Downhill demesne is not really a demesne in the true Irish sense of the word in that it is not surrounded on all sides by a wall. True, there is an imposing jagged cliff boundary which is walled – more likely to protect people and livestock inside from falling 120 feet rather than to deter intruders. The southern end of the demesne is marked by the A2, Mussenden Road. It does include most of the features associated with a traditional demesne. So, yes, there is a walled garden, and, yes, there is a mausoleum, and, yes, although it is small compared to many, the demesne does squeeze in an arboretum into its south east corner.

Every Demesne needed to have a *"lord"*[32]. Downhill was originally the manor of an Englishman, Frederick Augustus Hervey. Born in 1730 into one of England's wealthiest families, Hervey inherited the title Earl of Bristol following the death from *"gout of the stomach"*[33] of his elder brother Augustus, the third earl, in 1779. By this time, Frederick was already well established in the Church of Ireland as Bishop of Derry, a role he had fulfilled since 1768, succeeding William Barnard.

The news of Hervey's translation from the bishopric of Cloyne to the richer pastures of Derry apparently arrived while the Earl was engaged in a game of leap-frog (he was 37 years old!). He is reported to have received the message with the words *"I will jump no more. I have beaten you all, for I have jumped from Cloyne to Derry"*. It was in this role that he earned the nicknames *"Earl Bishop"* and *"Edifying Bishop"*. There is no doubt that Hervey was an energetic

---

32 With the exception of a Royal Demesne which belonged to the crown.

33 Likely, some form of bowel or colon cancer.

man, something of a visionary and a very skilful financial manager. Whether his investments helped to advance the cause of the Church of Ireland is a matter of debate.

The Earl Bishop travelled extensively and acquired a large collection of works of art and literature over the years. In need of a suitable home for himself and his hoard, he commissioned the building of Downhill House in 1772, by which time he had been married to Elizabeth Davers for twenty years and had fathered seven children by her.

Although his contribution to the advancement of the Church directly is doubtful to say the least, Hervey was instrumental in the development of infrastructure in the county of Londonderry. Without his drive, and cash, it is possible that many roads would not have been built. Certainly, the north coast would not have developed in the nineteenth century, agriculturally or commercially were it not for the earlier investment and support of the Edifying Bishop. He financed the building of Derry's first bridge over the Foyle. Probably in a case unique for its day, Hervey also gave financial support to the Roman Catholic church, donating £200 towards the construction of St. Columba's church in 1783. His money paid for the four capitals on the Corinthian columns that border the high altar. The church has many Renaissance-style features and it is possible that Hervey who had spent a considerable time in Rome, also contributed architectural advice.

In his later life, Hervey became more and more political in his thinking, writing and actions, working alongside members of the Roman Catholic church attempting to create a common shared oath of allegiance. He spent less and less time at Downhill. In 1791 he returned to his birthplace at Ickworth in Suffolk, where he built a large mansion on his extensive estate and never lived in Northern Ireland again.

Opinion is sharply divided on his legacy. Those who benefited directly from his benevolence, such as farmers and fishermen were generally positive, but his absence from Ireland for long periods as well as his outrageous behaviour resulted in harsh, but generally fair words about him. Hervey's contemporary, James Caulfield, the 1st Earl of Charlemont called him *"a bad father"* and *"a worse husband"* acknowledging the *"shallow stream"* of his genius as *"rapid, noisy"* but ultimately *"useless"*[34]. Sir Jonah Barrington, himself never too far

---

34 To be fair, the two men were fierce rivals with no love lost between them.

from criticism described the Earl Bishop as a man of *"extensive learning ... but eccentric mind"*. Another critic wrote that Hervey was more Middle Age prince-bishop than eighteenth-century divine.

But what of Hervey's Demesne at Downhill? With a budget of around £80,000, architect Michael Shanahan[35] had plenty of opportunity to indulge in extravagances. Hervey's initial income as Bishop of Derry was around £7,000 annually, but when additional sources of revenue such as tenants dues were factored in, the Earl Bishop was worth nearer £15,000 a year – a figure that rose to more than double that following the deaths of his two brothers.

Shanahan had the money to spend, but Hervey was very much in control of how it was spent. The architect and his wife (as housekeeper) lived on site and communicated with Hervey constantly. This was a period of strong political ambition and the Bishop needed a mansion or castle befitting a man of state. Downhill grew with Hervey's ambitions. It began in 1776 as a five-bayed villa, grand enough to serve as a retreat with a fantastic seascape beyond, but soon becoming inadequate for Hervey's needs.

The Bishop used Downhill for lengthy political meetings and gatherings – sometimes involving overnight stays. The addition of a large east wing which became known as the Curate's Corridor provided *"barrack-style"* accommodation for many of the single men who stayed here.

Hervey was very actively associated with the Volunteer Movement for many years. Some say that aspects of the interior design of Downhill were added later to reflect the Bishop's feelings and to serve as positive icons for those he entertained and lobbied in his expanding mansion. Fashion in the 1770's had moved upwards – ceilings became more and more elaborate, with walls kept as blank canvases – ideal if you happened to be an ardent collector of paintings, as Hervey was.

Records reveal that the Bishop employed local artisan craftsmen when he could, but was not afraid to seek contracts with traders from all over Europe when they could not be sourced on the island of Ireland. The latter turned out to be very much the minority – Ireland had rather more highly skilled craftsmen in the

---

35 Hervey is also believed to have met noted architects James Wyatt and Charles Cameron whilst in Italy as part of a *"Grand Tour"*. Many suggest Wyatt as the designer of original plans and Cameron as a consultant, but in the absence of real proof, Shanahan as a confirmed architect in-house (forgive the pun) gets the credit.

eighteenth century than many texts acknowledge.

Of the items imported, one, a carved marble chimney-piece, attributed to the Italian Lorenzo Cardelli, was auctioned at Sotheby's in 2007 for £72,500. Unfortunately, much of the rest of the original Downhill House has been lost forever. Much of it in a major fire in 1851, with more of the interior being irreparably damaged immediately after the Second World War when the roof was stripped of lead and ultimately removed altogether.

Michael Shanahan completed his contract with Hervey in 1787, by which time a library, two galleries and a billiard room had been completed. The Bishop called the Library his *"lounging room"*, at a time when the concept of a *"lounge"* was barely known.

In 1782 Frederick ordered the construction of another building – a grand library close to the cliff-tops. By the time of its completion in 1785, the Bishop no longer had a wife – the marriage, often difficult, had come to an end three years earlier, and a reported relationship with a cousin, Frideswide Mussenden had ended with her untimely death at just 22 years of age. The new structure, built to look identical to the Temple of Vesta at Tivoli near Rome became an instant memorial to the dead young lady – Mussenden Temple was born.

A stunning library retreat on its ground floor, a little known extra is that the basement, accessed via a separate external door overlooking the sea, was carefully designed to include a permanent fire to prevent damp from encroaching the precious works of literature. It also featured an area purposefully added for the benefit of visiting Catholic priests giving them a much appreciated space to conduct Mass.

Around the base of Hervey's temple is the Latin inscription:

Suave, mari magno turbantibus aequora ventis

e terra magnum alterius spectare laborem

which broadly translates into English as:

It is pleasant safely to behold the shore

The troubled sailor and hear the tempests roar.

When Hervey chose these words, from the Roman poet and philosopher, Titus Lucretius Carus, it most certainly would have been pleasant to behold the shore *safely* from the comfort of the warm library, but his memorial to Frideswide runs the very real risk of disappearing over the precipice one day. Erosion is a constant worry along much of the Northern Irish Coast, even here at Downhill Demesne where the hard basalt cliffs are still prone to crumbling. Some pin the blame firmly on the railway works carried out in 1846. This included the digging of a 1,000 foot tunnel immediately beneath Hervey's memorial and blasting away a cliff face nearby using 3,600 pounds of gunpowder. When Mussenden Temple was completed in 1785, a cart track encircled it, now it balances precariously, only the meticulous underpinning and stabilising work of the National Trust has prevented it toppling over the edge already. Even they cannot guarantee the long-term future of this iconic landmark.

Mussenden Temple is one of the most photographed places in the whole of Ireland. Be careful taking shots from the side – don't be tempted to cross the wall. The beach below is a good place to take a picture from – but not if you've just gone over the edge.

The Earl Bishop became increasing restless following the death of Frideswide and in 1791 returned to his larger estate in Suffolk. He continued to travel extensively and succumbed to gout in July 1803 whilst in his beloved Italy. The house at Downhill passed to his nephew Henry Bruce (Frideswide's brother) and remained in the Bruce family until 1946. For the next four years the interiors were steadily stripped away and sold off. Only a roofless shell of the once-grand mansion remains.

Or does it? In 2012, students at the Northern Regional College in Ballymoney completed a project to produce an interactive 3D-model of the original house[36]. The video brings Downhill to life again.

When you visit Downhill, don't miss out on the other notable features within the demesne. Look out for the strange carvings on the Bishop's Gate. Try to identify as many different types of tree as you can in the small but wonderful arboretum. Don't miss the most recent addition – albeit over 100 years ago. There can't be too many public "bog gardens" and this one has some a stunning collection of irises. And, keep an eye out for the walled garden, the icehouse and mausoleum. Should you want to follow a more regimented trail the National Trust have one

---

36 Watch a video of it here: https://www.youtube.com/watch?v=wwFqc54A6jA

on their website[37] for you.

Hervey was a flawed bishop in many respects, but it is hard to be critical of his sensitivity to the economic needs of the people in his bishopric. He provided jobs at a time when work was scarce, farmland at low rents, roads to help people get around and showed sensitivity for those choosing to worship in different ways to him. He was incredibly wealthy, spent prolifically but died with a healthy bank balance and three noteworthy estates.

Having spent some time with a man of faith who developed strong political leanings, we'll move a little further on in time and a few miles east to a woman who never shied from expressing her convictions, a rising in the early spring and the important town of Newtownards.

Further Reading:

S. Price, The Earl Bishop, Great Sea (2014)

B. Fothergill, The Mitred Earl, Pimlico (1988)

---

37 Download it here:
   https://www.nationaltrust.org.uk/downhill-demesne-and-hezlett-house/trails/downhill-demesne-walk

E is for Eilis and Embroidery

Frederick Hervey's expansion into the political arena through his vocal and financial support of the Irish Volunteer Movement coincided with the break-up of his marriage in 1782. Elizabeth Bloxham's political life began whilst still a teenager just over a hundred years later.

Elizabeth, like her contemporary C.S. Lewis *"tweaked"* her name from time to time, favouring Eilis, the Irish equivalent of her first name in her early writings. Her story is told here not due to political allegiance – I don't do politics remember – but because of her connection with an important town near to the County Down coastline – Newtownards.

Bessie (as she was known through childhood) was born and raised in County Mayo, firstly inland at Claremorris and then onto the coast at Westport[38] so when her first job came along her move north-east to Newtownards took her into Northern Ireland, but gave her town and coastal living which she was well familiar with.

Before she left County Mayo Elizabeth got an unexpected introduction to politics. She had forged a, some might say unlikely, friendship with two male boat-building brothers. Bessie had been raised a Protestant amongst a fiercely Catholic community and the brothers were Catholic too. That didn't seem to bother any of them as they shared an interest in literature and exchanged books regularly. On one occasion, the brothers showed Elizabeth a poem written inside a *"paper"*. Bessie loved the poem and ended up borrowing the whole paper, against the advice of the two young men.

The paper turned out to be a copy of *United Irishman* – a nationalist newspaper. Before long, Elizabeth was not only reading it, but penning articles for the newspaper, perhaps enhancing her Irish nationalist credentials by adopting the first name of Eilis for these pieces. When the newspaper folded under the threat of libel action in 1906, its co-founder Arthur Griffiths didn't hesitate to offer Eilis work on his new weekly publication - *Sinn Féin*.

---

38 Where she lived on the Westport Demesne following her father's retirement from the Royal Irish Constabulary.

By 1911 Eilis was living and working as a *"domestic economy instructress"* in Newtownards. Her writing was getting her noticed, by other periodicals *and* the authorities. In turn she was noticing things more for herself, leading to her championing women's rights and ultimately becoming a founding member of *Cumann na mBan*, the *"Irishwomen's Council"* in the spring of 1914.

Bloxham was essentially a libertarian seeking peace and harmony in co-existence. Her first home in Newtownards was at 14 Victoria Avenue where her landlady, 55-year old Mary Ann Sloan was a member of the Presbyterian church. After attending the regular Sunday service at Newtownards Parish Church in February 1912, Eilis was moved to write a letter to the Newtownards Chronicle. Many see this as the beginnings of her radicalisation, but the letter itself began *"I wish to protest in the strongest possible manner against the use of the pulpit for political speeches"*. Far from being an advocate of violence, she described murders as *"dastardly"* and accused the priest himself of attempting to *"stir up political bitterness"*. It was an angry letter, but not a call to action, rather, an appeal for the church to rein in its involvement in partisan politics. Protestant and Catholic worship the same God – when they take up arms against one another, He cannot possibly be "with" both sides.

One particular conversation illustrates this conflict of interest well. Whilst lodging at Victoria Avenue, Elizabeth began an exchange of ideas with the daily bread deliveryman. He was one of the first Orangemen the young teacher had the opportunity to engage with regularly. Bloxham advocated Home Rule, while Johnny the bread van driver was a staunch Loyalist. What irked Elizabeth most, wasn't Johnnies politics, it was the way he changed after *"the Rising"*.

Prior to Easter 1916 Newtownards was a place where Catholic, Protestant, Presbyterian and the like held and freely voiced different views, but did so in a largely tolerant environment. More than three-quarters of the 27,999 residents of the Newtownards District Electoral Area described themselves as Protestant or *"Other Christian"* with just one in twelve being Catholic. What was exceptional about Eilis was her membership of the Protestant church combined with being a *"Home Ruler"*. This aroused the curiosity of the likes of Johnny the bread van driver who was always keen to elicit views from the mouth of Bloxham – until the Easter Rising.

In September 1914 the third Irish Home Rule Bill passed into law, but the onset of war led to its deferment. Elizabeth was, by this time, actively campaigning for

Cumann na mBan, whose published aims included advancing the cause of Irish liberty and supporting the arming and equipping a body of Irish men for the defence of Ireland. Bloxham attracted much attention and support, even at a time when most of the young men of Newtownards, and elsewhere, were signing up to join the fight against the Kaiser. True, some members of Cumann na mBan saw that you couldn't support both causes and left the fledgling organisation, but Elizabeth stuck with it, facing up to criticism from other women's rights groups that Cumann na mBan was just a collection of *"slave women"*. Elizabeth travelled all over Ireland campaigning for her beliefs, but was home in Newtownards at the time of the Easter Rising[39] – becoming aware of the nature of events from reading the newspaper at home in Victoria Avenue. Immediately afterwards the mood of people towards Elizabeth changed. Johnny no longer attempted conversation and would look the other way. Those that did confront Eilis got the same retort *"I only wish I had been in Dublin to give the Volunteers any help that was in my power"*. Many years later she acknowledged the *"great agony of spirit in Ireland at that time"*.

At the end of the Summer Term, Elizabeth was dismissed from her teaching position. No reason was given in her notice letter, but Elizabeth admitted later it came as no surprise since her views outraged *"popular feeling"* and *"some such repercussion (was) bound to ensue"*. She found herself ostracised by former colleagues and associates and left Newtownards with her resolve strengthened as a result of the reaction she endured.

Newtownards at that time was, like so many other communities, very much focused on the trials of war overseas. The Orangemen of the town even cancelled their 1st July parades in 1915 and 1916 because of the war, bringing it back in 1917 as a joint commemoration to include the loss of so many Ards men at war. Nowadays, the Somme Museum at Conlig a couple of miles north of Newtownards is a natural focal point for those wanting to learn more of Newtownards involvement in the Somme campaign and more widely. Why Conlig? The site, in the grounds of the Clandeboye Estate was formerly where soldiers of the 108th Brigade were trained.

Also in the grounds of the same estate is Helen's Tower, a folly dedicated to the

---

39 The six-day uprising led to the deaths of over 450 people, with a further 2,600 injured and 3,500 people taken prisoner by the British, about half of whom were interred. Ninety of the failed revolts organisers were sentenced to death, and by 12th May 15 executions had already been carried out.

mother of Frederick Hamilton-Temple-Blackwood, Baron Dufferin and Clandeboye. Frederick inherited the estate whilst still a child of 15 when his father died from an accidental overdose of morphine in 1841. Born Helen Sheridan, Frederick's mother had a literary pedigree. Her grandfather was Irish writer Richard Brinsley Sheridan and her mother was the novelist Caroline Henrietta Callendar, youngest daughter of the fifth Earl of Antrim.

Frederick's estate was managed by his mother until he reached maturity. He was well known locally for his efforts to support local people by providing employment and low-rent homes at a time when Ireland was still reeling from the effects of the Great Famine. Profoundly influenced by Helen, in 1848 Lord Dufferin commissioned Scottish architect William Burn to construct a building in her honour. Opinions differ as to when Helen's Tower was completed. It may have been as early as 1850 or as much as seventeen years later, by which time Helen had remarried (briefly[40]) and been widowed for a second time. The three-storey tower contained a single (but rather grand) room on each level connected via a stone turret stairway.

Unsurprisingly, given Helen's literary background, the new tower attracted the attention of several notable writers of the period. Alfred Lord Tennyson said it stood *"dominant over sea and land"* acknowledging further that *"son's love built me"* and adding that the tower holds *"Mother's love in letter'd gold"*. This was a reference to the many texts inscribed within the tower. In his own offering, Robert Browning wrote, almost prophetically *"The Tower of Hate is outworn, far and strange"*, and that this *"loves rock-built tower, shall fear no change"*. Many poems were etched onto bronze tablets (not quite *"letter'd gold"*) and fixed to the granite walls

Should it appeal to you, Helen's Tower is now a very upmarket holiday let. Near the village of Thiepval in north-eastern France is the Ulster Memorial Tower, a very similar structure, based on Helen's Tower and erected in 1921 as the first official memorial on the Western Front. An indication of the poverty that existed in Newtownards and North Down at that time is that all attempts to raise money by public subscription for a memorial at home proved unsuccessful and the first memorial to the dead of the First World War was erected indignantly in March

---

40 Her long-time friend George Hay, Earl of Gifford was critically injured protecting a workman from a falling tree in the grounds of his estate at Yester Castle in Scotland. Helen immediately arranged to marry him. George died from his injuries two months following their wedding.

1924 by a small group of out-of-work ex-servicemen, who took advantage of a particularly heavy snowfall to build their own nine-foot-high snow memorial. The authorities took a dim view, fining four men half a crown plus costs for causing an obstruction[41].

Newtownards was recently revealed to be within the second-most desirable area to live in Northern Ireland. On average, its residents are some of the wealthiest in Ulster and property prices are amongst the highest. How times have changed over the last century. In Elizabeth Bloxham's day, most lived in rented accommodation and worked full-time to make ends meet. At the time of the most recent census, two thirds were owner-occupiers, with half of them already owning their homes outright, and less than one in twenty described themselves as unemployed.

So what, if anything has changed?

The independent town really developed during the industrial revolution period. Factories, shops, schools and churches were interspersed with homes, parkland and a large workhouse built to the west of the town which opened just in time for the Great Famine. In the twentieth century, the big development that affected Newtownards came in transport, public and private. Belfast was becoming increasingly cramped, but needed more workers. Newtownards had room to expand, and good connections by road or rail – it became a relatively prosperous and affluent commuter town, more than doubling in size in the last forty years of the twentieth century.

The 1918 *Belfast Street Directory* described Newtownards as *"populous and prosperous"*. Where was the wealth coming from? Nearby Belfast had the nickname of *Linenopolis* as one of the world's biggest centres for textile manufacturing. Newtownards specialised in a very particular branch of this industry – handkerchiefs.

The same directory commented *"the leading industries of the town are weaving, embroidery, hemstitching, printing and finishing of handkerchiefs"*. Samuel Lewis's 1837 *Topographical Dictionary of Ireland* noted *"the weaving of damask is carried on to a small extent; about 600 looms are employed in weaving muslin, and 20 in weaving coarse linen for domestic use"*. This was followed by the revelation that *"more than 1000 females are constantly employed in*

---

41 A permanent memorial site and obelisk was donated to the town by the Marquis of Londonderry in 1934. It stands on the site of the old bowling green in Court Square.

embroidering muslin", almost all of which was shipped to merchants in Glasgow. The *Belfast Post Office Directory* published six years later added *"weaving of muslin employs a large number of the male population"*. The town and its immediate environment had no fewer than thirty distinct manufacturers of muslin at the time[42]. George Bassett wrote in his 1886 *County Down Guide and Directory* that *"A highly cultivated farming country ... helps materially to maintain its (Newtownards) prosperity"*, also noting that brewing, a once-grand business in the town had ceased, but new industries had arisen including *"a tape and twine factory, a linen factory, handkerchief printing works, bleach works, a woollen factory, bed-quilt factory and hosiery, shirt and skirt factories"*, all contributing to what Bassett called *"a first-rate town"*. None of these journals mentioned the importance of *"out-working"*. Much of the finishing of handkerchiefs and the like was done by women and girls in their own homes, with workers paid per piece. Wages were often low and hours long, with no pay during periods of sickness or confinement. Tasks such as *"over-seaming, vice-folding and thread drawing"* were all carried out in the homes of widows and spinsters or where the man was out of work or busy in a lowly-paid job such as an agricultural labourer as many where in and around Newtownards at that time[43].

According to Thomas Walter Freeman, wages in places such as Newtownards were so low that firms in Scotland found it cost effective to ship raw yard to Northern Ireland for weaving before returning it to Scotland to be bleached and finished, ready to be shipped again and sold in Ireland[44].

Homeworkers around the time of the Great Famine earned as little as 10 pennies per day embroidering things like pocket handkerchiefs and pre-stamped muslin collars. For those unable to embroider, clipping jobs were available. This was even less well paid and involved removing loose threads with scissors – fail to spot one and you risked not getting paid. James Godkin's 1870 book *The Land-War in Ireland* painted the scene in Newtownards very nicely for us:

---

42 There were also 11 straw bonnet makers, giving an indication of the size and relative wealth of the town in that period.

43 According to the 1912 *Report of the Committee on the Conditions of Employment in the Linen and other making up trades in the North of Ireland.*

44 See Pre-famine Ireland: A Study in Historical Geography, Manchester University Press (1957) p86

"although there are no great mills sending forth columns of smoke, Newtownards is really a manufacturing town. Those clean, regular streets, with their two-storey houses, uniform as a district in the east of London, are inhabited by weavers. In each house there is one loom at least, in most two or three, and in some as many as six".

Godkin went on to describe what he witnessed in the home of one weaver:

"I saw one man working at a piece of plaid of six colours, a colour on every shuttle. With the help of his wife, who assisted in winding, he was able to earn only eight shillings a week by very diligent work from early morning till night".

He also noted the beginning of the demise of the town's embroidery heritage:

"The trade of muslin embroidery once flourished here ... but it has so fallen off that now the best hands, plying the needle unceasingly during the long, long day, can earn only three or four shillings a week".

***

When Elizabeth Bloxham was starting her career in Newtownards, the town was getting its first glimpses of a very new and exciting form of transportation – the flying machine. In June 1911, Belfast engineer Harry Ferguson gave a demonstration flight as part of the annual North Down Agricultural Society's Show in Newtownards. It attracted great interest. For traders, the route to Scotland, England and Wales was costly involving rail and/or road as well as crossing the difficult Irish Sea. If Newtownards could transport freight by air? Well, that would open up whole new markets and opportunities, wouldn't it? Pessimists reminded optimists that Newtownards was always intended to be a port itself, and had never gone beyond being a busy(ish) market town. The optimists set about finding a suitable site for an airfield. The Marquis of Londonderry was president of the Agricultural Society and major landowner in the area, and he stepped up to provide a field for planes to use.

The First World War saw tremendous advances in aviation, but heralded a lengthy pause in commercial ambition, and it was 1934 before Newtownards finally got an airfield of its own – the first civil airport in the Province. The Marquis of Londonderry, who once again had put up the money and gifted the site talked eagerly of Newtownards as a base for flights not only to the rest of the British Isles and Europe, but across the entire globe.

It wasn't to be.

Four years later, a second airport opened at Sydenham. This was just a handful of miles nearer to Belfast, but, being established by the Belfast powerhouse of Shorts, whose huge factory was next door, it took away most of the commercial business Newtownards had worked so hard to bring in over the previous four years, making it the seventh busiest airport in the whole of the British Isles and second only to Croydon for carrying freight.

Once again war intervened. Newtownards was requisitioned for military use. The site was enlarged and some improvements were made to hangars, living quarters and runways. From the perspective of the Luftwaffe, Newtownards became a bigger target. In April 1941 a single raid killed thirteen soldiers[45] of 70th (Young Soldiers) Battalion Royal Inniskilling Fusiliers. Some of these soldiers weren't old enough for front line service and were used for homeland defence instead. The youngest was 16. A memorial stone stands in Court Square in the centre of the town.

Requisitioned sites were returned to their previous owners following the war in an assortment of conditions. Billy Butlin, for example, drew up contracts with the UK government ensuring that his holiday camps were handed back to him in better condition than pre-war, all at the tax-payer's expense. The same was not true at Newtownards where Lord Londonderry had to dig deep into his pockets before the airport could operate commercially once again.

For a short while in the 1950's the Airport operated the fastest ever car+passenger connecting service between Northern Ireland and Scotland. For a return fare of under £100 a family of four could fly, with their car, between Castle Kennedy near Stranraer and Newtownards in just 17 minutes.

Roll-on Roll-off car ferries plus competition from the airport at Belfast saw the commercial side of Newtownards Airport fall into steady and rapid decline, so that by the 1960's only a newly-formed Flying Club operated regularly from Newtownards. The Ulster Flying Club continues to this day and has expanded to become Northern Ireland's largest flying school.

Newtownards is very much a modern town with much to commend it. As a "flagship" town for the administrative district of Ards and North Down it is correctly identified as a place where residents tend to live longer lives, have

---

45 According to entries in the Unit's War Diary, 10 were killed that night and another three died from their injuries the following day. A fourteenth officer who was on leave, died during the Belfast Blitz on the same night.

"*better*" qualifications and a job, but pay more for their homes in comparison with the rest of Northern Ireland.

Before we leave the town of Ards as it is known affectionately by locals, we have a final call at Whitespots Country Park adjacent to the Somme Museum. This is the site of a once-prosperous lead mine which was worked from the 1840's until 1910. Be aware that the name is not white-spots, but whites-pots. Why? In the old Ulster-Scots dialect, "*whites*" was a term for lead or other metals, while "*pots*" were mine shafts. In the 1850's the mine was yielding a third of all the lead in Northern Ireland. The shafts are flooded and capped, but some of the old mine buildings are still *in-situ* and observable.

The park is very much a work-in-progress and care should be taken around the old exposed spoil heaps, where museum-quality crystalline specimens are often found. With more than 70 acres of attractive woodland and connecting pathways to Helen's Tower and on to Ballygrot, this is well worth a visit, particularly when combined with a call at the Somme Museum.

Elizabeth Bloxham may or may not approve of the way her old town has turned out. Neither do we know for sure what successive Marquesses of Londonderry feel about the town that has received so much investment. Regardless of what you may think about its political and economic history, I reckon you'll rather like the place.

And now, we leave Newtownards and head north to a river that passes through his ancestral seat.

Further Reading:

You can read Elizabeth Bloxham's full 38-page statement to the Bureau of Military History by downloading it freely from
http://www.bureauofmilitaryhistory.ie/reels/bmh/BMH.WS0632.pdf

J. Hanna & D. Quail, Old Newtownards, Stenlake (2004)

F is for Foyle

Elizabeth Bloxham campaigned vigorously for Home Rule, but when you read her journals, you'll likely find a woman who deeply wanted an end to division and for peoples of all backgrounds and allegiances to get along well together.

Literally on the boundary between Northern Ireland and County Donegal in the Irish Republic is the River Foyle. Its waters enter the sea at Lough Foyle, with the western bank in the republic and the eastern bank in the north. My point?

The river is formed from a confluence of two rivers – the Finn and Mourne. The former brings water from Lough Finn in County Donegal with the latter originating in County Tyrone, between Strabane and Newtownstewart.

So, the Foyle symbolises both division and unity. Perhaps we should look more closely at its own *"troubles"*.

The City of Derry has three bridges over the river. Each of them with its own story of challenges. The Foyle, for its size is considered to have one of the most energetic flows in Europe. This means that constructing any crossing poses great difficulty.

Working downstream, the first of Londonderry's bridges is the somewhat strangely-built Craigavon Bridge. Known locally as the *"Blue Bridge"*, it is the oldest of the three, but actually is the third bridge to span the Foyle.

The Earl Hervey Bridge was fully completed in 1792 (Yes, the same Earl Bishop we met earlier) and was the result of a collaboration between the Bishop and an American bridge builder Lemuel Cox[46]. The total cost was £16,594 – a hefty sum for a bridge at that time with the price being inflated by the exclusive use of American timber and labour. Hervey himself put forward £1,000 towards the cost as well as sending his own architect, Shanahan to Switzerland to survey bridges in the country most well known for its expertise in this field.

---

46 Raised in Dorchester, Massachusetts, Cox had strong associations with the American Royalist movement. He was imprisoned in 1775 and supported the building of a gunpowder mill in Andover, Massachusetts for General George Washington in 1776. His first bridge linked Boston with Charlestown. He began accepting work overseas in 1789. His Derry bridge was the first of six he built in Ireland.

Cox arrived in Londonderry with a party of 25 workmen in 1790 and had the first phase of the 1,068 foot bridge open to those able to walk across the following year.

United Irishman Thomas Russell wrote of the bridge in his diaries noting wryly that Cox was presented with an engraved tea caddy during the opening ceremony. The man from Boston, like most Americans had not consumed any tea since the 1773 Boston Tea Party. Hervey received a gold box and the Freedom of the City. A second irony was that American biographers failed to exploit the opportunity to recognise the achievement of one of their own, especially after the renowned London engineers Milne and Payne had surveyed the fast-flowing 900-foot wide river and declared it impossible to span.

The bridge was extremely useful for the next twenty four years until strong winds pushed great blocks of ice which struck it in February 1814[47], destroying a section of over 300 feet. Analysts have concluded the bridge had been weakened when the original drawbridge section – installed to placate the people from Strabane who had vigorously campaigned against the bridge[48] – was modified a few years earlier. Sections were recovered from the Foyle over the next 80 years but not were kept. All that remains is a model, built in Switzerland, presumably at Shanahan's request, which is presently in the British Museum. Unfortunately, it is likely that the 19-foot model, made by John Conrad in 1772 bears little resemblance to the bridge designed and installed by Cox and his American team.

Derry had to wait until 1863 for its second bridge, even though plans had been in place for over 30 years. This time the structure was built with an iron frame. The Carlisle Bridge, named after the Lord Lieutenant at the time, took four years to complete but revolutionised transport and commerce in the north-west of Ireland for a single reason – it allowed trains across the Foyle for the first time. But it wasn't a straightforward affair. Railway companies on either side of the bridge used different gauge lines – Irish Standard (5 foot 3 inches) on one side and a narrow, 3 foot gauge on the other. So a mixed gauge track had to be laid

---

47 Some online sources date this event to 1813, even 1862, but the 1837 *Topographical Dictionary of Ireland* confirms 6th February 1814, as do several newspapers from that month.

48 Their argument was based on historic rights of free passage and the belief that the bridge would restrict their ability to trade.

on the bridge to allow goods to cross in either direction. You see, no fewer than four different railway companies operated lines in and out of Londonderry at the time. The Great Northern and Northern Counties companies operated in Northern Ireland connecting Derry with Belfast amongst others, while the County Donegal and Londonderry & Lough Swilly companies operated services connecting Derry with all points west of the city.

The bridge was a double-decker, with a second, upper tier for pedestrians and road vehicles and cost £90,000. Like its predecessor, some of the costs were recovered by the collection of tolls for a while.

This bridge provided much-needed communications links across the Foyle until 1933 when Derry got its third bridge – the aforementioned Craigavon. Controversial from its opening, the bridge was named after the first Prime Minister of Northern Ireland, Unionist politician James Craig, also known as Lord Craigavon. A view held by many was, and still is, that when "*building bridges*" it's wise to avoid antagonising those on either side. Perhaps the "*blue*" nickname has more to do with avoiding the official name and less to do with the choice of paint colour?

The Craigavon Bridge retained the double-decker principle of its forerunner, with rail services running on the lower tier at first. All this required complex and expensive management with turntables at both ends of the bridge. Once uncoupled from their engines, goods wagons were then hauled over the Foyle using a system of chains and winches. It will probably come as no surprise that after Lord Beeching's report led to the axing of a third of all rail lines, the lower tier was converted to a second road deck.

The Foyle divides Londonderry into a predominantly Catholic zone to the west, whilst east of the river, many of the population are Protestant. In 1992[49], local sculptor Maurice Hannon erected *Hands Across the Divide*, a thought-provoking installation, albeit on a traffic roundabout, showing two life-size figures standing facing one another atop a pair of stone walls reaching out to touch fingertips – almost. Hannon's optimistic work in many ways symbolises how tantalisingly close the prospect of peaceful co-existence is for many, yet, whilst any "*gap*" remains, the fragile relationship between both sides struggles on.

A different kind of gap created problems with the building of Derry's blue bridge.

---

49 Exactly twenty years after the deaths of 28 civilians in the western *Bogside* area of Derry in the events that became known later as *Bloody Sunday*.

Engineers responsible for sinking the main supporting piers, couldn't locate firm foundations below the water where they'd expected to find them, resulting in the cylindrical columns being driven to a depth of 23 yards below high water – quite a bit lower than originally planned. The 420-yard, five span bridge eventually cost just over a quarter of a million pounds – peanuts in comparison with the £4.2 million required to refurbish and repaint the bridge at the start of the new millennium.

Moving a third of a mile north, is a newer symbol of reconciliation. Completed in 2011, the Peace Bridge is a cycle and foot bridge connecting the predominantly Unionist *Waterside* area of Londonderry with the largely nationalist *Cityside* of Derry. Built at a cost of £14 million pounds the s-shaped bridge is 771 feet long and just 13 feet wide and its design was reputedly inspired by the sweeping shape of one of the stone walls in Hannon's sculpture further south. Amazingly, using 500-ton floating cranes, the self-supporting suspension bridge was completed in just eighteen months. It would have been less, but work was suspended twice for a while. Firstly, the particularly cold winter of 2010/11 required construction to be halted for three weeks, and secondly, a pause was ordered so as not to interfere with the salmon-spawning season.

Whether or not the Peace Bridge has *"radically changed"*[50] people's perceptions of Londonderry is open to debate. What is beyond dispute is that it is a popular focal point for many public events that for a time at least, draw people from all communities and persuasions together.

The third of Derry's Foyle bridges is also the one nearest to the opening of the Lough. As well as being the city's third bridge, the Foyle Bridge is also one of three bridges still in existence bearing the same name[51]. This one was completed and opened in 1984, four years after work commenced on what would be, and still is, the bridge with the longest central span in the whole of the island of Ireland.

It is this bridge that carries most traffic over the river – often peaking at over 30,000 vehicles every day on its four-lane dual-carriageway. With that amount of

---

50 As recorded on the Northern Ireland tourism website (February 2018)

51 A second Foyle Bridge is an iron railway bridge near the village of Porthall, and the third is a concrete road bridge between Lifford and Strabane, more commonly known as the Lifford Bridge but which was officially named the Foyle Bridge when it opened in 1964.

work, wear-and-tear is inevitable, but I doubt that when the original construction bill of nearly £16 million pounds was paid, anyone anticipated having to shell out a further £10.6 million pounds for essential repairs just twenty years later.

The central section measures 767 feet (about the length of two football pitches) with the total length of the bridge being not far short of 1,000 yards. The bridge is well elevated and bow-shaped to allow shipping to pass beneath through Lough Foyle's narrow deep-water channel. Road traffic joining the bridge from the east do so on the curiously-named Madam's Bank Road, whilst those arriving from the west must pass Boom Hall. What's the link?

The Foyle Bridge stands near to *Madam's Bank*, broadly where a defensive boom had been erected in 1689 as part of the three month siege of Londonderry. By the time the armed merchant ship *Mountjoy* rammed and broke through the boom bringing in vital supplies, some claim that half of Derry's 8,000 population died during those three months. The *Mountjoy's* master Michael Browning, lost his life in the action and is commemorated on a memorial tablet embedded within the city walls, paid for by a former occupant of Boom Hall also a merchant shipman. Boom Hall itself was built around 90 years after the siege as the seat of the Alexander family, who retained it until James Dupre Alexander sold the entire 125-acre estate which included extensive stables, a walled garden and woodland, to Daniel Baird. The hall passed through various hands until the Royal Navy requisitioned it in World War II. Since then it has fallen into serious disrepair and has a very uncertain future.

To the north of Madam's Bank and Boom Hall Lough Foyle opens out and is a haven for wide varieties of wildlife, with sandbanks, beaches, mudflats, shingle and boulders supporting a richly diverse range of species and habitat. Before it does so, the port of Londonderry stands on the east bank of the river.

The city was granted a charter to manage its own port by King Charles II in 1664. Within 100 years, the port was handling up to 67 ships and carrying goods and emigrants all over the world. Many of the landmarks associated with the port's heyday are long gone, but clues remain. Shipquay Street is one good example. This road led to the Shipquay, close to the western end of the new Peace Bridge. The Queen's Quay, once bustling with incoming and outgoing passengers, is now a lively centre for leisure, entertainment and retail. The only tall ships you'll see here nowadays are those docked to coincide with some cultural festival or another. To find out more about the history of the Port of Derry, a visit to the Harbour Museum in the former offices of the Corporation, situated in the old Guildhall would once have been highly recommended. Unfortunately the museum closed whilst renovations of the Guildhall were carried out, and has yet to reopen.

Londonderry is renowned for being a walled city, of which a full chapter to itself near the end of the book, but for now we're off into County Down to visit a very different wall.

Further Reading:

A. Farrington, The Natural History of Lough Foyle, Hodges (1951)

R. Doherty, The Siege of Derry 1689, History Press (2010)

G is for Granite

Walls are generally built to keep things in – or out. The walls of the City of Derry, for example were laid early in the seventeenth century with the intention of defending the early Scots and English settlers from unwanted invaders. Nowadays it not only symbolises the troubled history of the city, but also serves as a focal point for tourism as one of the great walled-city walks of Europe.

In the Mourne Mountains is a rather different wall that also turns out to draw a lot of visitors every year who turn up to walk its 22-mile length as it winds its way over no fewer than fifteen[52] of the areas great hills.

This isn't a wall to protect land from people. The wall completely surrounds the Silent Valley reservoir and its main water catchment areas and is there to keep livestock out and thus reduce the risk of contamination.

Built using age-old dry-stone wall construction methods over a period of 18 years, the Belfast Water Commissioners had just one thought – functionality. To get all the jobs done, including the building of the reservoir would require a workforce of up to 2,000 in one of the remotest and wildest areas of Northern Ireland. So, what did they do to make life a little bit easier for the workers?

They erected a village for them to live in.

A little way to the west of the reservoir (inside the boundary wall) is all that remains of Watertown. It was meant to provide all that could be needed so the village had shops, dance hall which doubled up as a cinema and small hospital as well as several hundred timber cottages. Boots could be repaired, provisions purchased, teeth pulled and boils lanced all without leaving the village. Should anything be required that was not available on site, the blue "*Tin Lizzie*"[53] van drove into Kilkeel twice a week. Watertown was even reputedly the first settlement in Ireland to have its own street lighting. The village had its own

---

52 Claimed by some to be 17.

53 A Ford Model T – with a top speed of 45mph and just two gears, the "van" could carry a maximum of 6 passengers. More than 15 million were manufactured and half of all the vehicles on the roads in 1920 were Model T's, many of them customised as this one may well have been.

policeman, the unfortunately named Constable Lawless. Although very little is left on the site of Watertown, Northern Ireland Water, who now manage the Silent Valley area, have an excellent visitors centre where the story of Watertown is revealed and many artefacts are displayed[54].

To illustrate the scale of wall-building, lets work on the figures. With an average height of 1.5 metres and running for 35 kilometres the 1 metre thick wall has an approximate total volume of 55,000 cubic metres. Taking 18 years to build, that amounts to almost 3,000 cubic metres of wall per year, or a length of 2km. Given that work was generally only possible for half of each year (in the months of April through October), we can estimate progress of the wall to have been about 50 metres every single working day.

The area enclosed by the Mourne Wall is now known as the Silent Valley. Prior to the wall and subsequent reservoir it was the Happy Valley. How and why did the name change? The answer is that it didn't completely. There is still a Happy Valley, just not the same size any more. As for the change to *Silent*, many stories circulate including the lack of sound from the workforce and machinery after the reservoir project was completed, and claims that the noise and subsequent landscape changes sent the resident bird population away, never to return.

The Silent Valley scheme was the brainchild of Luke Livingstone Macassey, consultant hydraulic engineer to the Belfast and District Water Commission. He'd already designed and built two reservoirs at Carrickfergus and Lisburn to provide for Belfast's rapidly expanding population[55] when he was asked again in 1890 to find a way to further increase water supply. Macassey immediately turned to the Mourne Mountains and proposed two schemes pledging that these would realistically provide more than 30 million gallons of water every day – far more than the City of Belfast would *ever* require[56].

Macassey's first plan involved diverting water from the Annalong and Kilkeel rivers along a pipeline directly to Belfast. His second, and more ambitious project was the Silent Valley reservoir scheme. The former was delivering water by 1905. Macassey died in 1908 and it would take a further 25 years for the

---

54 For more information visit https://www.niwater.com/the-silent-valley-trails/

55 Between 1810 and 1890 the population of Belfast increased from 25,000 tenfold.

56 He was obviously a very busy man. The same year he submitted proposals for an undersea rail link between Stranraer and Belfast.

Silent Valley project to be completed.

With parts of the Mourne Wall, Northern Ireland's longest listed structure by the way, now over a century old, the need for repairs is inevitable. Part of the problem is that the wall is now such a popular destination for hill walkers that it has had to take more pressure than anticipated. A yearly challenge walk event became so popular that it had to be stopped due to fears that the volume of *"traffic"* was damaging parts of the wall. Also, a section of over 20 yards on Slieve Meelmore was badly damaged by lightning some years ago. In 2017, work commenced on replacing fallen and damaged stones on a 3-mile stretch of the wall between Slieve Loughshannagh and Slieve Meelmore. As before, a team of local stone masons was used, from the Kilkeel-based firm of Thomas Rooney & Sons. In just one month, 530 stones were raised back into place.

The Wall has provided a natural focus for hikers and ramblers. The challenge of completing a full circuit in 24 hours is irresistible to many. But the mountains drew people long before the wall was even started. Take Lewis Moore of the Yorkshire Ramblers' Club, for example. He wrote in 1901 of *"a mighty crescent"* with *"steadfast horns"* describing the Mountains of Mourne as *"the most important and attractive of the ancient kingdom's natural charms"*. Describing the panoramic view having ascended the Devil's Coach Road on Slieve Beg, a little way east of the Happy Valley, he wrote

"Opposite are the twin peaks of Slieve Bearnagh, a beautiful mountain, the Castor and Pollux of Mourne, and as the eye follows the valley of the Kilkeel river southward, Slieve Mweel. Beg, Slieve Lough Shannagh, the Carn Mountain, the north and south peaks of Slieve Muck, and Ben Crom stand brown and desolate, but grand and glorious, backed by ridge upon ridge, until Slieve Ban and Slieve Dermot are lost in the haze hovering above the blue waters of Carlingford".[57]

The Devil's Coach Road is a difficult ascent, far more of a scramble than a walk – so much so that hiking organisations often recommend that a helmet be worn at all times. The Mourne Wall walk is certainly strenuous and not for the faint-hearted but far less dangerous – provided you follow a few essential rules.[58]

---

57 All extracts copyright Moore, L. (1901) The Ancient Kingdom Of Mourne. Yorkshire Ramblers' Club Journal Volume 1 Number 3: pp155-172. Leeds: YRC reproduced here with thanks.

58 Download an essential safety leaflet here
http://www.walkni.com/useful-info/walk-safely-and-responsibly/

Waterproof walking boots are vital, not just to get through much of the boggy terrain, but to give proper ankle and foot support on sloping uneven ground – don't expect to be following wide well maintained footpaths. A piece in the *Irish Times* initially misleadingly described how the wall *"undulates gracefully through and over the Mourne Mountains"* before more realistically summing it up accurately as being *"like the tracks of some Stone Age rollercoaster"*. Consider the former quote to represent how it looks, while the latter represents how it feels and you won't be far out. An online commentator wrote last year that the challenge walk took over 12 hours and that he used up all 5 litres of water before the end of the walk. Another called it gruelling and stunningly beautiful at the same time – you have been warned.

Should you attempt the Mourne Wall Challenge Walk, you will be rewarded with views from 7 of Northern Ireland's 10 highest peaks, including Slieve Donard, the highest of them all with an elevation of 853 metres – provided you time your attack to coincide with good weather. Look out for the Isle of Man to the south east, Belfast and beyond to the north west and in the distance to your south you may even view the Wicklow Mountains and Dublin.

For most, walking the entire circuit of the Mourne Wall will be too much, so here is a far-less strenuous alternative, that takes in the Silent Valley Reservoir as well as a short section of the dry-stone wall. The Silent Valley Nature Trail is a two and a half kilometre circular walk through the Kilkeel River valley. It has a well-maintained all-weather surface, no steps, heavy gates or stiles and is pretty much level making it accessible to most[59]. You'll never be too far away from toilets, a cafe and information centre or the car park, making this a trail that will leave you unlikely to be calling out a mountain rescue team. The trail will take you past Watertown and the old railway line that served it as well as the wall of the giant Silent Valley Reservoir dam. You'll see a modern oak forest as well as a thousand year old wood, open heathland and muddy bog (but you won't have to walk through it), riverbanks and the shores of lakes – no wonder the organisation *Walk Northern Ireland* enthusiastically call the nature trail experience *"a sort of mini-Mourne"*.

The reservoir is considered to be a remarkable feat of engineering. Before I

---

59 For more information download the leaflet:
    http://www.walkni.com/walks/136/silent-valley-nature-trail/

explain why, we should also remember that several of the 2,000 or so local men and boys that worked on its construction between 1923 and 1933 lost their lives there. These included 18-year-old John Murphy who was killed when a tunnel collapsed in August 1929. He had only just moved from a mine in Scotland, having been persuaded to leave by his mother following a fatal accident there. Another, Mick Synnott, died when the steam crane he was driving overturned. Mick pushed his colleague out of one side of the cab to safety, sacrificing his own life. A memorial stone was laid near to the reservoir in 2006.

A pioneering method of engineering was required to prevent water from leaking out below the dam. This involved digging a 212-foot long trench using compressed air and the sinking of several cast-iron lined shafts. Only the fittest men could take on this work, and even these had to spend time in "*the Gazoon*", a decompression chamber, at the end of each shift in order to prevent them from an attack of the bends.

The completed reservoir with a capacity of 3 billion gallons was officially opened by the first Governor of Northern Ireland, James Hamilton the third Duke of Abercorn, in May 1933. The project had cost £1.35 million, nine lives and the loss of most of the Happy Valley forever.

In our tour around the Mourne Wall we've touched on just a few of the Mourne's great mountains – the tip of the iceberg, perhaps. Let's move on to examine them all more closely now.

Further Reading:

R. Lovett's 1888 book, Irish Pictures Drawn with Pen and Pencil has fantastic drawings of the Mourne Mountains and is availably freely from
https://archive.org/details/irishpictures00lovegoog

L. McKay's 1922 book, The Mountains of Mourne, their charm and their people is also freely available to read or download from
https://archive.org/details/mountainsofmourn00mcka

H is for Hewitt

Louise McKay began her lovely eulogy to the Mourne Mountains with these lines:

"There is one spot on earth, how dearly I love it,

'Tis a star that doth beckon wherever I roam,

And my thoughts often wander in loyal devotion

To the home of my childhood – to Kin'ly Mourne".

The *Irish News* reviewed the book, acknowledging McKay's awareness of *"the Kingdom of Mourne; its wide spaces thinly peopled, it's humble hamlets, it's wee towns (and) it's picturesque little capital"*. I can't compete with the author's local knowledge, or descriptive prowess, so please read her book, but what I can do is take you on a short tour of McKay's *Kingdom* passing over each of the Mountains on the way.

To be known as a Hewitt, two criteria have to be met – both must apply. Firstly, the summit must be officially surveyed as being at least 2,000 feet above sea level, and secondly, it must have a relative height of at least 30 metres, in other words it must be at least 98 feet higher than its immediate surroundings. The latter is particularly significant when considering plateaus and neighbouring or *"twin"* peaks.

The name *Hewitt* comes from the author and compiler Dave Hewitt who took Alan Dawson's work *The Relative Hills of Britain* and expanded it to include all of Ireland as well as England and Wales from Dawson's first publication. Hewitt also changed the name given by Dawson – *Sweats*[60], using his own surname instead, thus maintaining consistency with the Scottish convention of naming mountains over 3,000 feet *Munros*, after Sir Hugh Munro who published a first list of such peaks in 1891.

Many thousands of hill-walkers collect or *"bag"* Munros. For a lot of them it has

---

60 Dawson's name is actually a clever acronym of **S**ummits **W**ales & **E**ngland **A**bove **T**wo thousand. Hewitt surpassed this by creating his own surname as an acronym of **H**ills **E**ngland **W**ales **I**reland **T**wo **T**housand.

become something of an obsession, relentlessly striving to ascend all 282 peaks. Northern Ireland has just 19 Hewitts to bag and 14 of them are in the Mountains of Mourne[61]. Seven are to the east of the Silent Valley reservoir, with the other seven to the west, so we'll tackle them in these two geographical groups, with those on the east, nearest to the coast first.

Slieve Donard is Northern Ireland's highest peak with an elevation of 2,790 feet. In Irish it is *Sliabh Dónairt* or *Dónairt's mountain* after a priest and follower of Saint Patrick who made the mountain his home. His story was retold by Historian John O'Donovan in 1834[62]. O'Donovan described Donart (sic) as *"a fierce and warlike pagan chief"* who was approached by a servant of Patrick requesting a donation to support the clergy. Donart pointed at a bull in a field saying it could be taken, knowing full well that *"twenty persons would be unable to drive that bull to any place"*.

Well, the servant *"goes to the field, and far from being able to drive home the mad bull"* narrowly avoids losing his own life. When Patrick heard of this, he gave the servant a halter, saying *"take this halter with you, and as soon as you go to the place where the bull is, he will put his head into it, and then walk home with you"*. Sure enough, when the servant returns to the field and offers the halter to the bull, the animal *"having laid aside his native ferocity, walked over to the servant, put his head into the halter, and then walked home with him, meek and silent as the lamb when led to the slaughter"*.

O'Donovan related how this enraged the *"pagan chief"* who furiously demanded that Patrick return his bull. Patrick apparently showed the remains of the slaughtered and salted animal and performed a miracle, restoring life to the bull. On seeing this *"the warlike Donnart became a meek and humble disciple, and ... was induced to resign his chieftainship, abandon his fortified residence, give up his savage amusements of hunting the elk and other wild animals of the plain, and to betake himself to fasting and praying on the highest apex of that wild and desolate range of mountains which formed the southern boundary of his*

61 A good map can be found at
    http://www.haroldstreet.org.uk/waypoints/download/?list=hewitts&area=ireland

62 As part of his compiled letters to the Ordnance Survey Headquarters in Dublin. You can read them all (in his own handwriting) at:
    http://www.askaboutireland.ie/aai-files/assets/ebooks/OSI-Letters/DOWN_14%20C%2013.pdf

kingdom". He remained ón the mountain for the rest of his days, conducting mass at one of the two rock cairns near the summit. Early nineteenth century writers noted their existence, but also that the Ordnance Survey men who camped atop Slieve Donard for several weeks in 1826, considerably altered them so as to make use of the stones for their own survey work.

The two much-disfigured stone cairns can still be seen at the summit. These predate the legendary tribal chief by some 2,500 – 3,500 years. As with so many places in Ireland, these are the stuff of legend. The story goes that one of the cairns covers a secret cave running all the way to the seashore near Newcastle and Saint Donard still lives inside.

For a short time in the sixteenth century an attempt was made to change Slieve Donard's name to Mount Malby. Given that this was the idea of Captain Nicholas Malby, an Englishman serving under Sir Henry Sidney, I think we can see why it didn't catch ón.

Should you wish to make your own *"pilgrimage"* to the top of Slieve Donard, although its the highest Hewitt, its not the hardest to ascend (or descend) with a reasonably maintained path to follow all the way. Having said that, it is a remote spot that has seen accidents including fatalities in the past. You have been warned (twice now!).

From the top of Slieve Donard, three close neighbours stand temptingly, each with its own glen to drop through before ascending.

Chimney Rock Mountain is to the south with the Bloody Bridge River valley in between. At 2,152 feet it is considerably lower than Slieve Donard, but don't let that fool you into believing it to be an easier ascent. Expect to scramble over boulders, across streams and through thick heather at times – and it gets pretty steep near the summit. This mountain has a tragic story behind it. A United States Air Force B26 training flight crashed into Chimney Rock on 10th April 1944 with the loss of five lives. A subsequent investigation concluded that pilot error in poor weather led to the accident, however, several commentators have noted the age of the plane and that it had been "retired" from active service, suggesting some sort of catastrophic technical failure. A memorial plaque was placed on the summit some years ago, but at the time of writing it has been removed for repair.

Slieve Commedagh is the nearest Hewitt, just a mile to the north west of Slieve

Donard. This is the second highest peak in the Mourne Mountains, just 80 metres lower than Slieve Donard. A Col, or saddle ridge connects the two meaning that a simultaneous attempt on the pair requires a drop of just 200 metres between the two. The Mourne Wall passes directly over the summit, as well as offering the most straightforward and accessible route from Slieve Donard. A stone tower forms part of the wall at the peak. One of the most popular routes for Slieve Commedagh and Slieve Donard involves starting from Donard Park in Newcastle. This has the advantage of a long-stay car park as well as giving climbers the reward of a complete ascent from sea level. A gentle walk beside the Glen River takes you through Donard Forest before emerging near to an old ice house[63]. The path to the two mountains now stretches out in front of you with the Mourne Wall in the distance. Take your time and take care as you approach the wall. The path is steep and rocky, and can be icy and slippery too. When you reach the wall you have three choices. Left will take you to the summit of Slieve Donard, while right will lead you to the top of Slieve Commedagh. From here you can also follow the path of the infamous Brandy Pad towards Hare's Gap along the col between Slieve Commedagh and Slieve Beg – a route well-trodden by smugglers.

Cove Mountain is almost due west of Slieve Donard and has a very interesting, if unimaginatively-named natural feature – *Cove Cave*. When is a cave not a cave? That's a tough one, especially when you consider that Cove Cave has two openings, one in the face of a buttress, and a second (safety note: only use this as an exit unless you are experienced climbers with all the gear) is higher up on the floor of a plateau. Some might say it is more of a tunnel than a cave. Having said that, Cove Cave is still a popular place with hill walkers. Visible from the footpath, access requires a difficult scrambling ascent over boulders and loose rocks. If you make it inside, don't let your new-found confidence get the better of you. The cave interior is dark, uneven, sloping and can be very wet. The rock face to the side may also look appealing, but leave it to the professionals to climb. To find Cove Cave, leave your vehicle in the car park at Carrick Little and use one of the many maps available in the nearby visitors centre and cafe[64]. One

---

63 The forest park has four waymarked walks. Download them all at:
http://www.walkni.com/d/walks/253/Map%20of%20Donard%20Forest.pdf

64 Most of the maps are available on the Walk Northern Ireland website. One that incorporates Cove Mountain is here:
http://www.walkni.com/d/walks/579/Central%20Mournes.pdf

of the most dramatic approaches to Cove Mountain includes a walk through the Devil's Coach Road, a huge gully in the side of Slieve Beg. This northern approach to Cove Mountain is possibly the most rewarding, but with sheer drops and misty conditions likely at the drop of a hat, it is a hike to be given the highest regard for personal safety.

Slievelamagan[65] is one of the so-called Mourne Seven Sevens, due to its height being over 700 metres along with six other peaks[66]. Most choose to tackle this challenging hike in conjunction with an assault on Slieve Beg and Cove Mountain, but the southerly approach from Ben Crom Dam is shorter, yet more draining. The reality is that whichever way you go, Slievelamagan is a tough climb. Don't forget you'll have to come back down too, leg muscles and tendons working as brakes is, if anything, harder on them than climbing up. The name itself translates as "by hands and feet" giving the clearest indication this is one of the hardest of the Mourne Mountains to conquer. But what a reward awaits. A columnist in the *Daily Telegraph* recently called this *"pyramid peak"* a *"scenic highlight"* offering *"a beautifully panoramic eyrie"*. A little way to the south, beyond the scars of age-old granite cutting is the Blue Lough *"a calm round tarn of remarkable picturesqueness"*. The latter quote is taken from Robert Lloyd Praeger's *Official Guide to County Down and the Mourne Mountains*, written for the Belfast and County Down Railway in 1900. Praeger described the extent of quarrying at the time, observing on the eastern face of Slievelamagan *"a busy colony of granite-cutters at work on the rough slope, splitting blocks of stone into slices with wedges and dressing them into window-sills and kerb-stones"*.

Just **Slieve Binnian** remains on our eastern tour of the Mourne's Hewitts. If you've been keeping count you'll realise we are only up to number six of seven peaks. That's because the *mountain of the little peak*, has not one, but two summits to reach. Binnian itself has an elevation of 2,451 feet, with the North Top at 2,224 feet. Older texts such as Fraser's 1844 *Handbook for Travellers in Ireland* use the name Slieve Bingian for the same place. Writing in 1901, Lewis

---

65 Sometimes separated into two words – Slieve Lamagan and often pronounced locally as *Lavigan*.

66 An annual challenge walk takes in all seven peaks in the following order: Slieve Donard 850m, Slieve Commedagh 765m, Slieve Lamagan 704m, Slieve Binnian 747m, Slieve Meelbeg 708m, Slieve Meelmore 704m, Slieve Bearnagh 727m

Moore of the Yorkshire Ramblers' Club contrasted Slieve Donard's *"isolated and dome-shaped"* elevation with Bingian's *"rocky and serrated"* ridges[67]. With the Mourne Wall passing right over the summit, no walking guide is needed here – just follow the granite-brick road if you want the easiest route to navigate. However, this is pretty step and other routes are available. In Irish *Sliabh Binneáin* means the *mountain of the little peak* – a reference to one of a pair of stone tors on each of the summits. Further granite tors are passed when following the well-trodden path between the two peaks. Slieve Binnian was once a major centre for quarrying with some very noteworthy legacy landmarks. To the east overlooking Annalong wood is the site of Douglas Crag, with the stone remains of the quarry-workers homes nearby. It is an eerily silent landscape with part-worked granite blocks littering the ground. Beneath the mountain, the Binnian Tunnel is one of those oft-overlooked pieces of engineering that warrant closer examination. Dug between 1947 and 1951 to divert water from the Annalong Valley to the Silent Valley Reservoir, the, eight foot square, two and a half mile long tunnel passes beneath half a mile of solid granite mountain! Over 150 men were employed on the task, split into two teams working from opposite ends. There were no technological navigating aids in those days, yet, when the teams finally cut through to meet up, their opposing centre-points were just two inches out from one another. The Silent Valley Visitors Centre has more information on the construction of the tunnel and operates a seasonal open-topped bus tour encompassing both ends of this incredible engineering success.

Moving on to the seven Hewitt peaks to the west of the reservoir, we'll start with the pair furthest from the coast – **Shanlieve** and **Eagle Mountain**. The two are so close to one another and linked by the Mourne Wall that most climb both together in a single trip. Eagle is the higher of the two and from its summit cairn offers (in good weather) unobstructed views of almost the entire Mourne range. Poor visibility is, unfortunately, a perennial problem in these parts, highlighted tragically in 2010 when three men died (the pilot and two passengers) after the helicopter they were flying in struck the west face of Shanlieve. Fog was so thick that hill walkers nearby heard the helicopter fly by and then crash but saw nothing until they found the burning wreckage just 100 feet or so below the

---

67 Moore, L. (1901) The Ancient Kingdom Of Mourne. Yorkshire Ramblers' Club Journal Volume 1 Number 3: pp155-172. Leeds: YRC

summit. Investigators found that a vital ground detection warning system was not switched on, but if the helicopter had been a little higher or a hundred yards further south, the accident would not have happened[68].

Eagle Mountain is higher, but attracts more hikers because of its imposing eastern cliffs overlooking the Pigeon Rock River valley and the Windy Gap. Consensus opinion is that the gap is so named due to the high likelihood of being caught by some particularly gusty weather rather than because of the way the snake-like river meanders through the valley. Most go with win-dee but I rather like wine-dee myself. Either way, don't confuse this Windy Gap with its namesake in the Dromara Hills[69] further inland. There are those that prefer their mountain views from the summits and others who like to look up to them – the mountains that is. From Windy Gap are some of the most spectacular views of the Western Mournes to be had.

Slieve Muck – the *hill of the pig*, gets your eyes peeled for signs of porcine life. Look carefully at the old dry stone walls here. The rounded granite boulders used here show two things – firstly, an awareness that building walls with many small gaps in them, allows a certain amount of wind to pass through, improving a wall's ability to withstand storm force winds. Secondly, these walls weren't built to mark out fields of crops, but to keep livestock in. You can guess the rest. But that's not the end of the story. In Irish, the word *muc* can indeed mean a pig, but it can also mean a *rounded hill*, as in the shape of a pig's back. Which, coincidentally or otherwise, is remarkably like the profile of Slieve Muck.

When I tell you to allow two hours to walk to the summit of Slieve Muck from the car park on the Banns Road beside Crocknafeola Wood and that you will be following a broad gravel track as well as the Mourne Wall (again!) for much of it, don't get thinking this is going to be easy. It isn't. A columnist in the *Irish Times* some years ago described having to resort to *"all fours"* for the steepest part of the ascent. But is the effort worth it? The view west over the Rostrevor Forest to Slieve Gullion in South Armagh is about as good as it gets. Save some energy too, you may well want to follow Batt's Wall (the Mourne Wall's kid brother) all the

---

68 Should you wish to read it, the official Air Accident Investigation Report can be downloaded from: www.gov.uk/aaib-reports/agusta-a109a-ii-n2nr-23-october-2010

69 For more information on the Dromara *"Windy Gap"*, visit: http://www.walkni.com/walks/2530/windy-gap-pad/

way over Pigeon Rock Mountain too. Pigeon Rock may not be a Hewitt at just 1750 feet elevation[70] but its too good to miss.

Slieve Loughshannagh is our next stop. This can also be reached from Slieve Muck, this time by following the Mourne Wall along a ridge northwards passing Lough Shannagh below to the east. In the summer months this is a popular introduction to the Mournes for families with children as the moorland is often dry and paths well defined should you choose not to follow the wall. For many, this is a stopping off point on the way to **Slieve Meelbeg** and **Slieve Meelmore** further along the same ridge (with a short col to traverse)[71]. These are two of the Mourne Seven Sevens and so command respect as challenging ascents, even with the wall to follow for much of the route. Meelbeg is often described as inferior to Meelmore, its slightly lower twin, but the views to the north-west in the direction of Belfast from Meelbeg are some of the finest to be had in the Western Mournes. Meelbeg and Meelmore are respectively, in Irish, the little mountain of the ants and the big mountain of the ants[72]. Neither are particularly little or large and I'm not aware of any hikers having nasty encounters with any biting, stinging or spraying creatures, but I'd pack some antiseptic cream just in case if I were you. Remember also that Meelbeg, the "*little*" mountain is actually the higher of the pair. Meelmore has a rather nice stone cairn on the summit to aim for.

Our final mountain is **Slieve Bearnagh,** the highest peak of the western Mournes at 2,435 feet. The *mountain of the gap*, can be approached from one of two gaps (or cols). To the west is *Pollaphuca* and on the opposite side is *Hare's Gap*. The Mourne Wall also crosses the summit from east to west. One commentator suggests Bearnagh to be possibly the only mountain requiring hands to leave pockets. I'm not sure whether that is due to the difficulty of the ascent or the

---

70 It doesn't even make it into the Marilyns list because it is classed as a minor summit.

71 Download a circular walking route here:
http://www.walkni.com/walks/576/meelmore-and-meelbeg/

72 As before, this is an oft-disputed translation of the word *miol*. Others argue them to be the little *bald* mountain and the big *bald* mountain respectively, due to neither having the granite tors commonly found on the summits elsewhere. For a full guide to place-names and their translations try this: http://www.mountaineering.ie/_files/Paul%20Tempan%20Irish%20Mountain%20Placenames%20-%20Feb%202012.pdf

urge to applaud the magnificent sights at the summit – or possibly both. Bearnagh is capped by a pair of distinctive granite tors, with a low dip, or gap, between them. It is this gap that gave the mountain its name, not the much larger gaps either side. Of all the points to stop and contemplate, perhaps it is on this peak that C.S. Lewis got some of his inspiration for the sprawling mountainous landscape of Narnia. He once wrote of his time here *"it made me feel that at any moment a giant might raise its head over the next ridge".* With its glacier scraped volcanic contours, strange conical tors, spiny ridges, forests, lakes and winding valleys it is easy to see how the view from Slieve Bearnagh could fuel the imagination.

For a summary of the geology of the Mourne Mountains, if you can bear a little dated terminology, we need to look no further than Lewis's 1837 *Topographical Directory of County Down*[73]:

"The Mourne mountains, extending from Dundrum bay to Carlingford bay, form a well- defined group, of which Slieve Donard is the summit, being, according to the Ordnance survey, 2796 feet above the level of the sea, and visible, in clear weather, from the mountains near Dublin : granite is its prevailing constituent. To the north of these mountains, Slieve Croob, composed of sienite, and Slieve Anisky, of hornblende, both in Lower Iveagh , constitute an elevated tract dependent upon, though at some distance from, the main group. Hornblende and primitive greenstone are abundant on the skirts of the granitic district. Mica slate has been noticed only in one instance. Exterior chains of transition rocks advance far to the west and north of this primitive tract, extending westward across Monaghan into Cavan, and on the north-east to the southern cape of Belfast Lough , and the peninsula of Ardes.

"The primitive nucleus bears but a very small proportion, in surface, to these exterior chains, which are principally occupied by grauwacke and grauwacke slate, In the Mourne Mountains and the adjoining districts an extensive formation of granite occurs, but without the varieties found in Wicklow, agreeing in character rather with the newer granite of the Wernerians: it

---

73 For an up-to-date explanation with diagrams (all 106 pages of it), download this: https://www.ringofgullion.org/publication/geological-field-guide-cooley-gullion-mourne-slieve-croob/

constitutes nearly the whole mass of the Mourne mountains, whence it passes across Carlingford bay into the county of Louth.

"On the north-west of these mountains, where they slope gradually into the plain, the same rock reaches Rathfriland, a table land of inconsiderable elevation. Within the boundaries now assigned, the granite is spread over a surface of 324 square miles, comprehending the highest ground in the North of Ireland. Among the accidental ingredients of this formation are crystallised hornblende, chiefly abounding in the porphyritic variety, and small reddish garnets in the granular : both varieties occur mingled together on the top of Slieve Donard. Water-worn pebbles, of porphyritic sienite, occasionally containing red crystals of feldspar and iron pyrites, are very frequent at the base of the Mourne mountains, between Rosstrevor and Newcastle: they have probably been derived from the disintegration of neighbouring masses of that rock, since, on the shore at Glassdrummin, a ledge of porphyritic sienite, evidently connected with the granitic mass of the adjoining mountain, projects into the sea.

"Greenstone slate rests against the acclivities of the Mourne mountains, but the strata never rise high, seldom exceeding 500 feet. Attempts have been made to quarry it for roofing, which it is thought would be successful if carried on with spirit. Feldspar porphyry occurs in the bed of the Finish , north- west of Slieve Croob, near Dromara, and in a decomposing state at Ballyroany, north-east of Rathfriland. Slieve Croob seems formed, on its north-east and south-east sides, of different varieties of sienite, some of them porphyritic and very beautiful : this rock crops out at intervals from Bakaderry to the top of Slieve Croob, occupying an elevation of about 900 feet."

Don't get carried away. Tackle these great mountains in a measured way. Some people spend a lifetime here, returning again and again. Remember also, we've only mentioned the 14 Hewitts, the Mourne range also has dozens of smaller peaks to conquer and many find that the best way to savour the sights of a mountain range is from the many valley floors that wind between the countless peaks. To get to the top of any mountain *the only way is up* they say. That's true, but there's often a variety of ways up, and, if anything you'll use more energy coming back down again. So, plan carefully, don't take on too much, too soon and enjoy the experience.

You'll certainly want some rest time after taking on the Mourne Mountains, and

64

perhaps a day trip to Bangor might be just the ticket.

Further Reading:

R. L. Praeger, Official Guide to County Down and the Mourne Mountains, Linenhall Press (1900) available free from www.archive.org

P. Dillon, The Mountains of Ireland, Ciccerone Press (2013)

I is for Inver Beg

The seaside town of Bangor has gone by many names throughout its long history. Taxation records from the fourteenth century identify the settlement of *Inver Bece*, with earlier documents using the similar name of *Inver Beg*. William Reeves 1847 *Ecclesiastical Antiquities of Down, Connor, and Dromore* identifies Bangor as *Benchair*, most likely derived from the old Irish *Beannchor*.

What these old names reveal is something about the people who lived here. *Beannchor* ultimately derives from Old Norse words meaning the *horned bay*, while *Inver Beg* is the *mouth of the Beg* – a small stream, now culverted and obscured from view by the modern town and marina. *Inver* is commonly seen in Scotland, Inverness being the most memorable example, and originated as the Scottish Irish word *inbhir*. So Bangor has both Scots and Viking ancestry to explore.

Before that, there is a further name to consider. According to several sources including John Gorton's 1833 *Topographical Dictionary of Great Britain and Ireland*, Bangor was also once known as the *Vale of Angels*. Gorton noted the founding of an abbey by Saint Comgall in the sixth century which once held up to 3,000 monks, but neglected to mention the reputed origin of the name. Apparently, Saint Patrick rested here and had an angelic vision which inspired Comgall, a soldier, to lay down his sword and found a monastery.

Comgall ran a highly-disciplined Abbey, with days and nights filled with prayer, manual labour, abstinence and fasting. Perhaps we can use his own words to discern his methodology:

"If the cultivator of the land and husbandman, when preparing the soil to commit to it the seed, does not consider his work all done when he has broken up the earth with the strong share, and by the action of the plough has reduced the stubborn soil, but further endeavours to cleanse the ground of unfruitful weeds, to clear it of injurious rubbish, the spreading shoots of thorns and brambles, fully persuaded that his land will never produce a good crop unless it be reclaimed from mischievous plants, . . . how much more does it behove us, who believe the hope of our fruits to be laid up, not on earth, but in heaven, to

cleanse from vicious passions the field of our heart".[74]

Now, to attempt to untangle the other names. It's true that the profile of Bangor Bay does somewhat resemble the shape of a bull's horns. However, *Beannchor* may simply derive from two Old Irish words *benn* and *cor*, meaning the erection of defensive barriers (or prongs) to protect the monastery. As with all things Irish, there is a folk story to murky the picture. According to legend, a pair of warriors returning from France with a shipload of cattle, found that the bovine creatures all shed their horns mysteriously. The area thus became *Trácht Bennchoir*, with *Trácht* meaning a *strand*, *benn* is a *horn* and *cor* can mean to *cast off*; so another possibility is that Bangor was originally *"the strand of the horn-casting"*.

Other theories have been published, including in the pages of the U*lster Journal of Archaeology* where the name of Bangor has been suggested to mean the blessed choir – a clear reference to the singing from the Abbey, or even the head of a curlew, although I'm at something of a loss to explain that one.

One final intriguing source is an ancient manuscript known as the *Antiphonary of Bangor*. A 36-page manuscript compiled in Latin, it has been dated to the year 691 CE. Because the manuscript's title is *Antiphonarium Monasterii Benchorensis* some use this to argue that Bangor was known as Beannchor or something similar before the Vikings first raided here a century or so later. However, they fail to appreciate the manuscript was not named until the seventeenth century, by which time the Scottish and English Plantation of Ulster was well under way.

Perhaps climbing the Mourne Mountains was easier than this after all?

What we can say with some certainty is that Comgall, the founder of the abbey was a local man, born in County Antrim. The Vikings had many raids into County Down and inflicted much damage to the monastery as well as stealing the relics amassed by Comgall before Abbot Malachy undertook extensive repairs and renovations in the twelfth century. The only part of this that still stands – Malachy's Wall is alongside the Gate Lodge and runs adjacent to Abbey Street. The church that stands on the site today, is much more recent with a nineteenth century main building and a seventeenth century steeple erected by the resident Ulster-Scots atop a fifteenth century tower. Much of the stone used in construction came from Malachy's much-neglected structure. The building has

---

74 Extracted from John Stevenson's Two Centuries of Life in Down: 1600 – 1800 (1920)

not functioned as a monastery since Henry VIII dissolved them all in the sixteenth century.

Bangor was a significant enough settlement in the thirteenth century to warrant its inclusion on the late fourteenth century *mappa mundi* [75]alongside Jerusalem (as you might have expected in the centre), the Garden of Eden, and just three other locations in the whole of the island of Ireland.

To understand how the modern town of Bangor took shape, we need to turn back to the seventeenth century. James Hamilton, originally from Ayrshire, was *"given"*[76] a great swathe of land including Bangor by James I in recognition of his loyalty throughout the Nine Years War. He immediately *planted* several families from the lowlands of Scotland to farm and work his lands in exchange for low rents. By the time of the Plantation of Ulster, Hamilton had already moved in to a grand house in Bangor along with 80 other Scottish and English families of farmers, craftsmen, clergymen and merchants. Hamilton's residence a *"fayre stone house"* of 60 feet by 22 feet, according to a report by the Plantation Commission in 1611, stood on the site of the current Town Hall. He didn't stay long, perhaps anticipating the need for a well-defended stronghold. The same report noted he was preparing to build another house three miles away in Holywood using *"two hundred thowsand of brickes with other materialles ready at the place, where there are some 20 houses inhabited with English and Scottes"*. in 1625 he moved to Killyleagh where he claimed the twelfth century castle and added substantially to it, including the fortification of large courtyard walls.

Hamilton was already in his eighties at the time of the 1641 Irish Rebellion. The coup ultimately failed, but not before the deaths of thousands of English and Scottish settlers. Hamilton had already gained support from the King to raise a regiment of 1,000 men so that Bangor was well defended and suffered much less badly than many other places.

On the seafront beside Bangor's very modern marina is the Old Custom House, built by Hamilton in 1637 as Bangor expanded rapidly following King James granting the town rights as a port in 1620. It is a strange sight looking cylindrical from one aspect and square from the opposite side, and has a strange history to

---

75 You can see it in Hereford Cathedral, England.

76 I use the term in quotes as many argue the land wasn't the Kings to *"give"*.

boot. Charles Monck, Surveyor-General at the time cruelly, but probably fairly observed it and wrote *"if it were finished it were the best custom house in Ireland"*. Nowadays, the tower house and tower serve as the resort's Visitor Information Centre, but the building has also been home to hot sea water baths, an antiques shop and private residence at various points.

When Anne Hamilton (daughter of James) married into the influential Ward family, Bangor soon benefited from further and long-standing investment. Colonel Robert Ward (1754 – 1831) ploughed his money into two large cotton mills and a financial and industrial infrastructure that included Bangor's first market house. This gave much-needed if low-paid work to over 300 local people but did very little to give Bangor any character or visual appeal. Writing in 1920, John Stevenson noted that many still lived in *"warm and durable"* *"mud or clay houses, well-roofed, roughcast on outer wall surfaces and lime-washed within"* dating back possibly as early as 1740 when a property seller recorded *"houses are built with stone and ruff-casted, not built with Mudd like the rest of Bangor houses"*.

Industrial Bangor in the first half of the nineteenth century was *"crowded and dirty"* according to one writer, the two steam-powered mills (the oldest on High Street, and the second, all five storeys of it, on the site of the McKee Clock Arena and sunken garden on Quay Street) belched out clouds of smoke and soot constantly over the rooftops. The town had an ever-increasing need for coal, both industrial and domestic, and the *Ferguson and Neill* family businesses catered well for that demand, in turn adding to the expanding commercial success of Bangor Harbour which had been built in 1757. Lewis's *Topographical Dictionary* had this to say:

"In 1831 it (Bangor) contained 563 houses, most of which are indifferently built, and is much frequented for sea-bathing during the summer. The streets are neither paved nor lighted, but are kept very clean and the inhabitants are but indifferently supplied with water".

The McKee Clock Tower was erected in 1915, following a most generous donation of £200 by James McKee of Hamilton Road a rate collector for the District Council. The tower was made by builder John McNeilly of Victoria Road from granite slabs quarried at Ballycullen near Newtownards to a design by Henry Bell, the town surveyor. McKee passed away four years later and a black granite slab first inscribed when the tower was completed in 1915, required an additional line. The full inscription reads:

8 JULY 1915
THIS STONE RECORDS THE APPRECIATION
OF THE BANGOR URBAN DISTRICT COUNCIL
FOR THE GENEROUS GIFT OF THIS CLOCK
TO HIS NATIVE TOWN BY
JAMES McKEE
THE ABOVE JAMES McKEE DIED ON 28TH APRIL 1919

In one of the three occasions[77] Bangor was bombed during World War II, the McKee Clock took a direct hit. The bomb failed to detonate and the tower suffered only minor damage – and didn't even stop the clock.

From the beginning of the twentieth century Bangor had begun a massive metamorphosis, from a noisy, dirty industrial town into a flourishing seaside resort. Mary Lowry had this to say about it in 1913[78]:

"The town of Bangor ... is a very popular and prosperous seaside town and a favourite holiday resort ... The change and improvement within the last ten years is remarkable, and every year seems to extend the town".

She described how:

"Almost every general shop shows festoons of sand shoes, cascades of little buckets and bunches of wooden spades to delight the heart of the young Belfastians. The smaller builders design some wondrous architecture on the sandy beach, while the older generation disport themselves in the blue waters of the bay".

And there she spelled out what caused Bangor to change – the rise of Belfast. As the City grew and its population (but by no means all of them) became more affluent with more free time, so the concept of holidays and day trips to the seaside took off. Belfastians could just hop on a train and be in Bangor in a

---

77 April 1941, Luftwaffe bombing left five dead and caused significant damage. September 1940, incendiary raid, started several fires, but no injuries or fatalities. January 1940, friendly fire attack from RFAS Serbol conducting exercises in Belfast Lough with live shells – damage to property, no loss of life.

78 Writing in her bestseller of the period – *The Story of Belfast.*

matter of minutes. The *Belfast and Ulster Towns Directory* for 1910 called Bangor *"the principal Sea Bathing Resort in the North of Ireland"* imploring visitors to take advantage of the very good outdoor bathing facilities. At this time, Bangor's residential population had increased by 80% to 9,000 in a decade, with the number swelling to over 20,000 in the summer months *"by the large number of visitors who take up temporary residence"*. The directory listed attraction after attraction, including *"an extensive promenade pier, from which passenger steamers ply in the summer months"*, the beautiful *"promenade which skirts the bay"*, with its *"marine gardens"*, as well as a fine 18-hole golf course, yachting centre, shops and hotels.

Proposals for constructing a pier at Bangor were first submitted in the form of a petition (or certificate) published in the 31st July 1813 edition of the *Belfast Monthly Magazine*. No fewer than 250 signatories put their names forward supporting the need for *"erecting piers at Bangor and Portnessock"*[79] so that *"in the course of the year, more passages may be made, than between Donaghadee and Portpatrick"*. Perhaps a pointer to the cosmopolitan interest in Bangor was that just five of those signing their names were actually from the town, with the rest originating in other parts of Ireland, Scotland, England, even one from the United States.

Lewis's *Topographical Dictionary of Ireland* establishes that the petition was not successful making mention of just *"A small pier … built about the year 1760, by means of a parliamentary grant of £500 to the corporation for promoting and carrying on the inland navigation of Ireland"*. The town did eventually get a pair of piers – North and South to go with the older Central pier, but the modern marina in stone and concrete has replaced the old timbers. But not before a large colony of black guillemots moved in around 1911, taking advantage of the decaying wood to nest beneath the North Pier – these are Bangor's famous *"penguins"*, who now happily continue to use the purposely designed concrete nesting boxes built into the reconstructed pier. Today more than 25 pairs of Bangor Penguins make their family homes in the walls of Bangor Marina. Don't expect to see them between the beginning of August and early January when they shed and grow new plumage and spent most of their time on the water.

Since 2005 the North Pier has been named the Eisenhower Pier and is now home to an extensive mosaic display telling the story of Bangor's role in the 1944 Normandy landings as well as other key events in the history of the seaside

---

79 Portnessock in Wigtownshire, Scotland.

resort. The General himself stayed in Bangor for two nights before addressing the large American fleet including three battleships and thirty thousand men assembled in Belfast Lough offshore from the town. A plaque marking the renaming of the pier by one of Eisenhower's granddaughters can be seen next to the lifeboat station.

Adjacent to the marina is Pickie Fun Park at the entrance to the marine gardens. Attractions include mini-golf, racing karts and a long-standing (should that be floating?) feature – the Bangor Swans, a relaxing pedalo water ride. This was the site of Pickie Pool, a large open-air (but not heated!) swimming pool with a high diving board. Opened in 1937, the pool was one of Bangor's landmarks sacrificed to make way for the new marina complex in the early 1980's. A recent addition to Bangor's rapidly expanding leisure facilities is the Aurora complex, which includes a large swimming pool (indoors and heated) as well as water slides and a gymnasium.

Look out for the *"Pastie Supper"* sculpture close to Pickie's Fun Park[80]. Don't confuse a Northern Irish *pastie* with a Cornish *pasty*. Ask for a pastie in Bangor or similar and you'll get something resembling a battered burger whose contents are likely to include minced pork, potatoes, onions and herbs. Traditionally these were a bright, almost scarily bright, pink inside, due to the addition of cochineal colouring, although this practice has almost disappeared from use. The bronze sculpture is shaped so that you can sit beside the pastie-eating man to offer a lovely photo opportunity, – which hundreds take advantage of every year. What most of them miss is the map of old Bangor on the back of the sculpture.

The renovated Queen's Parade, new marina and all-round clean-up of the town centre have all contributed to the position Bangor finds itself in today, as officially the most desirable place to live in Northern Ireland[81]. Some residents jokingly (or not?) refer to this change in demographics as resulting in two types of Bangor residents – the *"have-nots"* and the *"have-yachts"*. For a time, the iconic Royal Hotel on Quay Street, a venue that once hosted Van Morrison amongst others and which rather immodestly called itself *"the spirit of Bangor"*, faced demolition and replacement with a 14-storey skyscraper hotel. After

---

80 I haven't included a specific location as he may well be on the move again following complaints that photographing him in his present location in front of the fun park may mean that playing children are inadvertently photographed without their consent.

81 In a 2007 survey conducted for UTV.

several years of uncertainty including four years of dereliction, the building is presently being remodelled as a set of luxury seaside apartments and restaurants. A plaque on the side of the building establishes it to be over 240 years old. It reads:

"Built by James Lyons in the year of our Lord 1773"

Lyons and his wife are commemorated on a gravestone in the grounds of Bangor Abbey. The inscription reveals that James died the following year aged around 60 years old.

Near to the Aurora complex is Bangor Castle, completed in 1852 at a cost of £9,000 as a home for Robert Edward Ward. The building includes the remains of Comgall's abbey and at one time boasted no less than 35 bedrooms as well as a very large, and well-used music saloon. The Ward/Hamilton family connection being represented by the inclusion of a great stained-glass panel picturing the Ward ancestry as far back as King Edward III[82]. It was a magnificent Gothic structure, but not to all tastes. Robert's daughter Matilda, later to become Lady Clanmorris observed *"there was not a comfortable room in the house"*.

For several decades the building, and its very large estate have been managed by the local borough council who now use parts of the castle for administrative purposes. Here you will also find the North Down Museum in what was originally the courtyard and stable block for Robert Wards three-storey limestone manor house. During the spring and summer months the Victorian Walled Garden is one of Bangor's must-see but less well known attractions. The gardens have been painstakingly restored to represent a typical garden from the Victorian era, with flowers, shrubs, herbs and vegetables.

Don't miss the museum's finest treasures. Thomas Raven's complete set of maps drawn up between 1625 and 1626 give a fascinating insight into Bangor and North Down in the early years of the Plantation era. These have been painstakingly digitised so that every last detail can be studied by visitors. Also look out for the Ballycroghan Swords found in a field on the edge of Bangor in 1949. These date from around 500 BCE.

---

82 The decline of the Hamilton's and their connection with the Wards is a complicated story including treachery and at least one case of poisoning. PRONI have thousands of family papers in their archives. A good place to start if you want more is here: https://www.nidirect.gov.uk/publications/introduction-ward-papers

An important artefact that forms the centrepiece of the museum's Bangor Abbey collection is the Bangor Bell. Reputedly discovered in1780 by the great grandfather of Lieutenant-Colonel John McCance (1843-1922), of Knocknagoney House, near Holywood. It had been buried beneath the grounds of the Abbey. There is general agreement that the bell was most likely hidden to avoid it being looted by Viking raiders. The 14-inch high bronze bell was crafted around 825 CE in a single piece, including the handle. It is decorated with an incised Celtic cross and intricate border-work and would have been used by the monks as a call to prayer. The bell does not have an internal clapper so monks would have to strike it with a hammer to make it ring out.

The rediscovered bell passed through several hands, including those of a Belfast doctor, before ending up in the Bangor Museum.

Bangor now has a second "*Bell*". Sited nearby is a 14-foot high Bangor Bell sculpture commissioned by Ards and North Down Borough Council and created by Cork based sculptor Holger C. Lönze. The bell has been carefully cast to be in the same proportions as the original, but this one, known as *Fluctus Angelorum* or the *Wave of Angels*, is designed to look like the surface of the ocean. These "waves" symbolise the epic sea voyage made by Columbanus, a contemporary of Comgall who sailed to Brittany in his fortieth year.

Dotted around Bangor are the remains of at least 25 ancient *Raths* – round earthen enclosures built as fortified residences for druidic chiefs. The largest of these is at Rath Gael and extends for more than two acres.

Before we leave Bangor, I am compelled to mention one final Hamilton – William, the poet of Bangor. I pass no judgement on the merits of his eighteenth century writing, but offer this extract from the September 1821 edition of the *Literary Journal*:

"Hamilton of Bangor is well known, and has been long justly appreciated as standing high among those secondary poets who dribble unmeaning love songs".

The journal went on to exemplify Hamilton's work with this passage:

"I'd be a miser too, nor give
An alms to keep a God alive"

describing it as one of a

"few absurd extravagances ... in the midst of surrounding nonsense". [83]

And with that, our time in Bangor is up, and we head along the coast to a neighbour and one-time fierce competitor.

Further Reading:

J. Stevenson, Two Centuries of Life in Down: 1600 – 1800, Linenhall Press (1920) is available online at https://archive.org/details/twocenturiesofli00stevuoft

A.G. Bell, Bangor: Then and Now, Colourpoint (2012)

---

83 Should you wish to find out for yourself, Hamilton's Poems on Several Occasions can be found online at: https://catalog.hathitrust.org/Record/100115209

J is for John, John, John and … John?

To tell the story of Donaghadee we will start with three men who shared a forename, John Smeaton and a pair of John Rennies.

The book *Two Centuries of Life in Down, 1600-1800*, written in 1920 by Stevenson (another John) notes

"By 1607 it was not uncommon for Scotch folk in days of favouring weather to ride, carrying wares for sale from Stranraer to Portpatrick, leave their horses there, cross the channel, hire horses at Donaghadee, ride to Newtownards, sell their produce, and, reversing the journey, reach homes round Loch Ryan by bedtime".

In a 1637 statement of customs revenues, Donaghadee was the third highest revenue provider in Ulster behind Carrickfergus and Bangor. It has never been a big town, but has a long history as an important port and harbour. It is the harbour and lighthouse that will be the focus of attention in this chapter.

Donaghadee had long been used as a haven for ships before Hugh Montgomery invested in the harbour's first true stone quay between 1616 and 1640. Montgomery was a Scot, a close friend of James Hamilton and a loyal supporter of King James I, resulting in the King granting him a large part of north-east Down. Like his acquaintance was doing down the road in Bangor, Montgomery lost no time in populating the Donaghadee area with Scots families.

Published in 1744, *The Antient and Present State of the County of Down* had this to say about Montgomery's quay at Donaghadee, calling it:

"a curving quay about 400 feet long and 22 feet wide built of uncemented stones"

It was this lack of cement that resulted in significant tidal damage over the years leading to the introduction of John Smeaton. It is well known that Smeaton took charge of the redevelopment of Portpatrick harbour in the 1770's. His plans make several specific references to the importance of the crossing between there and Donaghadee, and although little documentary evidence exists, the widely-held view is that it was Smeaton who advised on the extensive renovations to Donaghadee's crumbling harbour that took place under the stewardship of landlord, Daniel Delacherois.

The possibility of a Smeaton connection is very plausible. Smeaton definitely constructed the harbour and piers at Portpatrick, which also went by the name of Port Montgomery, being land owned by the same Montgomery family that had been planted in Donaghadee and operated a trade route between the two harbours. What makes this author doubtful, besides the fact that the Delacherois upgrade needed replacing itself after just forty years, is the lack of any evidence of personal involvement from within Smeaton's own writings. The surveyor was a meticulous note-taker and keeper of records, yet there is no mention of any plans for Donaghadee in his published writings. Now you know why the chapter title included a question mark.

Our next two Johns can be introduced without any such doubts.

John Rennie Senior was a Scottish civil engineer with an impressive *curriculum vitae*. As a young man he commenced his career working for James Watt in Staffordshire before setting up his own civil engineering business and digging many canals, including work on the revised Royal Canal between Dublin and the River Shannon. He also designed and/or built no fewer than four of London's Thames bridges including the critically-acclaimed and much-copied Waterloo Bridge, combining stone with cast-iron in ways not seen before. Rennie somehow found time to engineer many docks and harbours including those at Dún Laoghaire, Holyhead, Portsmouth and Hull before Donaghadee. He lived to witness Arthur Hill, the Third Marquess of Downshire lay the foundation stone of the new harbour on 1st August 1821, but died two months later.

Rennie's design was for a deep-water harbour, necessary to allow safe passage for the Irish Mail Packet Service running between Donaghadee and Portpatrick nineteen nautical miles away. It was a strange, but effective design, with a curved southern pier and a shorter northern breakwater that has no direct land access. To achieve this required considerable blasting of stone from the sea-bed, much of which was reused to form the seaward faces of the two independent jaw-like piers.

John Rennie's oldest son, our next John, took over the Donaghadee Harbour project working alongside renowned Scottish engineer David Logan, whose own credits included assisting Robert Stevenson's construction of a lighthouse on the treacherous Bell Rock off Scotland's east coast.

In a perhaps unwise attempt to keep the peace with local fishermen, John Rennie, the younger, agreed to leave the old crumbling quay in place. It was finally removed in 1833, perhaps in a less than satisfactory manner, leading to surveyor, Royal Navy Captain George Evans to report despondently in 1840 "*I found a quantity of large stones extending from just inside the entrance*" concluding "*Donaghadee, in its present contracted and shallow state, will not admit of larger steamers than those now employed*". And then, possibly in two sentences he wrote off any possibility of future investment, writing "*it is evident, however, that it is too small to be of any service as a harbour or refuge. It will always require an annual expenditure to keep it up, and has not capacity for admitting that length of vessel which alone could ensure regularity and safety in conveying the mails across the sea*".

Perhaps we should be thankful.

If Donaghadee had proved to be more viable as a port for larger steam-powered ships, it might have grown into a town the size of, say, Larne. Don't get me wrong, there's nothing wrong with Larne, as you may have read in my Antrim Coast guide. Donaghadee today, is a very attractive small seaside harbour town (or largish village) with a lovely harbour and lighthouse.

The lighthouse was a later addition to the South Pier, being completed between 1834 and 1836. At first the fifty-foot high tower remained undressed – bare, pale grey limestone exposed to the elements. It took almost forty years before it was painted to look how it appears today, brilliant white with a black plinth. It also took 30 years for the keeper to be granted accommodation on the pier itself, prior to 1864, he had to live in a rented home in the village itself.

A century after being built, however, Donaghadee Lighthouse was the setting for a first – the first unwatched electric light in the whole of Ireland, and 20,000 times brighter to boot!

Donaghadee itself has an interesting legacy feature. Blasting the seabed in the 1820's needed a lot of dynamite, which in turn needed a place to store it safely and keep it dry. These were the earliest days of archaeology, and it is extremely unlikely that permission would be granted these days, but Rennie's engineers utilised Donaghadee's ancient (probably Norman at least) *motte*, and built a castellated structure on top of what is now known locally as "*the moat*". This tower, described as a "*castellated powder magazine*" by Lewis was also acknowledged by the same writer as being erected on the top of "*a rath, seventy feet high with a large platform on its summit commanding a fine view of the channel and surrounding country".* A second *"lofty"* tower was built around the same time, at the western end of Donaghadee, forming part of the village church, paid for by Captain Daniel Delacherois, whose family also donated a very heavy bell for the tower at the same time.

The Ulster-Scots connection with Donaghadee is not a story of one-way traffic. The daily packet ship to Portpatrick often carried young couples, aware that a minister in the Scottish town would marry them without the need for banns to be published or residency proved. According to some sources, the entire marriage formalities could be completed in the time it took the mail boat to unload, pick up the post for Ulster and disembark for the return trip to Donaghadee with the newly-weds on board.

Modern Donaghadee is a quiet, relatively peaceful resort, whose calm belies a past with periodic episodes of violent upheaval. It was here in the 1660's that Presbyterian Covenanters on the run from persecution in their native Scotland, found that they fared no better and often faced arrest and imprisonment. The town's Norman motte and bailey are clear indicators that the settlement had to be defended long before.

In fact, this is the site of a Bronze Age rath – and the scene of many struggles with Viking raiders, before being further raised and strengthened by a twelfth century Norman landholder. To tell his family story, we need to take a short trip offshore.

Due north of Donaghadee are a group of three islands – known as the Copeland Islands. They comprise, Copeland Island – the largest of the three, Lighthouse Island – which used to have one, but not any more, and Mew Island, which does still have a lighthouse. William and Henry Copland (also recorded as de Couplan) were known to be tenants of John de Courcy, with land including Donaghadee and these islands, but as with so many place-name origins, the story isn't quite so simple. At about the time of the Coplands, we find the islands documented in Norse as *Kaupmanna-eyjar* which broadly translates as the *merchants islands*. Documents from the period certainly support the belief that these islands served as trading posts for the Vikings. By 1575 this name had become *Copmans Iles* on at least one map[84]. The generally accepted view is that although there are

---

84 The name *Hellayn Harrons* was also seen at this time – *Kidney Islands*, the rough shape of the main island.

clear similarities between *Copmans* and *Copeland*, the two names were being used independently of one another.

The islands themselves are no longer inhabited. The last humans left shortly after the end of the Second World War. Prior to that, up to 100 hardy folk lived on these islands, making a living from farming and/or fishing and selling their wares in Donaghadee and neighbouring communities.

Returning to Donaghadee, and the subject of conflict, 1798 saw opposition to British rule come to a head with what became known as the Irish Rebellion. In County Down, Pike Sunday (10th June) bands of United Irishmen from Donaghadee, Bangor, Ballywater and Greyabbey marched on Newtownards[85] in an attempt to occupy the town. They met with intense musket-fire and were repelled, suffering many casualties.

For the last hundred years or so, Donaghadee has settled quietly into a nice little rhythm alongside Bangor, its busy, bustling seaside neighbour. If its tranquillity but not isolation you are looking for, this could be just the seaside resort for you.

One final venue, with something of a history is *Grace Neill's* – a pub and restaurant which lauds itself as the oldest surviving inn in Northern Ireland. It first opened in 1611 as the *"King's Arms"*, keeping that name until 1918 when its landlady died at the age of 98, after owning the inn for over 70 years and it was decided to rename the pub in her honour. Grace was known to be a strong-spirited woman who smoked a clay pipe and often greeted customers with a kiss and a hug.

We've now recorded a few encounters with Vikings and Normans along the Down Coast, so lets leave the King's Arms and head for the King's Castle and continue the theme by travelling south to the village of Ardglass.

Further Reading:

R. Frame & K. Simms, Colony & Frontier in Medieval Ireland, Continnuum (1995)

H. Allen, Donaghadee: An Illustrated History, White Row Press (2006)

---

85 They were led by Henry Monro, a man with local knowledge – he was a shopkeeper in the town. He survived the failed attack, but was captured and hanged a few days later.

K is for Käng's Kessel

It may look like Norse but the expression above is actually Ulster-Scots and means the *King's Castle*. This particular castle is in the coastal fishing village of Ardglass south-east of Downpatrick.

But it is a Norman Castle, dating from the twelfth century.

And, nowadays, extensively renovated it is a nursing home.

In 1833, the *Dublin Penny Journal* had this to say about it:

> "(King's Castle is) the largest of the **many** ancient castles of Ardglass"

The emphasis is my addition. How many villages can you think of with *many* castles? Time to dig a little deeper.

Let's start by looking at what Lewis recorded in 1837 on the subject:

> "there are many good houses in front of the harbour, adjoining which is a long range of building in the castellated style, called the New Works, although they are so old that nothing is known either of the time or the purpose of their erection. They form together a line of fortifications, 250 feet in length from east to west, and 24 feet in breadth, close to the shore; the walls are three feet in thickness and strengthened with three towers, one in the centre and one at each extremity. These buildings were originally divided into thirty-six apartments, eighteen on the ground floor and eighteen above, with a staircase in the centre; each of the lower apartments had a small arched door and a large square window, which renders it probable that they had been shops occupied by merchants at some very early period, possibly by the company of traders that settled here in the reign of Hen. IV. About the year 1789, Lord Chas. Fitzgerald, son of the Duke of Leinster, who was then proprietor, caused that portion of the building between the central and the western tower to be enlarged in the rear, and raised to the height of three stories in the castellated style; and from that time it has been called **Ardglass Castle**, and has been the residence of the proprietor of the estate. It was formerly called Horn Castle, either from a great quantity of horns found on the spot, or from a high pillar which stood on its summit previously to its being roofed; and near it is another castle, called **Cow'd**

Castle, signifying the want of horns, from a word in the Scottish dialect, of which many phrases are still in use in the province.

*In a direct line with Ardglass Castle, and due west of it, are Cow'd Castle above noticed, and **Margaret's Castle**, both square ancient structures having the lower stories arched with stone; and on the north-west side of the town, on a considerable elevation, are two other castles, about 20 feet distant from each other, the larger of which is called **King's Castle** and the smaller the **Tower**; they have been partly rebuilt and connected with a handsome pile of building in the castellated style. **Jordan's Castle**, previously noticed, is an elegant building, 70 feet high, standing in the centre of the town, and having at the entrance a well of excellent water".*

I make that *six* castles in a village of around 2,000 inhabitants!

That 1833 Dublin news-sheet also had this to say about the **King's Castle** "*It was a fortress of considerable size and strength; but is at present much dilapidated and falling to decay*". There were once a pair of towers on the Kildare Street site, dating from at least the fourteenth century, and possibly earlier. King's Castle is mentioned in accounts of the 1641 Lecale Rebellion. In *A History of Ireland and her People*, Eleanor Hull wrote "*The old English settlers – the Russells, Fitzsimons and Savages of Ardes and Lecale – took part in the dreadful work, considering themselves part of the native than of the new population*". The Russells she referred to were well established and influential in the area at the time[86]. Writing shortly after the events of 1641, the well-known Royalist Sir James Ware noted "*O Neal … had resolved to send some forces for Lecale, under the conduct of his son, to seize on the King's Castle of Ardglass*". Ware was talking about Con Óg O'Neill who fought alongside many of the Anglo-Irish Catholics at the time including George Russell. Ardglass saw many bloody skirmishes over the following twelve years before Sir James Montgomery finally overwhelmed resistance in the name of Cromwell.

A descendant of George, Charles Russell, a successful corn merchant of Killough, acquired the crumbling King's Castle shortly after part of it collapsed in 1830 and restored it extensively. Before it became a care home, the castle had also been a private residence and religious retreat.

George Henry Bassett's 1886 *County Down Guide and Directory* gave a timely

---

86 There is much more on the Russells in Burke's 1845 *Genealogical and Heraldic Dictionary*, available freely online.

update on the condition of the castles:

"there are several remaining in good condition ... Jordan's Castle is the most interesting. It stands in the centre of the village. Simon Jordan, the owner, in the 17th century successfully defended himself in it for three years against the assaults of Con O'Neill's followers. He was relieved by Lord Mountjoy on the 17th of June, 1611. Horn Castle was once occupied by Major Beauclerc, the descendant of William Ogilvie, who bought Ardglass from Lord Lecale, one of the Leinster family. It is now untenanted. King's Castle, beautifully situated on the hillside, is at present tenanted by Mr. Charles Russell, J.P. A smaller castle, standing near it, and called "The Tower," was joined to King's Castle, forming a structure of imposing dimensions. Cow'd Castle, is so called to preserve an affinity with Horn Castle, and Margaret's Castle are still in evidence".

Jordan's Castle has not always been known by that name. In 1911, whilst in a poor condition, it was acquired by Belfast antiquarian, philanthropist and prominent solicitor, Francis Joseph Bigger, who called it Castle Shane as part of a transformation into a traditional Irish-style seat. Bigger had a wealth of traditional Ulster artefacts amongst his antiques and used his new four-storey home to adorn the walls with images of Irish chieftains. He entertained friends and neighbours frequently in the castle, all part of his desire for a return of Ulster culture in an area long-dominated by planted Scots and Englishmen. The name itself was homage to Shane O'Neill who had substantially reinforced the castle in 1565, in readiness to resist the forces of Queen Elizabeth. At this time, the town and port of Ardglass was, broadly speaking, loyal to the crown but the landowners and farmers of Lecale generally put loyalty to Dublin first.

The castle dates from around 1420, at which time Ardglass was developing a reputation as a major trading port – sending out potatoes, barley and oats from local farms and bringing in fish, particularly herring and timber. Jordan's Castle, built originally as one of the ports defensive structures, soon found a practical use – as a warehouse when Drogheda merchant, Thomas Jordan took out a lease on the castle and added an extensive storage building beside the four-storey town centre building. The Dublin Penny Journal considered this to be the most important of the castles in Ardglass – calling it the town's *citadel*.

Under the ownership of Francis Bigger, Jordan's Castle became a public monument and a popular visitor attraction. A guidebook published in 1929 tells of the strange assortment of items from his collection on display, including whale bones, muskets, badger traps and horn cups. The same book also gave a brief description of the Castle's interior of *"four superimposed single chambers, each about 20 feet by 13 feet"*. The *"unfloored"* ground level chamber reveals *"the irregular surface of of the outcropping rock"*, the suggestion being this was always a store-house, whereas the first floor with its original stone floor was probably always the *"main room"*.

Frank Bigger died in 1926 leaving his castle and museum to the government. Since then Jordan's Castle has been open to visitors, only closing its doors recently. The building is protected as a scheduled monument, but the museum and its contents have an uncertain future.

On the corner of Green Road and Castle Place, is a less well-preserved tower – **Margaret's Castle**. Just two storeys are still standing and the wall that connected it to its neighbouring towers is long gone. In the days before preservation orders, a cottage was built alongside, utilising part of one of the stone walls. You won't be surprised when I tell you it goes by the name of Margaret's Cottage and as a bed and breakfast facility, it can't be faulted for positioning if you fancy touring all of the castles of Ardglass.

Dozens of sources, in print and online will all tell you the castle itself dates from the fifteenth century, originally had at least three stories, was in a ruinous state by the nineteenth century, but who was Margaret? There's a reason no other texts identify the castle with a particular female, but here's my theory. Jenico D'Artois[87], a Frenchman had become prominent in the Ardglass area from 1401. He died in 1426. His grand-daughter and heiress was called Margaret, so it seems very likely the castle was named either by her, or by her father in her honour.

Directly over the main road from Margaret's Castle is **Cowd Castle**. Like it's neighbour doubts over the origin of its name continue. The popular view is that it is some form of homage to cattle, with the nearby harbour being used regularly to transport herds to and from market. A survey conducted in 1885 found that more than 54,000 *"milch"* or dairy cows were kept in the area as well as 150,000 other cattle – presumably bred for meat. This castle too has lost its head and has no public access, but it stands at the roadside at the entrance to a very popular golf course and to be fair, all there is to see is from the exterior anyway. Whether it should be called Cow'd, Choud or Cowd is open to debate,

---

87 Various spellings of both names exist, including Janico and Dartasso.

but then, so is the use of the word *"castle"* for this structure called *"remarkable"* by at least one reputed student of archaeology[88]. You see, a castle should really serve two purposes. Firstly, it must provide adequate defence, and secondly, it should be habitable. There are several reasons why Cowd meets neither criteria. The interior contains no evidence of ever having either fireplaces or latrines, both considered essential to sustain life in the period Cowd was built. As for defence, there are no murder-holes, or machicolations just arrow loops, but even these only provide partial cover and do not overlook the *"castle's"* weakest point of entry – its doorway. Some have even suggested Cowd was never intended as a castle but as a lighthouse, yet no evidence has been found to support this. There was never any attempt to make a substantial platform from which to light a beacon, or even build a permanent staircase to reach it – both would have been essential if the tower was to serve as a harbour light.

As for **Ardglass Castle** – there's no argument about it being in Ardglass. But a castle? Only in name. Let's leave it to Lewis's *Topographical Dictionary of Ireland* to make a start on explaining it all. In his 1837 publication Samuel Lewis described:

"a long range of building in the castellated style, called the New Works, although they are so old that nothing is known either of the time or the purpose of their erection. They form together a line of fortifications, 250 feet in length from east to west, and 24 feet in breadth, close to the shore; the walls are three feet in thickness and strengthened with three towers, one in the centre and one at each extremity. These buildings were originally divided into thirty-six apartments, eighteen on the ground floor and eighteen above, with a staircase in the centre; each of the lower apartments had a small arched door and a large square window, which renders it probable that they had been shops occupied by merchants at some very early period, possibly by the company of traders that settled here in the reign of Henry IV. About the year 1789, Lord Charles Fitzgerald, son of the Duke of Leinster, who was then proprietor, caused that portion of the building between the central and the western tower to be enlarged in the rear, and raised to the height of three stories in the castellated style; and from that time it has been called Ardglass Castle, and has been the residence of the proprietor of the estate".

Again, we have a structure that has gone by more than one name. But that's not the end of it. Lewis added:

---

88 Said T.E. McNeill, author of *Castles in Ireland*, amongst others.

"It was formerly called Horn Castle, either from a great quantity of horns found on the spot, or from a high pillar which stood on its summit previously to its being roofed".

So there you have it – Ardglass Castle was actually a row of castellated warehouses, and never the towns defensive fortress its name implies. Some have been generous and suggested it to be one of the earliest examples of a shopping complex or perhaps an indoor market space, but the buildings that now form part of the adjoining golf course's club house formed little deterrent to potential invaders bar the arrow loops on the first floor. We have the *Dublin Penny Journal* to thank once again for a detailed description of the complex in 1833:

"Here is also a long range of castellated houses, called by the inhabitants the New-works, and said to have been erected by Shane O'Neil about the year 1570. It stands boldly on a rocky shore of the bay, which washes it on the east and north sides, and extends 250 feet (76 m) in length, and in breadth only 24; the thickness of the walls being three feet. Its design is uniform and elegant, consisting of three square towers, one in the centre and one at each end, each tower containing three apartments 10 feet (3.0 m) square; the intermediate space is occupied by a range of 15 arched door-ways of cut stone, and 16 square windows--a doorway and a window being placed alternately next to each other all along the range, an arrangement which leaves no doubt that they were designed for shops or merchant's ware-rooms. There is a story over the shops, containing the same number of apartments, and each has its own separate stone staircase. The rooms on the ground floor were seven feet high; the upper rooms six feet and a half; and in each of these was a small water-closet, the flue of which runs down through the walls, and is washed at the bottom by the sea. They have no fire-place; and the merchants, as it would appear, were in the habit of using Horn Castle as their kitchen and dining hall. On the seaside there are no windows or apertures, except narrow loop-holes, a circumstance which, together with the centre and flanking towers, shows the secondary purpose of the building to have been a fortress, to protect the merchants from piratical assailants".

A painting from the eighteenth century, a copy of which is displayed in the Golf Club, shows a long three-towered building in ruins. The north wall is shown clearly as battlements, of which just a fragment remains today. The picture also reveals the building to have at least fifteen access points – not what you'd think of for a defensive fortress. As regards warehouse space, this was impressive. The entire building was around 240 feet by 20 feet. Allowing for the structure to have three storeys at one end, but only a single storey at the opposite end, this still gives an estimated 10,000 square feet of floorspace - comparable with say, a small supermarket in modern terms.

Finally, we shouldn't leave our tour of the Castles of Ardglass without mentioning the youngest of them all – constructed on perhaps the oldest settlement site in the area. **Isabella's Tower** was built atop the highest point overlooking the bay, a conical hill, known as *"the Ward"*. In 1851, fearing that his young daughter would die unless he did something drastic, Aubrey Beauclerk of Ardglass Castle had a tower built for her to convalesce from her tuberculosis. Isabella clearly benefited from the retreat, living another 79 years – which is more than can be said for her father who died three years after completing his folly[89].

The tower is a curious design of two storeys. The lower floor is octagonal and contains a spiral staircase to give access to a single-roomed upper floor, with this tier being conical and having four windows. The 27-foot-high stone folly is, in itself, unremarkable, but the hill it stands on revealed a remarkable surprise when excavations for the Beauclerk *"castle"* began.

It turned out this vantage point, the top of Ardglass, with views stretching out in all directions, was not a natural hill at all, but a Bronze Age burial mound. Furthermore it had long been known that King John visited and stayed in Ardglass in the year 1210, at which point it is believed the Ward was topped by a wooden fort, of which no evidence remains. With these reminders possibly in mind, the authorities listed the building in 1978. Prior to that, between 1885 and 1908 the tower had been leased out and used as a lookout tower for the Ardglass Coastguard. It was bought by a local man in 1999, with the intention of developing the site as tourist accommodation. When that plan didn't materialise, he attempted to sell the tower in a novel way – advertising it for sale on *Gumtree* – for just £15,000.

Ardglass itself almost certainly derived it's name from this artificial mound - *Ard*

---

89 There is a second folly in the town. The *"Eye of Ardglass"* dates from the eighteenth century and was also reputedly built as a retreat – this time by a husband for his sick wife. It is on private property and cannot be accessed, but a good view of it can be had from Green Road.

Ghlais, means the *green height*. And there we must leave Ardglass – that once-thriving harbour, with a centuries-old fishing heritage, and travel to County Londonderry and a market down with a peculiar name, a folly tower of its own to climb and the birthplace of a very well-known song.

Further Reading:

E. Hull, A History of Ireland and her People, Phoenix (1926)

J. O'Laverty, An Historical Account of the Diocese of Down and Connor, Duffy (1878)

L is for a Leaping Dog and Londonderry Air

Limavady is less than four miles inland from the south-eastern shore of Lough Foyle and is something of a boom-town. Twice as many people live here as did forty years ago.

Why?

Since the 1970's Limavady has been in transformation. The old town has continually grown outwards to the south-east where over 1,300 new homes were added in the final years of the last millennium. Simultaneously, the town's retail sector has been redeveloped and new industries brought in, providing jobs for most of those choosing to live in this popular town. For those prepared to commute, Derry and Coleraine are just 17 and 14 miles away respectively, both well served by road and rail.

With all that recent growth of a *"new town"*, it might seem strange to find that Limavady first got the *Newtown* tag more than four hundred years ago.

We'll look at the ancient history of *Léim a' Mhadaidh*, the place of the leaping dog later on, suffice to say, there was already a well-established settlement here prior to the Plantation of Ulster. Sir Thomas Phillips was granted 13,000 acres of land including the Limavady area in 1610 and proceeded to immediately develop the *Newtown of Limavady*[90]. By 1622, the fledgling community, centred on a crossroads comprised 18 cottage homes, an inn and the obligatory cross, flagpole and stocks. A Royal Charter granted by King James I in 1613 gave the new town the right to send two men to Parliament as well as to be led by a Provost supported by twelve Burgesses. Perhaps more important for the future growth of Limavady, the King's Charter also granted the town rights to hold a weekly market, an annual fair on 1st July and to build a school.

Initial growth was temporary. Under siege in 1641, the townspeople, men, women and some juveniles, joined ranks with Captain Phillips small army and

---

90 The name *Newtownlimavady* was retained until 1875, when, at the request of the population, it was agreed to shorten it to *Limavady*.

successfully repelled the Irish *"invaders"*[91] for over six months, including a particularly difficult winter. They were not able to hold out against a second wave though, and the entire town was burned. The Irish proceeded to rebuild Limavady, only for the forces of James II to capture the town and burn it to the ground once again less than fifty years later.

The oldest buildings in present-day Limavady hail from the second rebuilding period shortly after 1688. Once again, we can be grateful for the *Topographical Dictionary* to give us some idea of the town in 1837. Lewis wrote:

"(the town) comprises four principal and several smaller streets; three of the streets are large and well-built. There is a handsome sessions-house, where the general sessions for the county are held in June and December, and petty sessions on alternate Tuesdays; adjoining it is a small bridewell".

Lewis use of the term *"bridewell"* for the town's police station establishes that it also served as a small prison and reform school. You'll recall the seventeenth century Charter allowed for a weekly market day – this had expanded to three days by this time. Mondays were for the selling of potatoes, flax, butter and cattle, with busy grain markets being held every Tuesday and Thursday. Similarly, the annual fair day had by then become five distinct fairs, one each in the months of February, March, June, July and October.

As for the composition of the townspeople in the nineteenth century, a trawl through Limavady's entries in a succession of Belfast & Ulster Street Directories uncovers an assortment of builders, solicitors, spirit merchants, auctioneers, haberdashers, carpenter, flax dealers, blacksmiths, whitesmiths, tinsmiths and at least one guano merchant – a gentleman by the name of Robert Douglas. His Guano and seed outlet expanded into a bakery and grocery store as the twentieth century began, but what could the folk of County Derry be doing with guano?

Robert Douglas was a well-known figure and Justice of the Peace in the town. His death in 1935 was felt by most in the community. As for his trade in guano, I can reveal that Peruvian seabird droppings are particularly high in phosphorus and nitrogen, making it a very effective fertiliser for farmers growing potatoes – of which there were (and still are) rather a lot in the area. Shiploads of the

---

91 In speech marks to respect the Irish view that it was their land in the first place.

manure came into Londonderry from South America for that very purpose[92], providing a lucrative business for the likes of Mr. Douglas.

I mentioned spirit merchants just now. Most people will be aware of Bushmills and its association with Irish Whiskey, but Limavady also has a long history of distilling whiskey. It began in 1608 with King James I granting Sir Thomas Phillips permission to distil whiskey. Not being people to rush impetuously into things, the folk of Limavady got round to establishing their first distillery a mere 142 years later when the Alexander family under the headship of John began whiskey production. And then, just like waiting for the bus, no sooner had Alexander commenced production, but William Small immediately followed suit, and a small still was also put into use within an inn in the town. None of these businesses was sustained, however and the town was left without the unmistakable scent of the *angel's share*[93] until David Cather[94] began production again from a new distillery beside Drumachose Church early in the nineteenth century. His son George took over the business but by 1859 it had closed down, possibly in part due to in-family tensions. William's daughter, Margaret being a patron of Limavady's *Total Abstinence Society*. Meanwhile, William Moody had commenced distillation in a former corn mill around 1821 before Peter Rankin took it over in the 1840's. For a while Roemill whiskey was a commercial success, perhaps in part due to its higher than average alcoholic strength, but this operation too had ceased by 1859. The building became a mill once again, before the Limavady Electricity Supply Company took it over in 1926 as a site for a water turbine to supply electricity to the growing town.

Limavady remained without a whiskey producer of its own until about 1880 – the folk of the town seemed to still be drinking the stuff though, a directory from 1877 lists no fewer than 20 spirit dealers in Limavady. The Cather family had also run a brewery in the town which was taken over (on a leasehold basis) by William Purcell in 1850. The Cathers decided to sell up entirely in 1864. The new owners being James Galloway & Co. By 1886, James Mclaughlin, managing the former brewery for the large Belfast firm of Young, King and Co was turning

---

92 It is alleged in some parts that South American guano was the most likely source of the dreadful potato blight that devastated crops and led to the deaths of millions.

93 A percentage of the barrelled whisky escapes by evaporation creating an instantly recognisable smell.

94 Or possibly, Cathar.

out around a quarter of a million gallons of Limavady whiskey annually.

By 1914, the whiskey giant – Distillers – in control, and like all commercial giants, when the going got tough, its smallest operations were sacrificed first. Limavady has not manufactured whiskey since. You'll find very little evidence in the town of it's whiskey heritage, even Distillery Road has been renamed – Alexander Road.

Lewis wrote of the *"environs of the town"* being *"extremely beautiful"* in 1837, while the compiler of the 1877 Street Directory mentioned earlier included the observation that the Roe Valley had been described as *"the garden of the North"*. Nowadays, the Limavady area continues to have plenty to offer those seeking open spaces and the call of the wild. Just to the west of Limavady, on the Derry side of the Roe are two man-made structures that provide good focal points for such calls.

Sampson's Tower is located in a small copse near the townland of Farlow a mile to the west of Limavady, but unfortunately is on private ground, so neither entry or immediate approach are possible without the land-owners prior consent, which is something of a shame given that the tower was paid for by public subscription in 1860 following the death in January of the previous year of Arthur Sampson, a prominent local fishmonger[95] and Justice of the Peace. The sandstone tower is an interesting combination of right angles and curves with forty-eight steps rising to the round turret. Nearby is the Ballykelly military airfield that made the headlines in 2006 when the flight crew of a Ryanair commercial trip, mistook it for Derry Airport and landed at the wrong place.

Moving just a little way south, crossing the railway and entering the townland of Moneyrannel is the site of *Rough Fort*. It can be found by joining the Moneyrannel Road off the A2 and looking for the National Trust signage. Northern Ireland has thousands of circular earthworks – *raths*, built by the early Christians as family homes, surrounded by raised a raised ring to retain livestock. The suffix *-fort* has been added to the names of many of these raths, some of which date from the Bronze Age, even though no real evidence exists that any of them ever served defensive purposes.

Continuing south-west of Limavady, Roe Valley Country Park has something for everyone (apart from sea-views, to be fair). Here you can get off the beaten

---

95 Not in the sense of owning a shop selling fish, but as regional agent for the London Worshipful Company of Fishmongers, a position he held for 40 years.

track and explore waterfalls, woods and considerable gorges. There are walking trails and cycle routes[96] to follow. The parks paths are well-marked with an excellent visitor centre as a focal point. Allow enough time to call in at the small but very informative industrial museum which tells much of the story of the growth of the fascinating town of Limavady.

Here in the park you will also find the place that legend says gave rise to the name of Limavady. Well, two different legends actually. The first one goes something like this. A local chieftain by the name of O'Cahan had a very loyal (and, by the sound of it, rather agile) dog, who on detecting the presence of unwanted invaders, miraculously leapt and cleared the River Roe gorge in order to alert others of the impeding danger. The second account is possibly even more dramatic. This time, O'Cahan himself, being chased by marauders, successfully jumped across the gorge in a feat that his pursuers were unable to match. This story is further corroborated, apparently, by the presence of a horseshoe-print in the rock near to the edge of the gorge. Whether either legend has any basis in fact is questionable, to say the least, but the town happily owned the story and took it for its name.

The Limavady area has been populated since the Bronze Age. Perhaps the finest evidence of 3,000 year old habitation locally was some *"treasure"* dug up in 1896 by two men ploughing a field just outside the town. The so-called *Broighter Gold* hoard comprised a beaten gold bowl, a beautifully decorated neck *torc*[97], more jewellery and an intricately-made model boat, amazingly surviving 3,000 years of ploughing without losing or breaking its mast, oars, bench seats and rudder – all the more remarkable when I reveal the model is just seven inches long. You can view the *Broighter Gold*, albeit in holographic form, at the Limavady Visitor Centre. The real thing is in Dublin's National Museum of Ireland. How it ended up there is something of a story.

After cleaning the mud and other debris from their discovery, the landowner, a farmer by the name of Gibson, sold the haul as a single lot to a Londonderry jeweller for an undisclosed sum – it is possible that Gibson had not realised he was selling solid gold items. Robert Day, a much-travelled antiquarian from Cork, instantly recognised the significance of the treasure, purchased it and

---

96 Route 93 of the National Cycle Network passes the park.

97 A two-piece solid neck collar, typically worn by high-ranking Celtic officials around the time of the first to eighth century BCE.

immediately sold the collection to the British Museum for £600. It may have remained there were it not for the interest of English archaeologist, Arthur Evans who published a paper describing the *Broighter Gold* in great detail. This caught the attention of the Royal Irish Academy who sought to have the hoard returned to Ireland.

It was a long drawn-out legal case, not without humorous moments, not least when the Judge read out his verdict. Treasure Trove law is complex but essentially centres around the principle that anything buried in the ground is intended to be found and dug up again at some time in the future. All such *treasure* is deemed to be the property of the Crown. The British Museum argued this not to be the case, claiming the artefacts were *votives* – gift offerings to the ancient gods, placed in the sea at a time when the area north-west of Limavady would have been under water. The case lasted for six years and cost a hefty sum, all for the Judge, Mr Justice Farwell to rule, somewhat cuttingly, that it was impossible for him to accept the finds as votive to a *seagod* by a chieftain *"both equally unknown"* when similar were *"hitherto unknown"*, and that they had been deposited in a sea *"not known to have existed"*. The *Broighter Gold* was awarded to King Edward VII, whose advisors deemed that the Dublin Museum was the best home. Of course, not all in the North of Ireland agreed, and efforts continue to this day to find the treasure a suitable home nearer to Limavady.

You've almost certainly seen the Broighter Gold without realising it. Some of the old-style one pound coins featured the torc collar design on the reverse and the boat featured on the back of a specially-minted silver one pound coin to mark the millennium.

*****

Jane Ross of Limavady is likely not someone whose name you've come across before. As far as I can ascertain, her name first appeared in print in 1855 in George Petrie's *The Ancient Music of Ireland*. Petrie acknowledged Ross *"a lady who has made a large collection of the popular unpublished melodies of the county"* who he identified as *"Miss J. Ross, of New Town, Limavady, in the County of Londonderry"* for her donation of a single song. Petrie noted *"The name of the tune unfortunately was not ascertained"*. It was almost forty years later that Katherine Tynan (later Hinkson) penned an *Irish Love Song* to fit the tune and it became known as *Londonderry Air* for the first time. It was not until 1913 that Frederic Weatherly's lyrics were set to the tune and *Danny Boy* was sung for the first time. It is hard to believe that this quintessential *traditional* Irish anthem is barely a century old – or that the words were written by a lawyer from Somerset, England.

The original tune itself is much older, and likely somewhat different to the version penned by Ross and Petrie, but it is probable that were it not for the efforts of a Limavady lady, Danny Boy and Londonderry Air might never have existed. Miss Ross, who first heard the tune being played on the violin by a blind fiddler in the Limavady market area in 1851, lived in the town for her entire life, much of it at 51, Main Street, where a blue plaque commemorates her. The fiddler, by the way, was a man by the name of Jimmy McCurry from nearby Myroe who was a regular on market days. The story goes that Jane paid *Blin' Jimmy* a florin (ten pence these days, but a generous tip back then) for his tune.

The Limavady area has so much more to explore, so we'll stick around for another chapter at least.

Further Reading

T. H. Mullin, Limavady and the Roe Valley, Limavady District Council (1983)

N. McGronagle, Limavady and the Roe Valley – Memories, Impact (2017)

M is for Magilligan, Martello and Maps

Travel due north from Limavady and you'll reach the sea at Magilligan Point. Here you will find a man-made structure that illustrates clearly how the coastline has changed over time. The Martello Tower here was established (along with dozens of others, including a non-identical twin across Lough Foyle at Greencastle[98]) supposedly in readiness for an impending invasion by Napoleon. The predicted French attack never materialised, which is a good thing as the 36-foot high tower took five years to complete, by which time Napoleon was in exile on St. Helena.

The name Martello Tower comes from Napoleon's birthplace – the island of Corsica. It was here at *Point Martella* in 1794 that the British navy struggled for days to capture a round stone flat-topped tower. Stories circulated, the design was copied and the source acknowledged (virtually) in the name given.

Martello Towers are often tapered, truncated cylinders, as is the case at Magilligan, the only Martello Tower in Northern Ireland, by the way. It was a clever design, allowing for good interior storage, an all-round firing position, but a smaller target from attackers offshore. A survey completed in 2017 concluded that *"Magilligan Martello Tower is in excellent condition and is probably one of the best preserved examples of its type anywhere in the U.K.".* [99] The interior is in as good a condition as the exterior. Unfortunately, at present access is only granted during the annual European Heritage Open Days weekend every September. But, check online regularly as there are plans to open regularly, at least through the summer season.

The tower has two floors, the ground floor (for which there is no exterior access), would have been a weapons and ammunition store, but also sits atop a natural spring providing any besieged residents with an unlimited fresh water supply. Upstairs, and accessed via a ladder and a doorway almost 10 feet off the ground was the living accommodation. And, people did live in it for a while, even though it was a windowless structure, requiring constant candlelight – one

---

98 Which is elliptical rather than cylindrical in shape.

99 Binevenagh Coast and Lowlands Defence Heritage Audit , quarto/Ulidia Heritage Services (April 2017)

family even raised children in the tower. On the flat roof top a 24-pound cannon was mounted on rails to give a full 36-degree firing option.

When it was completed in 1817, the sandstone tower, with walls some 8 feet thick, stood amongst dunes at the water's edge. Tides, winds and river estuary deposits cause this coastline to be dynamic – not just in appearance, but in shape, position and composition. Where there are dunes now was a sandy beach fifty years ago, and in some places would have been under water fifty years before that. The Magilligan Martello Tower seems to be slowly but steadily creeping inland (perhaps that ought to be that the coastline is slowly but steadily creeping away), which is good news for its long-term prospects.

The name Magilligan is a corruption of *Mac Giollagain*, successors of the *Ó Cathaín* clan who'd ruled the area since the twelfth century. Perhaps, it is unremarkable that this beautiful peninsula over which countless bloody feuds have erupted should nowadays be the site of an incredibly diverse nature reserve, dozens of military sites, a prison and an active weapons firing range[100].

Should you visit the dunes nature reserve? Certainly, but be aware this is a fragile landscape, with designated areas specifically protected to exclude the possibility of damage by human intervention. Fences may be there to protect the environment from you, and they may also be present for your own good – remember the military fire live ammunition around here[101].

Look out for signs of rabbits amongst the dunes. These were introduced here long ago, in part as a deliberate environmental management strategy – rabbits help to restrict the encroachment of larger shrubs and trees and thus protect the native dune vegetation, but also as an economic resource – skins being sold for their fur, and the meat as a rich-source of protein. In the 1950's a terrible myxomatosis epidemic wiped out almost all of the rabbit population throughout Great Britain and Ireland. Terrible for the rabbits on two counts. Firstly less than one in one thousand escaped with their lives – in many parts none at all. Secondly, this was no random outbreak – the virus was introduced intentionally, in South-East England, from where, as you might expect, it spread uncontrollably, as a pest-control strategy. Thankfully, with rabbits being what

---

100Not to mention caravan parks and a golf course.

101A short walk encompassing aspects of the nature reserve and the Martello Tower can be found here: http://www.walkni.com/walks/161/magilligan-point/

they are, populations have now recovered, and *harvesting* of them is now controlled. In some places cattle and sheep have been introduced as their grazing routines have a similar positive effect on dune ecosystems.

When making your way through the dunes, stick to the boardwalks. The native marram grass serves a critical purpose, binding the dunes together. Once it has been trampled, the loose exposed sand blows away with the wind, and before you know it the dune is lost.

Look out for *grey* dunes – these are the older, more mature dunes, farthest away from the sea. They take their name from a thin greyish layer of decaying plants that forms on top of the sand. Here you will find an abundance of wildlife – with sand barely visible. In the summer months, the purple flowers of wild thyme give a most attractive appearance, as do the taller yellow flowers of Lady's Bedstraw which can be seen here from June through to September. These dunes would be great for introducing children (with magnifying glasses etc.) to the strange and wonderful microclimate of these ancient dunes. Get them to spot and count (but not collect!) brown-lipped snails which are particularly abundant here.

As you approach the beach, look out for the youngest *embryo* dunes. These lead a harsh, fragile and often temporary existence. Being closest to the sea this is where salinity and acidity are at their highest. Only the toughest couch grass can grow here to bind the fledgling dunes together, with the result that a single wind storm or high tide can take an embryo dune away entirely.

The natural vegetation of this area, believe it or not, is forest. Without the introduction of rabbits initially, and livestock latterly, birch, oak, hazel and willow would thrive here – and they do a little way inland, where a forest ecosystem is rich with insect and birdlife.

Magilligan does seem to have something for just about everyone.

Given the dynamic nature of the coastline here, it might not be one of the first locations you'd think of for mapping out the island of Ireland and yet this area served a critical role.

This particular story began in 1824 when a House of Commons committee recommended a new mapping project covering the whole of Ireland using a standard scale of six inches to the mile. The considerable expense involved would, to some extent, be ultimately affrayed by the availability of more accurate taxation levels.

A notable by-product, and now in print, of the mapping programme was that the considerable memoirs containing a unique record of pre-famine life were far more extensive in compiling details of land-holdings, livelihoods, buildings, population and lifestyles than even the most modern online census.

Survey work commenced in 1830 and the first section to be mapped was an eight mile stretch of Lough Foyle coastline running from Magilligan Point to Ballykelly near Limavady. This *"baseline"* was chosen as it was unusually flat and straight. All of the rest of Ireland was then mapped relative to that critical first line. This wasn't just pioneering work in an Irish sense – prior to these incredibly-detailed and accurate maps, nothing like them had been produced anywhere else in the world, making this part of County Derry, the first of the first.

The Ordnance Survey of Ireland was founded under the direction of an Irishman, Thomas Spring Rice, but following intervention by the Duke of Wellington himself, Rice's preferred Irish team of surveyors were turned away in favour of groups formed from within the British Army. The Duke argued that Irish surveyors were not suitably qualified for the task, many believe his hidden motive was to produce maps strategically beneficial to the British Armed Forces, a prospect enhanced by using the military themselves.

Thomas Colby was directing the Ordnance Survey in England at the time, and, as a former officer in the Royal Engineers, he seemed to be the ideal man to lead the project. In 1803, an accident with an exploding pistol had left Colby without his left hand and he had to endure the remainder of his life with a piece of the gun lodged in his skull. Officers from the Royal Engineers together with three companies of Royal Sappers and Miners worked alongside locally-employed civil servants, scholars, fieldwork labourers and clerks for over twenty years on the project, with a total final cost of just under a million pounds.

In those days everything was done manually, there was no GPS, no satellite imagery, no optical laser sights and the like, just lots of people with heavy boxes of hand-tooled instruments prepared to camp out on mountain tops, cliff-edges and windswept shorelines in the name of work. A single brass and wood theodolite, for example weighed as much as 28 kg – more than a sack of spuds!

The detail achieved was awesome, and the accuracy no less impressive. Each map included administrative boundaries, transport routes (roads, paths, what few railways existed, canals and river routes), settlements were often set down identifying notable individual buildings such as mills, churches, poorhouses and inns. Vegetation was annotated, distinction made between agricultural land and wilderness, plain and bog. Take woodland for example. In earlier maps a wooded area might be shown in green with a tree icon and a name perhaps. Now, for the first time, the mapping of woodland was detailed, conifers could be told apart from broadleaved deciduous woodland, natural forests from plantations, even mature woodland from recently-planted.

And, perhaps the most astounding fact of all, with the advent of more modern technologies it has been possible to confirm this very first mapping of the Magilligan Point stretch – a task that took over fourteen months[102] back in the nineteenth century – had been completed accurate to within a single inch[103].

The initial eight-mile *baseline* is, therefore something of international significance. Both ends of the Lough Foyle Baseline are marked by base towers, named conveniently, North and South. The North Tower is on private land – in a farmer's field in Ballymullholland, while the South Tower near to the Drummond Hotel in Ballykelly is more readily accessible. Don't look up for them – even topped with iron railings, each is only about four feet high. A third tower at Minearny is also on private ground, and a fourth, that was positioned near the northern end of the line at Mount Sandy was the victim of coastal erosion many years ago.

Perhaps the best way to appreciate this remarkable *"line"* between a pair of seemingly pointless towers that barely get off the ground, is to get off the ground yourself. Take a hike (or drive the car) to the top of nearby Binevenagh Mountain where you'll find the Gortmore Picnic Area which overlooks Lough Foyle. Here is a commemorative plaque, with the following detailed inscription:

"The Survey of Ireland

The Lough Foyle Base Measurement

---

102 Work commenced on 6th September 1827 and was completed on 20th November the following year. The total number of actual days worked was only around 60, with most of the time being lost to seasonal conditions and respect for farmer's needs.

103 See the Binevenagh Defence Heritage Audit for more details of the 1960 re-measurement.

Between the years 1824 and 1846 a major survey of Ireland was carried out by the Ordnance Survey under the direction of Major General Thomas F. Colby. Colby calculated that the most important part of the triangulation for the survey was the determination of scale by means of the precise measurement of a base. In 1824 he selected a site on the flat eastern shore of Lough Foyle for a base which was to be the longest of its kind and measured by methods to a standard of accuracy never before achieved anywhere in the world.

Colby devised an original apparatus for the measurement - a compensation bar of iron and brass about 10 feet long between the pivots, the total length of which was unaffected by temperature changes. Measurement of the base commenced on 6 September 1827, initially under Colby's supervision but later under the direction of Lieutenant Thomas Drummond one of the Ordnance Survey's leading mathematicians. Work was completed on 20 November 1828 having taken the most part of two summers to complete. The length of the base, levelled and reduced to the adjoining sea level, was 41,640.8873 feet or nearly 8 miles. In 1960 the Ordnance Survey of Northern Ireland remeasured the base using electronic equipment; the difference was approximately 1 inch - surely a tribute to the accuracy of the 19th century surveyors.

A base at Salisbury Plain was measured in 1849 using the same apparatus and methods perfected by Colby in Ireland and is connected to the Lough Foyle Base through the principal triangulation network. To preserve the site the Government acquired the land and erected three base towers that can still be seen today. The North Base Tower at Ballymulholland and Minearny Base Tower at Minearny are surrounded by private land and are not readily accessible to the public. South Base Tower, situated at the rear of the Kings Lane Estate in Ballykelly Village, can be visited."

Shortly after the first map's completion and publication Thomas Creevey, an Englishman and Member of Parliament for Downton in Wiltshire was moved to write *"most beautiful it was"*, also acknowledging the detail *"which is ten times more minute than that of England"*[104]. It was a remarkable achievement, all stemming from that first line of almost eight miles, measured by Colby and his team with the aid of his innovative Compensation Bars so accurately.

Although Magilligan Point cannot claim to be the location for the first manned

---

104 Found in *Creevey's Life and Times*, a collection of letters and papers, first published in 1934

flight in Ireland, the first man to build AND fly a plane in Ireland, did come here to test his planes. Harry Ferguson had designed and assembled his own flying machine in Belfast and, according to the *Belfast Telegraph* successfully "*made a splendid flight of 130 yards*" on the final day of 1909. The following year he had produced a two-seater and was flying regular, using the long sandy beach at Magilligan for take-off and landing of his 35 horsepower aircraft. Not every flight went smoothly. There were reports of narrow escapes for the young Ferguson in 1910 and again in 1912. He never lost interest in aviation, but went on to make his fortune in agricultural machinery – including tractors. Yes, THAT Ferguson!

He is known to have made several flights over Coleraine, including taking passengers to see the town from the air. We'll head over there now for a closer look ourselves.

Further Reading:

Department of the Environment for Northern Ireland, Shifting Sands: A Study of the Coast of Northern Ireland from Magilligan to Larne, HMSO (1991)

A. Day & P. McWilliams, Ordnance Survey Memoirs of Ireland: Volume 11 – County Londonderry, Institute of Irish Studies (1991)

N is for the Nook of the Ferns

Some people say that Coleraine is the last place to buy a house in Northern Ireland. Why? It is a bright, vibrant town, with a strong local economy and is incredibly popular with visitors and residents alike. But those factors combine to give Coleraine the highest house prices in the whole of Northern Ireland.

You can argue that it is not a coastal town, but the River Bann, or to be strictly accurate, the *Lower* Bann passes immediately to the west of Coleraine, separating Londonderry's second largest town from Killowen. With the sea just three miles away AND a busy marina it would be remiss to exclude it from this guide.

The Irish name for Coleraine, *Cúil Rathain* means the Nook of the Ferns. According to a ninth century text, Saint Patrick was looking for somewhere to establish a church alongside the river when he came across some young boys burning a small patch of ferns – needless to say he chose that particular "nook".

Coleraine has a long history as a port in its own right, but owes much of its more modern economic prosperity (the past two hundred years, say) to the production of linen, some of which fed the ever-expanding industrial mills of Belfast while most of it was of such a high quality that as Samuel Lewis put it *"this place has long been celebrated for its trade in the finer linens"*. Writing in his *Topographical Dictionary* he established that Coleraine was a focal point for many localised centres of linen production, identifying the following townlands *"Gorton, Ballydivitt, Macosquin, Drumcroon, Mullamore, Keeley, Aghadowey, Rusbrook, Collans, Mullycarrie, Island Effrick, Castle Roe, Greenfield and other places"* all following hot on the heels of the first *bleach-green*[105] established at Ballybritain in 1734.

And yet, Captain Nicholas Pynnar[106] who surveyed Coleraine, not once but twice

---

105 An outdoor area, almost always grassed, for laying out linen to whiten, or "bleach" in the sunlight.

106 A former military engineer, who arrived in Ireland around 1600 and stayed. With no men to lead after his company was disbanded in March 1604 he was pensioned off with an income of four shillings a day – enough to sustain him until the Plantation of

between 1618 and 1625 had found *"that part of the town which is unbuilt is so dirty that no man is able to go into it, especially what is called, and should be, the market-place"* and on his return *"The town of Coleraine is in the same state as at the last survey; only three houses are added, which are built by private individuals, the society allowing them £20 a piece. The walls and ramparts are built of sods; they do begin to decay, on account of their narrowness; the bulwarks are exceedingly little, and the town is so poorly inhabited that there are not men enough to man the sixth part of the wall"*.

By 1910, the Belfast and Ulster Towns Directory was calling Coleraine *"one of the most prosperous towns in the North of Ireland"* citing *"extensive distilleries, a weaving factory, also a shirt and collar factory (and) one of the most important salmon fisheries in Ireland"*. Not exactly a one-horse town was it?

There were two distilleries in Coleraine. To the west of the Bann, on Captain Street in Killowen, a small outlet produced whiskey for a while in the early part of the nineteenth century, and again, briefly, under the ownership of the Distillers Company in the 1920's. Bought out by the owners of Bushmills, the premises were used for storage only, until demolition in 1969. The much larger operation began in a converted mill on New Market Street. Defying the Irish convention of the extra *"e"*, Coleraine Whisky was an instant success – after ten years of ageing the first production run. By 1845, the triple-distilled malt was being supplied to parliament for serving in the House of Commons. From that point on, bottles had a prominent HC on the label. Writing in 1887 in *The Whisky Distilleries of the United Kingdom*, Alfred Barnard, who had toured 162 distilleries in the previous two years, and so, ought to be in a position to comment, wrote this: *"for cleanliness, order, and regularity, we have seen no distillery to beat this"*. As with its neighbour across the river, once Bushmills took over, production gradually fell away and ceased for good in 1964. All that still stands is a stone wall and a rather nice gated archway that can be seen from Lime Market Street.

Commercial salmon fishing has also disappeared from the Coleraine area. Poor stock management (i.e. overfishing) led to the almost total disappearance of salmon from the Lower Bann. Furthermore, changes to the river flow itself, in the interests of humans, spoiled the fast-flowing well-oxygenated streams required to keep the exhausted salmon alive. Nowadays, there are enough salmon around to keep those prepared to pay anything up to £60 a day for an

Ulster began six years later.

angling permit happy, but the times when stocks were so good that a citadel was built, not to defend the town, but to *"oversee the fishing"* are long gone. At least the salmon outlived the structure which was started in 1650, grew at the rate of a foot a year for twelve years, before further building was abandoned and the mini-castle was demolished without ever being completed.

Coleraine had a castle, briefly. More likely, it had several castles on the same site over many centuries. The earliest known one was built around the same time as the first bridge over the River Bann, Drumtarsey Castle, on the Killowen side of the river, but only lasted a few decades, being made from wood, it was easily burned to the ground.

Overfishing started in the very early years of the Plantation of Ulster. King James I had persuaded many of his loyal followers to move to Coleraine on the strength of the salmon population available and the newly-planted wasted no time in artificially diverting the river near to Castleroe and famously (perhaps that ought to be infamously) netted a haul of 62 tons of salmon in a single day.

This seventeenth century *"settler colony with privileged relations with the metropolis and a determination to remain part of the United Kingdom of Great Britain and Ireland, no matter what the majority in Ireland wished"*[107] weren't exactly welcomed with open arms. In 1642, for example, the town was besieged for six weeks. The Irish weren't able to penetrate the defensive fortifications – utilising the wide river to the west and digging a deep ditch, four feet wide, and the same deep, with raised ramparts, six feet high and sixteen feet thick on all other fronts. There were only two entrances – heavily guarded drawbridges at the Blind Gate facing south and King's Gate pointing east, located close to where Blindgate Street and Kingsgate Street are nowadays. Don't go looking for any physical evidence, though. All that remains of any of it is a short section of the northern rampart which can be seen behind the church of St Patrick.

As a Plantation town, Coleraine saw a rapid transformation into a port of great renown. In 1637, the Surveyor General's report included this notable statement about Coleraine as *"'port of the greatest consequence in the kingdom for coast business"*.

Modern landmarks serving as reminders of Coleraine's history include the *Diamond* – a market square, that is neither diamond or square, but rectangular. The old Market House once stood here where the Town Hall now faces the

---

107 The words of Dr. P. M. Clayton, writing in *Was Ireland a Colony?* Published in 2005.

market. This building is also home to a very good museum, which unfortunately does not open all year round so check online before committing to visit.

In the most part, it is the street names that establish where key features of the town once were. For instance, the Dominican Abbey was on Abbey Street, and you've probably already figured out what stood on Jail Street. Perhaps the easiest way to tour the older parts of Coleraine is to make use of a guided walk created in 2013 and called the Coleraine 400 Heritage Trail. You can find copies of it online, as well as guides who will happily escort you around the trail, usually for a small fee.

To the north of the town is the modern and attractive marina. Nearby, and often overlooked, is the Guy Wilson Daffodil Garden, named in honour of a former daffodil breeder (no, I didn't know either!) who died in 1962, and whose work, especially in conserving several types of Northern Irish daffodils, is featured in his garden. Obviously, there is an optimal period for visiting a daffodil garden, so pick your dates wisely. The collection is laid out in grounds that were once a stone quarry. With a mixture of winding paths, landscaped lawns and a myriad of daffodil beds from all over the world – this really has to be seen in the spring.

Thankfully, the *"dirty"* tag of the early seventeenth century has long been shaken off. Coleraine regularly features as finalist in such competitions as *Ulster in Bloom* and *Best Kept Town* and manages innovative schemes to reinvigorate tired spaces. The Cornfield Project is one such example, taking waste ground between two housing estates and creating community gardens, allotments and recreation space for young people.

It's time to leave the nook of the ferns behind, now we've a tower to climb.

Further Reading:

N. Pierce, Coleraine: A Short History, Brehon Press (2008)

T. Parkhill & V. Pollock, Coleraine in Old Photographs, Sutton (2000)

O is for an Open & Shut Case

In April 2014 the BBC News website ran the following headline:

County Down Monument Closed to the Public

The news caused shock waves throughout Northern Ireland. This was the iconic *Scrabo Tower* whose door was being locked. A place that can be seen for miles around. A tower to climb with your children and then them with theirs, was being closed, apparently for good.

The Northern Ireland Environment Agency expressed regret at the decision to close *"for the foreseeable future"* explaining *"the tower (was) very vulnerable to wet and windy weather"* and despite *"works costing hundreds of thousands of pounds over the last 30 years … the tower continues to suffer serious water ingress"*. The Agency also revealed a serious risk to public health when, for *"the second time in five years, this (the water) has damaged the electrical supply and lighting"*.

People feared the end of this 41 metre high landmark that has stood overlooking North Down for more than 160 years.

In scenes reminiscent of the film *Jaws*, the Mayor of Newtownards, Steven McIlveen and Strangford Member of Parliament Jim Shannon, both pushed for an early re-opening. In June, and, it turned out, somewhat prematurely the *Belfast Telegraph* ran a story under the headline:

Scrabo Tower to Reopen This Month

It didn't.

Hopes were raised briefly when it was announced the tower would be opened on a temporary test basis including the annual Heritage Open days in September 2016. But that was it. At the end of the short trial run, the door was once again locked and bolted tight.

Then came better news. After more repairs and the announcement of a partnership agreement with the National Trust, a press release stated the tower would finally open again – on Friday 30th June 2017.

It didn't.

With one day to go, the *Belfast Telegraph* had to inform disappointed readers:

"*Scrabo Tower in Newtownards will remain closed for the foreseeable future*"

It opened the following Friday.

What's my point?

The tower is now officially open, with an entrance fee, but is prone to short-term closures, particularly, it seems off-peak days and seasons. Therefore, if you intend going so that you can climb all 122 steps and take in the amazing views from the top, I'd ring or email first.

The story behind the tower's construction is a fascinating one. It was erected as a memorial to Charles William Stewart, the third Marquess of Londonderry, whose main home in Northern Ireland (he had others in County Durham and London) was Mount Stewart on the eastern shore of Strangford Lough. By the time of his death in March 1854, he had taken the surname Vane – his second wife Lady Frances Anne Vane-Tempest was an immensely wealthy heiress, so you can make your own mind up why he ditched Stewart in favour of Vane. During the years of the Great Famine, the "*planted*" Irish Landlords response, was, to say the least, mixed. On the one hand, some, like Robert Jocelyn, the third Earl of Roden, served soup and porridge to his County Down tenants and their families for a nominal fee. The Earl of Charlemont recognised the extensive failure of the potato crop and served a rent abatement notice to his tenants in Counties Tyrone and Armagh. On the other hand, others faced fierce criticism for their apparent ignorance or lack of empathy. Charles Vane, found himself the subject of both praise and anger. Some tenants, most of them Catholic by faith, were helped to leave County Down and set up new homes and lives in Seaham where Lord Londonderry, himself a prominent Orangeman had a considerable estate, but there were others who would afterwards reflect on Vane's apparent meanness. The tenth wealthiest man in Britain at the time spent £150,000 on property renovations at the same time as finding £30 to donate to famine relief efforts.

Enough of Londonderry's tenants wanted to show there appreciation for his benevolent spirit that a meeting was called shortly after his death to consider the best way to go about this. A monument was agreed on pretty swiftly, but agreement could not be reached as to where it ought to be positioned. Some wanted Scrabo Hill, but others preferred a town centre location in Newtownards. It took a second meeting in Belfast almost a year after the Earl's death to settle in favour of the hill top.

As for the nature of the monument itself, a competition was announced with a small cash prize available for the winner. The memorial would ideally by a tower or obelisk and had to be able to be completed for a maximum cost of £2,000.

By the time the competition closed in February 1856, four entries were deemed to be worthy of consideration. A stone obelisk designed by William Barre, the prominent architect from Newry was announced as winner. All the remaining designs were towers. James Boyd, the Belfast surveyor and architect was awarded second place, with Assistant County Surveyor, Daniel Hanna[108] coming in third. Charles Lanyon submitted an entry, possibly drawn up by an underling, and, briefly, had to contend with last place.

Barre didn't have long to savour the victory, especially over Lanyon, a long-time rival. When McLaughlin and Harvey, the North Belfast engineering firm stated the obelisk could not be erected for less than £2,400 the Newry man was disqualified. Neither of the two runners-up could meet the cost requirement either. That left Lanyon. To cries of *"fix!"* from a very disgruntled Barr, Lanyon persuaded the committee that his tower could be built within the cost limit.

It couldn't.

That became abundantly clear in mid-build when the design had to be altered to save money. The tower should have been taller than 125 feet with larger turrets and buttress walls. Things had to be sacrificed in the name of economy. The final bill still came in more than £1,000 over the agreed budget.

You can see William Barre's granite and sandstone obelisk for yourself by travelling across the border to the town of Monaghan. Barre offered a scaled-down version of his design as a monument to commemorate Lieutenant Colonel Thomas Vesey Dawson of the town, who had also died – in his case in battle - in 1854.

On Scrabo Hill, in scenes more often seen at state funerals and the like, the foundation stone was laid on 6th March 1857 by the new Marquess and Marchioness flanked by the Bishop of Down and many of Ireland's landowners

---

108 Most sources incorrectly name the Belfast surveyor as *Hanus*.

and politicians. All of them were led to the top of Scrabo Hill by a lone highland piper.

A large glass jar was built into the foundations. Its contents included a beautifully inscribed scroll, copies of regional and national newspapers, the recently-completed six inches to the mile Ordnance Survey map of County Down, coins of the realm and a list naming all 600 subscribers, *"tenantry and friends"*[109] who contributed towards the cost of the tower - with Emperor Napoleon III of France at the top.

Two types of stone were used in construction, both quarried from the hillside itself. The metre-thick outer walls are made using the darker dolerite rock, from the higher part of the hill, while the staircase, window lintels and dressings, roof and quoins make use of the sandstone found in the lower part of the hill. The quarried south face is still clearly visible. It was from here that most of the stone for Dundrum Castle was taken. The monastery at Greyabbey was also built (in 1193) from this red sandstone, whose distinctive colour is a result of iron oxide covering the sand producing a rich deep colour that has been much sought-after. It is also a very versatile stone, its tone making it desirable for decorative features such as lintels and quoins, while its structure makes it relatively easy to quarry and shape, whilst still being one of the stronger stones and most resistant to the elements. George Bassett noted in his 1886 directory of County Down *"many of the finest houses of the county gentry are of this stone"*.

For those with an interest in geology, the hill's South Quarry reveals much of its past life as one of Northern Ireland's most active volcanoes. Prehistoric fossilised dinosaur bones have also been exposed here as well as those of ancient scorpions, providing physical evidence of times long ago when this part of world was super-hot desert.

This 500-foot-high volcanic plug with a history exceeding 200 million years in the making, is also the site of one of Ireland's oldest human settlements, and one of the largest unearthed. It is the highest point for miles around, so with full circle visibility, the *"craggy hill"* would have been the logical site to develop a community that could be defended from raiders. Bassett simply wrote *"remains of a large cairn are visible on Scrabo Hill"*. The cairn and attached burial chamber were sacrificed by over-zealous treasure-seekers a few years later, believing the

---

109 From the stone panel inscription above the north door.

hill concealed a massive Viking treasure hoard, the summit was excavated – with explosives. A more conventional archaeological dig carried out in 1968 established this was indeed a large Bronze Age settlement of more than a dozen 10-metre diameter hut circles, enclosed as a hill fort 300 feet by 120 feet with a single narrow entrance to the east.

Before we proceed, there is another controversy that ought to be given some attention. Thanks to the diligence of the late Norman Nevin MBE, and the online availability of his excellent *Story of Comber*[110] I became aware that the memorial to the Marquess may very well have the wrong name. Nevin, noting Walter Harris's use of *Scraba* as opposed to Scrabo in his 1744 epic history of County Down, suggested the former meaning *"the high ground"* seemed more appropriate than the latter which meant *"the sward of the cows"*. Only two years prior to the erection of the tower, James Carruthers, writing in the Ulster Journal of Archaeology used the term Scraba Mountain, not *Scrabo* and Henry Joy, writing in 1817 suggested an *"invisible enemy"* may be hiding *"on the top of Scraba Hill"*. A guide book to Ireland, written in 1837 also advised readers that *"ascending Scraba Hill"* offers *"delightful"* views of Newtownards. So which should it be? Since Scrabo tower went up, the traditional spelling pretty much faded out of use, but as most locals will tell you, *Scrabo* is pronounced *Scrabba*![111]

Some say you can predict the weather using the tower. The system goes something like this. Look in the direction of Scrabo Tower. If you can't see it, that's because its raining. If you can, then rain is on the way!

For over 100 years Scrabo Tower was a family home. The first tenant was William McKay a former foreman from the quarry, whose wife raised eight children in the tower. Their grand-daughters, Elizabeth, Jan and Agnes Millin were the last. The three sisters ran a very popular tea room in the tower for many years, only leaving the tower of their birth in 1966.

Nowadays Scrabo Tower is the focal point for Scrabo Country Park, with many walking trails encompassing the former quarry sites and some outstanding hazel and beech woodland to explore. It can get very busy here in the summer months, so why not time your visit to coincide with the spring season when

---

110 Download it free from: http://www.comberhistory.com/

111 Tower is, of course *tar* locally.

Killynether Wood is a carpet of bluebells and anemones, or on a bright day following snowfall for the most brilliant white winter views? To the south-east the Ards Peninsula stretches out a long finger towards the Irish Sea. Let's see what it has to offer.

Further Reading:

D. Kirk, A Year in Scrabo Country, Cottage Publications (2014)

C. Vane, Memoirs and Correspondence of Viscount Castlereagh, several volumes published around 1850 widely available to read online

P is for Peninsula

There seem to be *two* qualifying rules for a piece of land to be accepted as a peninsula. It must either be not quite, an island, being almost completely surrounded by water, *or* it must project out into a body of water. The Ards Peninsula qualifies on both counts with over 40 miles of water-line, half of it Irish Sea coastline, and the rest banking onto the inland waters of Strangford Lough and Straits. At its widest, the projection is just over 6 miles, with an average west-east girth of a little over 3 miles.

With well over 250 square miles of countryside, coastline, abbeys, castles, villages and harbours to explore, there's plenty to get to know around here. With that in mind, *Aird Uladh* – the *Peninsula of the Ulstermen[112]*, will take up this and the next chapter.

Where the Ards Peninsula starts and ends is something we'll have to consider. As an administrative region it is best described by including everywhere on Strangford Lough East of Newtownards, and everywhere on the coast south of Donaghadee. Since we've already looked at both of these towns, that seems like a good definition to use to me.

Let's start with one of Northern Ireland's very best (and it has quite a few) sandy beaches – and a vivid reminder of the Holocaust.

Ballyrolly Farm outside **Millisle** may seem an unlikely place to focus on the Nazi's systematic persecution and extermination of the Jewish people. In 1938, the German occupation of Czechoslovakia began. The Jewish community there had seen it coming to some extent and plans had been drawn with leaders of overseas synagogues to evacuate as many children as possible. Members of the Jewish community in and around Belfast[113] collected enough money together to take out an extended lease of an unoccupied 70-acre flax-bleaching farm - *Ballyrolly*, which they quickly set to, converting it into suitable accommodation

---

112 *Ulaid* was a Middle Age kingdom of North-East Ireland, that incorporated most of the modern Counties of Antrim, Down and extended further south and east.

113 A home *"for the aid of Jewish refugees"* in North Belfast was already being used, but had already exceeded capacity.

for up to 80 refugee children at a time. Cowsheds became dormitories and a stable was turned into a dining room. Other farm buildings were brought back into operational use, so that the children could learn agricultural methods during their stay on the farm. The older ones took on the heavy labour, while the younger children sowed seeds and supported in other ways. Before long, a fully self-sufficient Kibbutz was established, moving one newspaper to report the story of Ulster's *"Haven from Hitler"*. Through the war years and a few beyond, an estimated 300 refugees from Czechoslovakia, Austria and Germany, part of the *Kindertransport* programme lived at Ballyrolly Farm. Most of the children attended classes at the school in Millisle, where they sat alongside local children for all lessons with the exception of their specialist English classes.

One woman was asked years later whether the children liked living on the farm. Her response was simply

"they liked living".

The last to leave moved away from Ballyrolly Farm in May 1948. Many of the buildings and artefacts have subsequently been lost to time. The farm itself, now McGill's has no visible signs this was once the Ulster Kibbutz. The nearby school has taken steps to preserve the memory of this remarkable achievement during the Holocaust[114] years. The *"Safe Haven"* garden is a public space near to the entrance of Millisle Primary School. The centrepiece is Ned Jackson Smyth's sculpture displaying a Star of David filled with many metallic leaves, some hollow, others silver and about half of them gold. Ned himself is from nearby Carrowdore, while the base for his work was crafted by Rodney Brown, a former pupil of the school. Once a year the school receives a case of oranges in the post – a gift from a kibbutz in Israel, partly to recognise the ongoing work of the school in preserving holocaust memories, but also as a thank you for nine years supporting Jewish children more than seventy years ago.

The origin of the name of Millisle has, to my knowledge, three possibilities. Given the history of flour and grain milling in the locality, the prefix *Mill-* likely needs no further explanation. As for *-isle*, one candidate raises the possibility of a dammed stream creating a mill pond that had an island with a single tree, but

---

114 Hitler's extermination campaign led to an estimated six million Jews being killed – less than one in three of the European population of Jews survived. The Nazis also targeted other groups including Jehovah's Witnesses, ethnic Poles, the *"incurably sick"* and the Roma population – these and others adding up to another five million murders under Hitler's orders.

cannot be verified from any maps available today, while another suggestion is that rocks off the coast were once marked as *Milles Isles* on ancient charts. Even though the latter is supported by the 1744 writing of Walter Harris and the former by widespread folklore, both seem unlikely. The existence of another village in Wigtownshire, Scotland, with exactly the same name, points to a possible corruption of Scots-Irish. The word *Innis* can be used to mean an island, but has also been frequently used for a meadow. Now, a meadowland with at least one mill does seem to fit the area rather well.

The mill-pond-island *"legend"* centred around a mill belonging to a family with firm Scottish roots – the Carmichaels. David and his brother William ran the family flour mills in the 1860's – a business with over 100 years of experience. They took ofter in 1854 following the death of their father. In 1867 David's wife Catherine, herself the daughter of a doctor from nearby Portaferry, gave birth to their first child – Amy Beatrice. Catherine had earlier been deeply affected by the many open-air prayer meetings held in Belfast's Botanic Gardens during that period and raised Amy and subsequent children to believe in God.

Amy Carmichael was brought up in a wealthy Presbyterian household in a small seaside community where it was not uncommon for more than 1,000 people to turn up to open-air summer services and prayer meetings. Bear in mind, the entire combined population of Millisle and Ballycopeland was less than 1,000 in those years after the Great Famine had caused so many deaths and forced countless others to flee. The Ballycopeland Presbyterian church had been built on land given by the Carmichael family, and enlarged with the support of donations from David and William. Her family home was *Mervue House,* an imposing grey stone[115] building on the corner of Abbey Road and Main Street in the *"little old-world village of whitewashed cottages on the shore of the Irish Sea"*. You cannot see this as it was demolished in 2002. A blue plaque was positioned on the nearest available building four years later – the Millisle Baptist Church.

The village school was built and opened during Amy's childhood, but her parents chose to use some of their considerable income by providing home tutors before sending here away to Harrogate Ladies College. The family left Millisle when Amy was 16, moving to Belfast where the Carmichael business expanded.

It is for her work as a missionary in India that Amy is remembered. She spent

---

115 Later painted white.

time in Japan and Sri Lanka (then known as Ceylon) before settling in the Tamil Nadu region of southern India. There she encountered many young girls living with daily *"physical and moral danger"* at the Hindu temples. Amy established the *Dohnavur Fellowship* in 1901 on the site of an existing mission school. From here, she led a campaign that liberated hundreds of children from abuse and forced changes to a system that had previously normalised child prostitution for generations. Amy died in India in 1951.

Back in the Millisle area, the **Ballycopeland Windmill** – the best example of a fully-functional four-sailed mill in Northern Ireland, is an excellent reminder that the Ards Peninsula's fertile soils and excellent microclimate have made it one of the most productive grain growing regions in the entire island of Ireland. At one time the peninsula had around 100 working mills powered by fresh air.

This one, fully restored and open as a tourist attraction since 1978 dates from around 220 years ago. The former miller's house has been converted into a visitor centre and includes a scale model of the mill itself showing the mechanics of milling. Access is free, but opening hours are limited as is wheelchair access.

Millisle is also undergoing something of a restoration. The Main Street has begun a long-term process of re-imaging, and the seafront area is being upgraded to bring into line with other nearby resorts boasting long promenades.

The resorts USP[116] is its lagoon. Adjacent to a sandy beach of almost 200 yards in length, with a car park, toilets, picnic tables and ice creams all just a stones-throw away, a stone barrier retains seawater after each high tide creating a safe environment for supervised swimming or just splashing around. A separate paddling pool for the little ones completes the arrangement – almost. Don't forget to look out for the seal sculptures dotted around. Better still, bring your binoculars – there's a colony of grey seals that spend much of their time on the nearby rocks.

Heading west out of Millisle on Abbey Road, we pass through **Carrowdore**[117] before arriving on the banks of Strangford Lough at **Greyabbey**. We mentioned the Grey Abbey briefly earlier, so now we'll have a look at the rather quirky little

---

116 Unique Selling Point

117 Take a look at the nineteenth century Carrowdore Castle as you pass. It is a private residence in a large park with surrounding woodland featuring a three-storey stone tower.

village itself. Writing in 1837, Samuel Lewis noted *"The village is pleasantly situated on Lough Strangford, and on the road from Portaferry to Belfast; and the neighbourhood is embellished with some elegant seats and beautiful scenery"*. Much more recently, it has become known as the *"wedding village of the peninsula"* for its wealth of retail outlets specialising in all things matrimonial. The village also has something of a reputation as being a centre for the antiques trade.

The Abbey is in the grounds of Grey Abbey House – the family seat of the Montgomery family since the very start of the Plantation in 1607. The house and gardens are in immaculate condition, but to view them properly, you'll need to be part of an invited group, such as a classic automobile club, or a cruise ship party. It is possible you've already had a look around and seen inside the grand house. Several movies and television programmes have filmed here including the recent production of *The Woman in White* and *The Frankenstein Chronicles*. The grounds surrounding the ruins of the Abbey are open to the public, free of charge. Here you can see one inhabitant that needs no invitation – the red squirrel. Grey Abbey has plenty of these instantly identifiable natives.

Just a couple of miles further north is another estate and house with Plantation roots. Mount Stewart is the family seat of the Vane-Tempest-Stewarts. It was on 28th November 1899 that Charles married Edith Chaplin, of Blankney in Lincolnshire. Edith became the Marchioness of Londonderry when her husband inherited the Marquess title on the death of his father in 1915. As Lord and Lady Londonderry the couple built a family at Mount Stewart, where they also hosted lavish parties of up to 2,500 people. Amongst those who were accommodated at Mount Stewart was Ulrich Friedrich Wilhelm Joachim von Ribbentrop who arrived from Germany in 1936 with a party of S.S. Officers. Charles has been roundly criticised for his *"support"* of the Nazis. A visit to Hitler in Berlin, for which he chose to take other family members including his youngest daughter Mairi, resulted in scornful public comment. Calling Hitler *"a rather agreeable and kindly man"* didn't help matters. His own family cousin, Winston Churchill, called him a *"half-wit"* and newspapers nicknamed him the *"Londonderry Herr"*. For many years, a gift from Von Ribbentrop stood on a mantelpiece, even when the house had opened to the public. As far as I know it is still there. The 18-inch tall porcelain statuette features a helmeted Nazi Stormtrooper holding a flag. Lord Londonderry, speaking in 1940, admitted *"I backed the wrong horse"*.

Edith's story is also controversial. Her relationship with Prime Minister Ramsay

MacDonald is still written about to this day, but we will focus on her Mount Stewart legacy – the magnificent gardens.

Armed with a seemingly bottomless purse, throughout the 1920's Edith worked tirelessly (as did a very large number of landscape gardeners, labourers and others) on the re-creation of the estates large garden area. She designed and had installed a shamrock garden, sunken garden and Menagerie. Mediterranean influences resulted in the magnificent Italian and Spanish gardens. The lake was cleaned and enlarged, lined with rhododendrons, azaleas and magnolias, and several trails through the extensive woodland were carefully laid out. There are many red squirrels here too by the way.

Following the death of her husband, Edith gifted the gardens to the National Trust to be used as a public space *"to be lived in and enjoyed"*. Whether you're drawn to Mount Stewart by the eighteenth-century vineyard, the efforts to restore a Victorian rose garden, or the quiet solitude that can be had strolling or sitting in the Mairi Garden where a fountain depicting the Londonderry's youngest child forms the centrepiece, you are sure to treasure your visit to a garden that regularly features in top gardens of the world lists.

This part of Northern Ireland is certainly not short of grand houses. There is one that even offers overnight accommodation – at premium prices. Advertised as part of the *Ulster Grand Tour*, guests staying at Ballywalter Park Mansion House are promised *"luxurious and highly individual bedrooms"* with *"hearty Irish breakfasts and delicious dinners"*[118].

The seaside village of **Ballywalter** was once known as Whitkirk, which in turn became anglicised to Whitechurch before the name it uses nowadays was adopted in the eighteenth century. At that time, Ballywalter was a busy fishing village, a few remnants of which remain even though the main industry has been tourism for a long time here. People come to Ballywalter to get away from the crowds, so don't tell too many others about the long wide sandy beach or the fantastic uninterrupted walk along the seashore (tides permitting) that can be enjoyed, often with peaceful serenity.

With some care, it is possible to continue south along the beach as far as **Ballyhalbert**. This is another village with an old name and a newer one. The village was recorded in the fourteenth century as Talbotyston – Talbot's town. By

---

118 https://ballywalterpark.com/historical-cultural-tours/

the Plantation years this had become Ballitalbot, which, over the years has been corrupted or softened depending on your point of view to Ballyhalbert. So forget any stories about who "*Albert*" was, we need to establish the origin of "*Talbot*".

The Talbots were a family of English descent, holding the title Earls of Shrewsbury, who had also been successive Barons of Cleuville in Normandy until their return to England with William the Conqueror. In French they had been known as Tailbois or Talebot.[119]

It was Richard Talbot who first set foot on Irish soil in 1174. Eleven years later his loyalty to the English King Henry II during the conquest of Ireland resulted in the granting of land and the harbour at Malahide north of Dublin. From there, he and his successors built further estates throughout the island, including at what would become Ballyhalbert.

Overlooking Ballyhalbert are two signs of man's existence here from long ago. The youngest is the motte, or locally the moat, which dates from the period of the Anglo-Norman invasion of these parts, and may even have been built on the orders of Richard Talbot himself. Not far away is a standing stone, possibly moved here from Scrabo Hill. This has been examined by archaeologists who suggest it was put in this position as much as 4,000 – 5,000 years ago. To find it, you'll need to make your way along the Moat Road from the main A2 road. The stone is in a field about 100 yards from the junction. There used to be three of these sandstone megaliths, no-one can say for sure what became of the other two[120].

A much more recent addition to Ballyhalbert was the military airfield, constructed between 1940 and June 1941. In those wartime days, the existence of an ancient windmill was no obstacle – the Clydesburn mill disappeared beneath concrete. More than 9,000 miles of runways were laid throughout the British Isles to service the needs of the military. was demolished during the process.

---

119 Perhaps with the French origin in mind, there are moves in the village (by petition) to officially change the recognised pronunciation of the village name from ending with a hard -*t* to a silent -*t*. In other words from al-*bert* to al-*bear.*

120 One was believed to be at the junction of two fields between Ballyhemlin and Ballyhalbert. When the fields were being merged into one, some 35 years or so ago, the egg-shaped stone, about six-feet long was removed and rolled away. It was last seen in a grass verge, but subsequent searches have not unearthed the rolling stone.

The station was known as RAF Ballyhalbert but was served by men and women from the United States, Poland and Commonwealth nations as well as Royal Air Force personnel. Look carefully through the graves in the nearby churchyards and you'll see that many of them served **and** lost their lives here.

We've already heard about General Eisenhower's time in Bangor. The Supreme Commander of the Allied Forces also visited Ballyhalbert on 19th May 1944.

Much of the site has been taken up by a holiday park for families enjoying this peaceful resort, but the control tower and some sections of concrete runway are still visible.

Ballyhalbert Bay once saw four ships sunk in the space of a few hours. The victims of stormy weather? No. Attacked by Viking longboats? Think again. Perhaps it was the French Navy or even a remnant from the Spanish Armada fleet? Still no. You might not think of this quiet corner of the County Down coast as being the scene of a U-boat attack, but it was. The steamship *Amber*, taking a cargo of coal from Troon to Dublin under the command of Captain Michael Montgomery encountered U-boat UC65 on 2nd May 1917. The German commander Otto Steinbrinck ordered Montgomery to abandon ship with his crew before scuttling the steamer. The wreck is in one piece, with a clean hole in the stern, lying in about 150 feet of water and is often visited by divers. A sister-ship the *Saint Mungo*, making the same journey, also laden with coal for Dublin suffered the same fate as did two vessels travelling in the opposite direction, the *Derrymore* and *Morion*. Steinbrinck reputedly sank 58 allied ships during the First World War before exhaustion forced him to leave active service.

A visit to Ballyhalbert ought to incorporate a walk along the seafront to Burr Point. Burial Island just a stone's throw offshore is named thus, due to this land being a Viking burial site. Why here? The Vikings were known to be excellent navigators – remember, they sailed to the Eastern shores of North America and back, long before Columbus. Burr Point[121] happens to be the most easterly land[122] on the island of Ireland, and is marked by a large circular all-weather steel and bronze sculpture incorporating a letter "E" - also the work of Ned Jackson Smyth.

---

121 Burr derives from the Irish word b*ior* meaning "*poin*t", so Burr Point literally means *point point*!

122 Strictly speaking the most easterly mainland – *Big Bow Meel Island*, 1000 yards off the same coast is a little further east.

Leaving Ballyhalbert, we criss-cross the peninsula once again, this time heading south-west to **Rubane** – the home of two places that share the name *Echlinville* - Ireland's newest distillery and a manor house offering luxury accommodation. The two can be combined for those with an interest in following the whiskey production from field to glass. The distillery and manor house both belong to the same business who offer those with enough time and money on their hands the opportunity to live for a short period in the manor house whilst spending the day taking part in every step of whiskey manufacturing – all the way through to bottling and tasting.

Echlinville is named after the Echlin family, of Scots descent but for nearly four hundred years prominent in the Ards. The neighbouring village of Rubane was used to rebrand the house – *Rubane House* – around 1850 when James Cleland acquired it and completed substantial alterations. In the latter half of the twentieth century, Rubane House was converted into a residential home for young Catholic boys in need of care. Operated by the De La Salle Brothers, the home took in boys from January 1951 until 1985 when it was forced to close as allegations of widespread abuse mounted. A recent inquiry found an all-too-familiar story of ongoing abuse with allegations being swept under the carpet for years. It is no surprise that the new owners have removed every possible trace of Rubane House's sorry past – including the name.

The distillery, built in brand new premises alongside the manor house prides itself in using traditional methods and barley grown in fields alongside the still. For a premium, customers can order their own casks of Single Malt or Irish Pot Still whiskey, even with bespoke bottling and labelling.

From Rubane we have two more places to call. **Kircubbin** on the bank of Strangford Lough is a short drive north-west and **Cloughey** on the coast is a little further in the opposite direction. Being the nearer of the two, we'll head for Kircubbin first.

The village of Kircubbin has gone by the names of *Cubynhillis* and *Kilcubin* suggesting the origin of the name may well be the Irish *Cill Ghobáin* where the latter part is a person[123] and *Cill* means Church. There had been a place of worship here as early as 1306 – the *Ecclesia de Sancti Medumy*. Unfortunately, in modern times there is no evidence of this building.

This is a place with a long and complicated history that a couple of paragraphs

---

123 Some suggest this is a little-known Benedictine monk whose name was *Goban*.

cannot possibly cover adequately. With that in mind, I'll just tell you about the village as it has been for the last hundred years or so.[124]

Until the 1950's Kircubbin was a busy commercial harbour, loading and unloading coal, corn and potatoes officially, and quite a lot of other *"stuff"* unofficially. In this respect, it was no different to most other ports throughout the British Isles - and smuggling still goes on today, but not much of it by boat.

Perhaps the most famous stories of smuggling in Strangford Lough are those recorded by W.G. Lyttle[125] in *"Daft Eddie"* a fictionalised serial first published in the *North Down Herald* at the end of the nineteenth century. Writing in 1890 Lyttle described Kircubbin thus:

> *"The village of Kirkcubbin is pleasantly situated upon the eastern shore of Strangford Lough, in the barony of Upper Ards, about eight Irish miles to the south-east of Newtownards. It lies almost directly opposite to Killinchy, from the shore of which may be distinctly seen the white houses of Kirkcubbin that stand near the water's edge".*

Lyttle's stories were all apparently based on local legends and had each had elements of truth behind them. He wrote of the fishing industry and subtly suggested that some of the boats were up to no good *"fishing boats arrived and departed without any interference in the way of either demanding or collecting dues from the owner"*. Tax avoidance in other words. Two landmarks were identified by Lyttle as being critical to the success of the smuggler's operations – *Black Neb* and *Doctor's Bay*. The writer had this to say about each of them:

> *"Black Neb is a dark spit of land covered with heather and whin at the south side of "The Doctor's Bay", a haunt of wild duck and the barnacle geese about 400 yards south of Kircubbin sea front ... a low dark sliver of heath, pointed like a dagger across Strangford Lough to the distant and misty Mountains of Mourne".*

These days the Doctor's Bay is more likely to be full of sailing boats than fishing boats, and should you venture onto Black Neb you'll probably encounter scrambling ramblers rather than raging smugglers.

---

124 An excellent place to start your personal dig into Kircubbin's past is here: http://www.ardspeninsula.com/kircubbin.html

125 Generally remembered as Wesley *Guard* Lyttle after his name was incorrectly printed in this way by the Belfast News-Letter after his death. Lyttle's middle name was actually *Greenhill*.

The village is surprisingly lively given the population is only just over 1,000. A recent effort to renovate the main shopping street and harbour area has made Kircubbin a smart little village in the middle of the Ards Peninsula.

Cloughey is another village with a fishing tradition, which these days is well known as a seaside resort, albeit a small one. Let's read what the 1886 *County Down Guide* had to say about it:

"Cloughey has a population of about 150. It is a fishing village in the barony of Upper Ards. 14 miles, Irish, from Downpatrick, and 4 miles, Irish, from Portaferry. The bay on which it stands, marked Cloghy on the map, forms a half circle, 2 ½ miles from point to point. The beach is clean sand and has only one obstruction, a small rock almost midway, called after some celebrated person of the name of Charlie. There is a good chance for surf-bathing. Nine fishing luggers belong to Cloughey, and about 30 row boat fishermen live here. The herring fishing is good off the coast in favorable seasons. There is a natural harbor with about 10 feet of water in spring tides. Coasting vessels discharge coal, and take in potatoes and paving stones. The land of the district is fair for tillage. Potatoes, oats and wheat are the principal crops. Kirkistown Castle is about half a mile from Cloughey. The landlord of the district, Mr. Montgomery, has lately had it repaired".

So, how does that compare with today? The most recent census established the population had risen to 1,075. The beach regular features in awards for cleanliness such as the Green Coast Awards. Volunteers, most of whom live locally, regularly walk the entire length of the beach from Ringboy to Slanes Point collecting litter and washed-up debris. The result is a beach that is sandy, wide and inviting, with a shallow slope into the sea making it a family-friendly bathing beach as well. Fishing is less of a commercial operation and more of a pastime for visitors these days, and its been a long time since the harbour saw any loads of coal. Keeping the beach clean is an ongoing matter, as is keeping the beach! Coastal erosion is a major issue along the Ards Peninsula. Look closely at the first Ordnance Survey maps and compare them with the most recent satellite images and the problem identifies itself. Where populations have grown near to the sea, so has the need to protect their vulnerable homes from the elements. It is the sea defences – walls, rock armour and the like that are diverting tidal energy onto nearby beaches and, literally, washing the sands away over time. Some scientists warn that without drastic measures, some beaches such as at Ballyhalbert and Cloughey could disappear completely.

The 1886 guide book also made reference to Kirkistown Castle, which itself is suffering from a completely different kind of erosion, but with the same cause as previously identified. The desirability of a home with both sea and castle view has led to property developers squeezing, or *eroding* the green-belt land around the castle, which once stood in solitude. What was once a green meadow to the west of the Castle is now a housing estate, and the seventeenth-century three-storey tower house which once had commanding views of the Irish Sea as far as the Isle of Man, now overlooks a holiday park in the foreground. But the good news is that after years of neglect, the building has been restored and is now open to the public.

Like so many other Ards Peninsula castles, this one was built as a home first, and defensive fortification second. To tell why the Savage family needed to build a tower house here in 1622 requires us to travel another 450 years backwards in time. It was John de Courcy who conquered almost all of County Down in 1170. He was faithfully supported by William Savage whose reward included the Ards Peninsula. Savage immediately built a castle at Ardkeen overlooking Strangford Lough and, on the site of the golf course at Cloughey he put up a second motte and bailey castle – almost certainly built from wood. A raised mound, known to locals as *"the moat"* is the only evidence that can be seen with the naked eye.

Until the Plantation of Ulster, this wooden structure was sufficient to deter raids from the ousted O'Neill clan. Roland Savage, whose own brothers had died at the hands of the O'Neills twenty years earlier, decided in 1622 to build something a little more defensible. He chose a site slightly further inland – *Kirkistown* and opted for a three-storey tower house surrounded on all sides by a *bawn* and stone walls flanked by round castellated towers. At nearby Ballygalget he built a second castle. It was said that a beacon lit on Kirkistown would be seen at Ballygalget, where a second beacon would then raise the alarm at Ardkeen on the other side of the peninsula.

By 1660, Kirkistown Castle was in the hands of Captain James McGill who invested heavily in improvements to the walls and gardens. McGill also built a windmill, of which, sadly, only the stump is left. McGill's granddaughter inherited the property and promptly[126] married a Savage, returning the castle to the family that built it.

---

126 She promptly married, but not a Savage – he was her second husband.

After passing into the hands of the Montgomery family, the castle became something of a ruin. By 1832 half of the roof was missing and many of the windows were broken[127]. The Presbyterian church took over in 1840 and converted the castle into a church briefly, before a farmer – James Kelly, took on a tenancy in 1880 and used the buildings to retain his livestock. In the twentieth century the tower house had a temporary resurgence as a popular dance-hall venue until the years immediately following World War II when the developments of housing and a cemetery threatened the future existence of the castle. Excavations undermined what little foundations existed and for a time the possibility of Kirkistown Castle disappearing completely was very real. Thankfully, it is now in the care of the regional authorities and steps have been taken to reinforce the structure.

A natural structure off the coast that disappears completely with every high tide is the South Rock. This has been the scene of countless shipwrecks over the centuries. Writing in 1744, Walter Harris warned

"beware of the South Rock on which many brave ships have perished"

adding ominously

"no (lifeboat) crew can save their lives … if the winds blow high".

By 1767 the Irish Government was being petitioned to erect a lighthouse. A second petition was submitted in 1783 followed by a third before Thomas Rogers was authorised to design and build a conical granite tower in 1793. Can you imagine the scale of the task? Every day, a boat set out from Newcastle to the South Rock a mile offshore from Cloughey. On board were 22 men, tools and granite blocks – some of them 5 feet long. The construction window each day was short – the time between mid-tides in theory gave twelve hours work time, but the weather frequently intervened. In the winter months progress proved to be impossible.

Not to be deterred, Rogers persevered and in March 1797 the South Rock lighthouse was illuminated for the first time. It continued warning (not always successfully) shipping for eighty years after which it was replaced by the South Rock Lightship. The lighthouse is still standing and can be seen (with binoculars) from the shore on a clear day.

The village of Cloughey is a great location for a day at the seaside or as a base

---

127 From the *Ardkeen Parish and Statistical Remarks*.

for touring the Ards Peninsula. It lies midway between two of the area's best known and most-visited locations. We'll visit them both in the second half of our peninsula tour.

Further Reading:

M. Taylor, Faraway Home, O'Brien Press (1999) is a work of fiction inspired by the *"Safe Haven"* at Millisle.

W.G. Lyttle, Daft Eddie or The Smugglers of Strangford Lough can be downloaded freely from the Ulster University website – search for "Daft Eddie".

Q is for a Quartet of Quays and Queens

Head north from Cloughey and you'll find yourself at Portavogie – a fishing village that has not only retained its age-old industry but expanded it – considerably! Fishing out of Portavogie has not always been plain sailing if you'll forgive the pun. Herring had long been a traditional seasonal catch when stocks appeared to be drying up in the first quarter of the nineteenth century. Fishermen were reporting having to travel farther out to sea and fish in ever-deeper waters to find herring, who, as it turns out, were avoiding them. Research shows the eighteenth century practice of igniting kelp had contributed to the destruction of herring spawn and damaged their offshore feeding beds, forcing the fish out to sea.

Nowadays the search for fish can take boats hundreds of miles out to sea, but when they return to Portavogie there is a modern industrial infrastructure ready and waiting for them. The large fishing fleet bring in prawns, herring and other fish where an evening auction takes place most days.

The 1886 County Down Guide reported Portavogie harbour as being home to *"about 40 fishing luggers"*. A pier was built in 1906 and the harbour as we can see it today dates from the 1950's with substantial alterations and enlargement works carried out in 1875 and 1985 effectively doubling the harbour capacity. Now only Kilkeel has a larger harbour and permanent fishing fleet in the whole of Northern Ireland. In 1985, Strangford Member of Parliament John Taylor informed the House of Commons that Portavogie was *"one of the major fishing fleets in Northern Ireland (with) 60 boats of more than 40 feet in length"*.

Portavogie is an interesting place to visit for many reasons. As an active fishing harbour, the comings and goings of various vessels, the frequent auctions and the opportunist seals hanging around for a share of the unwanted catch all make for entertaining and informative times. Beside the harbour there is a memorial to the fishermen of Portavogie whose lives were lost in tragedies at sea – a vivid reminder of the danger faced daily by these hardy folk.

All around Portavogie the shore is lined with millions of scallop shells – discarded by the processing plants. Some say they give the beaches character, others call it littering. Nowadays, with local stocks diminishing, almost all of the

Chlamys Opercularis or **Queen** Scallops landed at Portavogie have been either dredged or trawled from the scallop-rich seabeds off the coast of the Isle of Man. The debate about the quality and flavour of fresh versus frozen scallops rumbles on. As a consumer, you're probably only going to get fresh if you dine out, or buy your own close to the point of landing. Even then you may well find the scallops have been frozen[128] at sea.

If its seafood you're after consuming then Portavogie has a couple of options available. Lucy's is a fish and chip shop with a reputation for preparing and serving delicious fish at very reasonable prices. The village's sole (did I just write that!) restaurant is the **Quays** which specialises in cooking meals from locally-source ingredients including locally caught crab and prawns as well as Portavogie-landed cod and mackerel.

Words painted on a lengthy wall mural remind of both the dedication of those who worked at sea, but also the threatened demise of an industry that began here with the arrival of Scots fishermen more than three hundred years ago. One side of the mural reads

LET NOT THE PROSPECT OF REWARD MY SOLE AMBITION BE

WHEN AT THE URGING OF THY CALL I LEAVE THE SHELTERED HARBOUR WALL

TO VENTURE ON LIFEs SEA

Alongside it is a poem by "Captain" James Moore of Portavogie who reminisces of *"that ancient fleet … with tapering masts and canvas furled"* where *"only ghosts in memory linger"*.

Nearby on a wall along Harbour Road a second large painted mural celebrates the life and achievements of footballer George Best who had a four-bedroomed detached home on Lemons Road in the latter years of his troubled life.

An excellent heritage trail can be followed if you'd like to take a tour around the whole of Portavogie. There's plenty to see and do, so allow at least a full day – better still, take your time and stay over[129].

---

128 Dry-packed scallops are frozen without any further additives. Wet-packed are treated with STTP (Sodium Tripolyphospate) prior to freezing. This artificially increases the weight as the scallop absorbs water during the freezing process.

129 http://www.visitardsandnorthdown.com/pdf/NMDT_Portavogie_Heritage_Trail.pdf

Moore's excellent *History of Portavogie* includes an account of the remarkable evangelical life of Sarah Currie Palmer. How this woman, born in Portaferry in 1880 to a family with a long association with Portavogie, came to be called a *"capable and forceful speaker"* by a newspaper in Pennsylvania, USA some 45 years later is a story that needs telling, regardless of your views of her faith.

Sarah's parents were James and Eliza, carpenter and seamstress respectively, who married in 1879 – Sarah being their first child a year later. She grew up in Portaferry and by 1899 was preaching in Presbyterian chapels across Ireland and as far away as England. Her father did some travelling of his own that year – emigrating to America. Eliza didn't follow him across the Atlantic for at least another two years. Sarah busied herself with her missionary work until both parents returned home, with tales of life in the United States. In August 1912, Sarah sailed from Londonderry aboard the Columbia, bound for New York and onward to a new role in Chicago at the Moody Bible Institute.

For the next 47 years Sarah preached across America. The Moody Bible Institute monthly magazines record her working in Pennsylvania, Illinois, Virginia, Michigan – often travelling overnight between appointments. Other newspapers show that she also addressed groups as far away as Alaska as well as making several voyages home where she preached often in Portavogie. In an incredibly active life, Sarah found the time to write *"The Story of my Life"* in 1917 and other works including *"Vera Dickson's Triumph"* followed later. When she passed away in August 1959 whilst staying with her sister in New York, her death warranted an obituary in the New York Times.

Having mentioned Portaferry, perhaps now is a good time to take the south road from Cloughey and spend a while there.

The 1886 *County Down Guide* asserted confidently that Portaferry *"deserves to be classed among the most charmingly picturesque places in Ireland"*. Today, one website calls it a *"beautiful little town"*[130], while the author of an online tribute to Portaferry gives it the ... *"Pearl of Loch Cuan"*[131]. The 1861 *Belfast Street Directory* clearly connected Portaferry as *"a thriving seaport and market town"* with its *"good quay, where vessels of light burthen can discharge their cargoes"*.

---

130 http://www.ardspeninsula.com/pferry.html

131 Ardrossan (Ayrshire) resident Danny Mathieson writing in 2008.

What was so *good* about this **quay** – at the place whose very name means the *"landing place of the ferry"*[132]? One dictionary defines a *quay* as a structure – usually stone, beside water for the loading and unloading of moored boats. By the middle of the nineteenth century, Portaferry had not one, but two stone quays, with a third added in the early part of the twentieth century. The oldest is the so-called *"Big Quay"* running almost the entire length of The Strand, with the *"Coal Quay"* located further south on Shore Road – the location of Portaferry's old salt pans. A smaller *"New Quay"* came much later.

Together, these quays gave nineteenth century Portaferry a material advantage over all its neighbours. It could provide adequate dock space for numerous vessels of all sizes and class, and its regular ferry service across the Lough straits gave meant it was readily accessible from Lecale as well as the Ards.

Just off The Strand is the Ropewalk. The traditional craft of rope-making involved laying out strands of fibre in as long a straight line as possible before pulling the strands taught together and twisting tightly to create a rope that is much stronger than the individual strands. At Portaferry this process was carried out in the open air along the 200 yard long lane[133] that took its name from the practice of walking with the strands of fibre to keep them from tangling before twisting. At the Lough end, production centred around a large building where the natural fibres and completed ropes were stored. This building, on the dog-leg of the lane, is now a popular café and bakery.

Opposite the café stands the remains of Portaferry Castle. A map of Portaferry produced around 1778 names it as Savage Castle, and the only other named road is Rock Savage Road, so this seems like a good time to talk about the Savages.

The story begins with William Savage – or more correctly William Le Sauvage, a Derbyshire Knight of Norman descent whose family had taken land in England as part of William the Conqueror's invasion force. William, in turn, was, as *A Genealogical History of the Savage Family in Ulster* put it *"one of the twenty-two Knights who fought by (Sir John) De Courcy in the subjugation of Ulster"*. Successive Lords Savage, loyal to the Crown *"swayed the North and held it*

---

132 An alternative view is that the name is, at least in part, an anglicised form of *Peireadh* - meaning *"rapid, treacherous whirlwinds"*.

133 Long enough for the requirements of most vessels, but not to meet the standard requirements of the Royal Navy – whose ropes had a standard length of 1,000 feet.

against the enemies of England". As the same text noted *"the descendants of almost all the other Anglo-Norman conquerors of Ulster the Mandvilles, Jordans, Chamberlains, Copelands, Martels, Ridals -were swept away or rendered utterly powerless (whereas) the SAVAGES still held their ancient inheritances in the ARDS, unsubdued"*.

By the sixteenth century, Rowland Savage, *Lord of the Little Ards* was established at Portaferry Castle, and his eldest son Patrick ensured the Savage dynasty would be further strengthened when he married into the influential Montgomery family. The Savage Castle at Portaferry is, as we've seen elsewhere, more tower house than castle, and comprises three storeys and an attic, all connected via a spiral staircase. The building is open to the public during the summer months. Next door, the former stable block serves as a Visitor Information Centre which includes a loft gallery area featuring displays celebrating the history of the Portaferry area.

More recently the family name most-often associated with the development of Portaferry is Nugent. What many do not realise is that this particular family are direct descendants of the Savage family. Andrew Savage was born in 1770. His grandfather, also Andrew, had married Margaret Nugent and so, in order to inherit the Nugent holdings and titles, grandson Andrew changed his surname from Savage to Nugent when he succeeded his father in 1797.[134] By 1800 he was a married man. Eight years later he served a term of office as High Sheriff of County Down. Nugent's inheritance included Portaferry House, *"a large country mansion in a restrained classical style"*[135] built originally for his grandfather and extended by his father. Andrew invested over £7,000 and brought in the services of William Farrell who added substantially to his country home, ideally situated to overlook both Portaferry and Strangford Lough. Location, location, location they say. Writing in Ireland Exhibited to England in 1823 A. Atkinson recalled a visit to the improved and extended 3,500-acre estate with

"commanding several interesting views, over the channel, to the isle of Man, the coast of Scotland, and the mountains of Mourne, in our own country. — The

---

134 Not every relative approved of the change. One uncle famously quipped that he *"would rather be an old savage than a new gent"*.

135 According to property consultant and estate agent Thomas Orr who handle the letting of the cellar apartment – for *just* £750 pcm you can live in a country mansion accessed via a half-mile driveway and with gardens, ponds, lakes and a deer park!

home view to the village of Strangford, over the Lough, which forms a wide crystal expanse in that place, although not so eminently distinguished by the grandeur of space, as the foreign views, is nevertheless an animated scene, and strongly picturesque. — To this rich character of the home view, the luxuriant and widely extended plantations of the demesne, largely contribute".

The completed house had five bays to the front, ionic columns and end piers for the central porch and a relatively new innovation – Wyatt windows[136] to the upper levels.

The house and most of the estate are not accessible to the public, but Nugent's Wood is. A wonderful walk from Portaferry along the banks of the Lough takes you into this beautiful wood where you may well see red squirrels or badgers before returning along the same footpath to Portaferry[137].

Once again, Samuel Lewis provides a succinct and useful description of the town in 1837. The entry for Portaferry in his *Topographical Dictionary* includes these observations

"It is now, owing to the exertions of the proprietor, Andrew Nugent, Esq., and the spirit of commercial enterprise in the principal townsmen, a place of considerable business, and increasing yearly in prosperity. It consists of a square and three principal streets, besides a range of good houses on the quay, which is built along the edge of the strait, chiefly at the expense of Mr. Nugent. The only public buildings are the market-house, a substantial old structure in the middle of the square, which in the disturbances of 1798 became a post of defence to the yeomanry of the town, who repulsed a body of the insurgents that attempted to take possession of it; the church of the parish of Ballyphilip, a neat building erected in 1787; a large and commodious Presbyterian meeting-house, and another for Wesleyan Methodists: at a little distance from the town is the R. C. chapel (a large building) for the parishes of Ballyphilip, Ballytrustan, Slane, and

---

136 This was not merely following fashion. James Wyatt had created a way to integrate larger single-panelled windows into buildings where previously two or even three separate windows were needed. At a time when window tax was paid according to the number of windows in a home rather than the amount of glass used, Wyatt windows saved the owner considerable amounts of tax each year.

137 The wood is in the care of the National Trust who also look after the trail: https://www.nationaltrust.org.uk/strangford-Lough/trails/nugents-wood-walk

Witter. The town is a constabulary police and a coast guard station. The market, on Saturday, is well supplied with provisions; fairs are held on Jan. 1st, Feb. 13th, Tuesday after May 12th, and Nov. 13th.

There is a distillery; and a brisk trade is carried on, chiefly with Liverpool, Glasgow, Dublin and Belfast, whither it sends wheat, barley, oats, potatoes and kelp, and receives in exchange timber, coal, and general merchandise".

Andrew Nugent died in 1846 and was succeeded by his eldest son Patrick and, in turn, his grandson, another Andrew in 1857. Further Nugents came and went until the house and estate was sold privately in the 1980's.

Lewis mentioned the market house, described in the 1861 Belfast Street Directory as *"a commodious building".* Andrew Savage had paid for its construction between 1749 and 1752 so that it could serve as a trading centre for a weekly market to be held in the square every Thursday[138]. It is the oldest surviving building in Portaferry. Built to a typical Irish market house style, the ground floor was largely open plan with a large versatile space and administrative rooms on the upper level. Over time the upstairs area has been a court room, meeting room, dance hall and the site of Portaferry's first bank – the penny bank.

Restoration of the market house was completed in 2017 at a cost of £350,000 ensuring the long-term future of this important building and community space.

The penny bank was founded by John Orr, a Presbyterian minister and founder of the town's temperance society. Saving money, even a penny at a time, was better than wasting it on liquor was his reasoning. Even though the town had more than thirty inns, a busy distillery and a thriving smuggling trade, the bank quickly built up a long list of regular subscribers.

To complete our *Quartet of Quays and Queens*, we need to visit one more **Queen**.

A much more recent innovation in Portaferry is the Queen's University Marine Laboratory. Situated in the rather grand three-storey house that was once home to the Portaferry branch of the Belfast Bank, the University has been based here since 1972. The Marine Laboratory is a working home for teams of biologists, engineers and modellers studying topics as diverse as sustainable energy

---

138 By the middle of the nineteenth century, this had moved to Saturday and has stayed there ever since.

methods to the effects of the introduction of alien invaders[139] on natural habitats. Seaweed research may not sound particularly attractive, but when you consider that kelp is not only a carbon-neutral crop (actually releasing oxygen and absorbing carbon dioxide) and can grow from seed to 10 feet in length in just six months, without any further external fertilisation or intervention – you can see why scientists are studying the possibility of large-scale offshore kelp production as an alternative to land-intensive agriculture.

The rather comfortable building on Lough Shore Road is not where most of the actual research is carried out – much of it is risky business on or below open-water, often in the notorious currents of Strangford Lough. And that is where we leave the Ards Peninsula in search of stories a little further south – some with tragic outcomes.

Further Reading:

George Francis Savage Armstrong's A Genealogical History of the Savage Family in Ulster, published in 1906, is widely available to download freely online in a variety of formats.

J. Moore, Portavogie – A History, April Sky Design (2004)

---

139 Examples include Japanese Sea Squirt – not little green men!

R is for Risks, Rescues, Rights, Riffles & Rapids

As we've already discovered, Newcastle is as good a place as any to establish a firm footing for any assault on the Mourne Mountains, but this seaside resort has much to offer in its own right and a long history to recount – often punctuated with the most catastrophic events.

The 1886 *County Down Guide and Directory* said that of Ireland's *"many beautiful watering places"*, *"there is not one surpassing Newcastle in extent and variety of attractions"*. Is the same true today. That's not for me to judge, but here are just a few of the attractions available should you head that way shortly.

For an active time, but with the security of expert support on hand, businesses like Newcastle-based *Outdoor Ireland North* offer walking and hiking tours, cycle rides to challenge even the fittest of biker as well as custom-built tours to suit your own requirements and budget. They're a versatile bunch, with a website that even promotes ballroom dancing!

For something closer to Newcastle, and (probably) a little less risky, the boating pond at Castle Park, right in the centre of the town, has (in season) more than 20 pedalo swans that can be taken out on the lake for a small charge. Go-karting is a little more adventurous (and pricier) and there is a fun crazy golf course to try out. On the outskirts of the town, Island Park has a nine-hole pitch-and-putt course and four tennis courts.

For golf enthusiasts, the Royal County Down Golf Club has rounds on its championship course available for visitors for the relatively low price of £70 of you can bear golfing in midwinter. Prices in the summer months are three times as much! A shorter course, the Annesley Links can be played for £45, even in high season.

Should you wish to spend your time in the water, but not on the open sea, Newcastle provides two options. The Tropicana Outdoor Heated Fun Pool offers everything from water slides to paddling pools, but remember this is quite an exposed site, expect it to be very busy when the weather is good, but if its quiet, there's probably a good reason. On the South Promenade (but only open in the summer season) is the open air rock pool – a much-loved feature of the seafront since 1933. The high-board is no longer there, but make the most of the opportunity to swim in Ireland's last remaining sea-water outdoor pool, as it is constantly threatened with closure.

One of the options for visitors to Newcastle in 1886 was Donard Lodge, residence at that time of Lady Annesley. The house had been built for William Annesley, the third Earl, between 1829 and 1832. Lady Annesley was his second wife, Priscilla, who lived at Donard Lodge for 53 years following the death of her husband. The Lodge was terribly damaged by fire in 1941 whilst in the "care" of the US Army. The building was eventually demolished in 1966.

William and Priscilla's grand-daughter Lady Mabel Annesley found fame in her own right as an artist and wood engraver. One of the books she provided illustrations for was Richard Rowley's 1924 collection of *County Down Songs*. Rowley, whose real name was Richard Valentine Williams, had been raised in Belfast before moving to Newcastle, where he lived for much of his adult life. His home in Newcastle, *Brook Cottage* on Bryansford Road has been demolished, but he is commemorated by the Rowley Path near to the Island Park and a housing estate – Rowley Meadows.

Brook Cottage itself made way for another housing estate – Brooklands, where a curious name given to the *Beers Bridge* needs further investigation. It has no direct connection to brewing, but owes its name as a tribute to William Beers, one-time customs officer in the town (so, an indirect link to brewing too) and also a former occupant of Brook Cottage.

Donard Lodge, by the way, was the centrepiece of a large estate that included Donard Forest – we mentioned it briefly in *H is for Hewitts*. There are several different walking/hiking trails in the forest[140], some of them pretty gruelling. If you feel even more energetic, a local orienteering group regularly *run* around in the woods and welcome new faces.

We've seen a few risky activities on land in and around Newcastle, but to be fair, we're talking risk to limbs and muscles, whereas the next activity, can and does lead to loss of life as we're about to find out.

Take a sobering walk along Newcastle's South Promenade, with one eye on the

---

140 Here's the link again: http://www.walkni.com/d/walks/253/Map%20of%20Donard%20Forest.pdf

open sea and the other making sure you don't miss a large rectangular black plaque (near to one of those seafront *"pay and display"* binocular platforms). This is a memorial to the 73 Newcastle and Annalong fishermen who drowned in a storm on Friday 13th January 1843 in Dundrum Bay – the very waters the memorial overlooks. In all 16 fishing boats, 10 from Newcastle and 6 from Annalong put out to sea in search for herring that morning. Things started well, a firm southerly wind carried the skiffs eight miles out to their preferred fishing grounds and lines were lowered. All of a sudden weather conditions changed dramatically. A fierce storm whipped up giant waves and brought freezing rain and then snow with it.

Some of the boats capsized almost immediately whilst men were washed overboard from boats that remained afloat. This was January, remember, and visibility was reduced to almost zero. Those in the icy waters stood no chance. In conditions such as these the bodies systems shut down in a matter of minutes. There was no chance of rescue. But that did not stop a boat leaving Annalong in an attempt to bring in some of those affected. Accounts vary, with some reporting that all twelve volunteer rescuers being amongst those who died.

Only two boats made it back to land that day. In all, 73 lives were lost, 46 of them residents of Newcastle. In their homes, 27 women became what they had feared almost every time their husbands put to sea - widows. More than 100 children of Newcastle lost a father that day.

Almost immediately a public subscription was established. The funds raised resulted in the building of a line of cottages - *Widow's Row*, providing homes for many of those most affected by the disaster. The public response had been immediate, as the Banner of Ulster reported, just a week after the disaster:

"£372 5s. has been collected in this town by William Beers, Esq., and William Waring, Esq., and £50 additional was collected in Belfast by other individuals. Messrs. Beers and Waring also collected in Lisburn, Hillsborough, and Ballynahinch, the sum of £41 4s. 6d. In Downpatrick and its vicinity nearly £150 was raised. The Board of Management of the Shipwrecked Fishermen and Mariners' Benevolent Society have granted the sum of £100 for the surviving and destitute relatives of the unfortunate fishermen lost at Annalong and Newcastle".

You can imagine the scene in so many homes in the days and months following the tragedy. Wives imploring their husbands and growing sons not to put to sea while men and boys, needing to put food on the table, struggled vainly to reassure. Disaster couldn't strike twice, could it?

It did.

Just two years later, as the Great Famine was beginning to strike, a boat left Newcastle on a regular run to Dundrum in search of mussels (bait for the lines on the skiffs that fished for herring). This job was typically carried out by the wives and children of the men who ventured farther out to sea in the more dangerous waters. On this occasion sixteen made the trip to Dundrum, some in the boat with others walking the short distance along the seafront. Having completed their task, the nine females and seven males decided to return to Newcastle together – all of them in the boat. Once again a gale force wind caught them and as the *Newry Telegraph* had to report the following day *"another melancholy calamity occurred"*. The newspaper described how *"the boat upset and all perished"* noting that *"some of them are mothers, brothers and sisters of those lost on the 13th January, 1843"*.

When you've contemplated the risks these ordinary family folk took and the price so many paid, leave the memorial and head back to the harbour area and have a good look at Maeve King's mosaic mural on the wall of the water treatment works. It depicts the scene inside one of the fishing boats on the day of that first disaster – it's chilling.

Finally, take a look at Widow's Row. The twelve whitewashed cottages are all protected as listed buildings, with at least one available as a holiday let – strong reminders that this seaside resort where holidaymakers take on risky activities including windsurfing, snorkelling, rock climbing and kayaking is a place where lives were risked (and lost) on a regular basis, just to earn a living.

Not every perilous episode on the seas has a tragic ending. Since 1826, the Newcastle area has had almost continuous lifeboat support available. I could fill the entire book with stories of bravery and courage, but will illustrate the qualities of the men and women who volunteer their lives on our behalf with just one account – the very first recorded.

On 6th March 1826 a strong gale and powerful waves combined to drive the barque *Richard Pope* into Dundrum Bay. The ship was making its way from Liverpool to Sierra Leone. Captain John Morris on seeing the ship floundering launched the lifeboat and made two unsuccessful attempts to reach the *Richard*

Pope. On both occasions his galley filled with water and he was forced to return to land. A second boatman, Alexander Douglas on sighting a rowing boat leave the barque and upturn tried valiantly to swim through the surf. Unfortunately he was unable to rescue any of the men – four of the five drowned and Douglas himself almost lost his own life. Rescue attempts continued through the night and the following morning, with the help of additional volunteers, the coastguard men were able to reach the stricken vessel and save ten lives. Captain Morris and boatman Douglas both received bravery medals for their parts in the rescue.

The Tidal Commissioners Reports establish the true scale of the dangers at sea. Between 1783 and 1845 no fewer than 66 vessels were lost in Newcastle's Dundrum Bay alone.

Since 1993, the RNLI lifeboat station has operated from the South Promenade where a new boathouse and slipway were erected on the site of an earlier coastguard hut and tractor house.

* * *

Having given some thought to *Risks* and *Rescues*, what about *Rights*? Florence Anne Lemon Balcombe may not be familiar to you, but you've probably come across her husband – Bram Stoker[141]. Florence was born in Falmouth, England, in 1858 but moved to Newcastle at 2 years of age. Her father was a military man[142] and this was the time of the Crimean War, so many connect her first name with Florence Nightingale. Whether or not this is fact, cannot be verified. There is no argument that she preferred to be called *"Florrie"*.

She married Stoker in Dublin in December 1878 after a lengthy relationship with Oscar Wilde. Florrie is mainly remembered for her vigorous campaign against the German producers of *Nosferatu* – a vampire movie with a remarkably similar storyline to her late husband's famous novel – *Dracula*. She was the sole rights holder to her late husband's works, including Dracula and had received no prior request to use the novel as the basis for a motion picture. The widow won her case and all prints of the film were ordered to be destroyed. They weren't, as you may well have seen, but she succeeded in severely restricting distribution of

---

141 See *"D is for Dracula"* in my *"Yorkshire Coast From A to Z"* book for more.

142 In 1860 he was promoted to Adjutant in the Royal South Down Light Infantry, becoming Major in 1875.

what she considered to be a flagrant unauthorised adaptation of Bram's novel. Florrie died in London in 1937, 25 years after her husband.

* * *

As for *Riffles and Rapids*, Newcastle owes its existence to the Shimna River which flows out into Dundrum Bay. Its not one of Northern Ireland's longer rivers, running just under 10 miles from the slopes of Ott Mountain to Newcastle, passing through the Fofanny Dam and Tollymore Forest Park on the way. The Shimna is what is sometimes known as a *spate* river – one that is prone to spells or *spates* of sudden flooding. At other times of the year, the river can be little more than a trickling stream that has been known to dry up completely at times.

With this kind of river, shallow islands or *riffles* often form in the flatter sections, particularly as the river nears the sea. The Shimna has plenty of these to view. Riffles are interesting, not just to observe the water flow and particularly the way that fish – in this river's case often salmon or trout – navigate their way upstream past these islands on their way to the traditional spawning grounds near the river's source, but also to see how the crafty angler finds a position a little way downstream from a large riffle, knowing full well that the microscopic lifeforms that live on, in and around the relative safety of a riffle, will often be carried away downstream into the waiting mouths of the aforementioned salmon or trout. These in turn are blissfully unaware the angler is ready to strike. It's a cruel old world.

I doubt you need me to tell you what rapids are, so I'll simply explain where you can view them on this particular river. If you are thinking of riding them in your canoe – stop reading this and take some expert advice first. These are challenging waters, especially after heavy rain, and not for the novice, or unaccompanied canoeist.

On foot, a beautiful meandering walk that takes in many of the Shimna's rapids and waterfalls, as well as the excellent stepping stones and a few bridges is the Mourne Way[143]. Bear in mind that you'll need at least two days to complete it – possibly longer if you are elderly, infirm or have children with you. Take your time, do it in stages, and leave yourself enough energy to enjoy your evenings

---

143 Download a free guide (with maps) here:
    www.activitybrochuresni.com/Download.ashx?id=35

back in Newcastle.

The main road to Newcastle from the North takes you through Dundrum where John de Courcy built one of his many castles.

The *County Down Guide and Directory* entry for Dundrum mentioned *"the remains of the castle built for Knights Templar ... in the twelfth century, are still extensive and are seen to great advantage from the North-eastern approach"*.

From the same text we get a brief chronology of the custodians of Dundrum:

"When the monasteries were dissolved, the castle and several townlands were given to the Earl of Kildare. The Magennises were for some time lords of the castle, but it was taken from them for disloyalty and given to the Earl of Ardglass, from whom it passed to Viscount Blundell, and became Lord Downshire's by inheritance".

With Dundrum already in ruins, the leader of one of Ireland's oldest clans, Phelim Magennis had built a tower house near the mouth of the Shimna River in 1588. His *"new"* castle thus gave the seaside town its name. At this time, Dundrum was known as Magenis Castle, although these were turbulent years with the fortification passing through several hands, sometimes by force and at others by trade. Phelim retook the castle briefly during the Civil War in 1642 but lost it along with his entire estate for his part in the failed insurrection. The Earl of Ardglass referred to was an Englishman, Thomas Cromwell who was given the title and land by Charles I as a reward for his support of the Crown during the Civil War. The castle at Dundrum was seen as a strategically important site, but exposed and vulnerable to attack from the disgruntled Irish, so, rather than risk losing it and having to retake it, in 1652, Oliver Cromwell order its demolition.

Viscount Blundell referred to above, was the second Blundell to take possession of Dundrum. Sir Francis Blundell had owned the castle briefly from 1636, whilst it was his son and heir, Montague who, as the first and only Viscount built an I-shaped mansion house in the grounds of the ruined castle. The Viscount died with no male heir to inherit the property and it passed through his daughter's descendants to the Marquess of Downshire, who in turn handed it to the authorities as a public monument.

* * *

Should you feel like a really strenuous trek, why not take a look at Saint Patrick's Way – the so-called Pilgrim's Walk[144]? The compilers of this 82 mile hike have worked hard to include as many stopovers as possible having some association or other with Patrick himself. Newcastle is one of the recommended overnight stops in the section of the walk that takes in the County Down Coast. Perhaps this is a good time to give some thought to the Saint himself and a few other legendary tales.

Further Reading:

D. Allwood Egerton, Artist and Aristocrat:The Life and Work of Lady Mabel Annesley, Ulster Historical Foundation (2010)

R. Rowley, Tales of Mourne, Duckworth (1937)

---

144 Download it here: http://www.visitmournemountains.co.uk/PilgrimWalk

S is for Snakes, Saints, Stirabout and a Spike

One of the best-known Saint Patrick stories is the one where he becomes surrounded by snakes during a 40-day fast on a hilltop. Patrick immediately orders that all serpents leave Ireland. In one version of the account a single snake remains which Patrick has to lure into a box before casting it into the sea.

Some people argue that the complete absence of snakes of any kind from Ireland is evidence to support the legend, while others including National Geographic Magazine's James Owen[145] point out that there is nothing in the fossil record, or from any other form of archaeological investigation to confirm the existence of any snakes whatsoever in Ireland since the time of the last ice age. Prior to the period of warming that signalled the end of the ice age 10,000 years ago, Ireland, like most of North and Western Europe was far too cold for any snakes to survive, and since then, the Irish Sea would have prevented snakes from reaching the island. Owen consulted Nigel Monaghan from the National Museum of Ireland. Monaghan's conclusion was emphatic

"At no time has there ever been any suggestion of snakes in Ireland. [There was] nothing for St. Patrick to banish".

Monaghan also explained that mainland Britain's adders and grass snakes had been able to slither across from western Europe via the land bridge that only disappeared 6,500 years ago.

Some say that the snakes in the Saint Patrick story are a metaphor for the druids in Ireland who fiercely resisted conversion to Patrick's brand of Christianity. Patrick is known to have spent time in the area around Downpatrick, with many claiming the snakes were driven out of the Mourne Mountain region by him, so did this area ever have a druid population?

Yes.

The *Mound of Down* is clearly visible and just a short walk downhill from Down

---

145 The full article can be read at
https://news.nationalgeographic.com/news/2014/03/140315-saint-patricks-day-2014-snakes-ireland-nation/

Cathedral. Both sites were built on in the twelfth century. The Mound was the scene of a motte and bailey structure enclosing several small wooden buildings, whilst a monastery was erected by John de Courcy in 1183. The latter was a short-lived building. An earthquake originating somewhere off the coast of north-west Wales apparently put paid to it in February 1247[146]. I say "*apparently*" because this is another of those legends with little material evidence to substantiate the story. The archivists of Down Cathedral make no mention of it in their historical timeline other than to dismiss the event as a myth.

The facts of the matter are that John de Courcy did invite a group of Benedictine Monks to come over from England and establish a monastery at Downpatrick and a house was built for them. In 1220 they petitioned King Henry III requesting funds to build a cathedral on the site, reporting that their House of Saint Patrick was being rebuilt following extensive damage.

By this time the hill on which the monks were living was well-enshrined as the legendary grave site of not only Patrick but two more Irish Saints – Columcille and Brigid. You may have heard the rhyme

> *"In Down three saints one grave do fill,*
> *Patrick, Brigid and Columcille".*

Once again, the evidence to support the claim of a triple grave for three of Ireland's most venerated saints is circumstantial. It is true that texts attributed to Columcille point to *"Saul of Patrick"* as being the resting place for Patrick himself and the *Book of Cuanu* , now lost but extensively quoted in the *Annals of Ulster* had this to say on the matter:

> *"The minna of Patrick were placed in a shrine at the end of three score years after Patrick's death by Columcille. Three splendid minna were found in his tomb; to wit, his Goblet, and the Angel's Gospel and the Bell of the Testament".*

The *minna*, or relics are consistent with the belongings of a priest of the time of Patrick. Goblets, or *cailech* an ancient word for *chalice* as the book recorded it were certainly in use, the biblical text needs no explanation, and bells were well-used as calls to prayer at that time. The custom of burying artefacts with bodies

---

146 D.A. Chart writing in *A Preliminary Survey of the Ancient Monuments of Northern Ireland* in 1940 said *"destruction by an earthquake occurred in 1245"*. The nearest confirmed earthquake took place two years later.

was a pagan ritual though.

Patrick was big on bells – employing a team of blacksmiths who forged and crafted bells, sometimes as many as fifty at a time, wherever he preached. The *Book of Cuano* also revealed that Columcille chose to place the goblet in Down, the bell went to Armagh, whilst the *Angel's Gospels* were, as you might expect, retained by the angels. The seven-inch iron bell (later covered in copper) is in the Museum of Ireland, but the whereabouts of the *"Down"* chalice – most likely crafted from a single piece of wood is not known.

Historian John O'Donovan wrote this on the subject of Patrick's effect on the Druids in Ireland (and in turn the Druid's influence on the Irish form of Christianity):

> *"Nothing is clearer than that Patrick engrafted Christianity on the pagan superstitions with so much skill that he won the people over to the Christian religion before they understood the exact difference between the two systems of beliefs; and much of this half pagan, half Christian religion will be found, not only in the Irish stories of the Middle Ages, but in the superstitions of the peasantry of the present day".*

O'Donovan was writing in the nineteenth century, so we can take his use of the term *peasantry* to be a reference to the general public. One example of a pagan superstition embraced by many modern Christians in Ireland is the Shamrock. This iconic symbol of good fortune was never mentioned in any of Patrick's writings, or those of his contemporaries.

Patrick and his followers did what they could to convert pagan worshippers. The fifteenth century *Book of Lecan* described how Patrick took 180 of the Druid texts and had them all burned – possibly explaining why so little literature of this ancient religion remains in Ireland. However, the Druids were certainly co-existing to some extent with the Benedictine monks and other early Christians in Downpatrick for some considerable time before disappearing almost entirely. Were these pagan peoples, many of whom venerated icons including those of serpents, the figurative snakes that Patrick purged from Ireland? We'll probably never know for sure.

To find out more about Saint Patrick in the Downpatrick area, two places stand out as locations to visit. The first is Down Cathedral.

The name of Downpatrick was not recorded prior to 1790. Up to that point settlements, of which there were many, tended to develop around the site of the present-day cathedral on a hill known as the *Duno*, so named after the *dún* or fort erected atop the mound. In the second century after Christ, the Greek geographer Ptolemy included *Dunum* in his short list of Irish towns.

The first cathedral was built in the thirteenth century and had a troubled existence, being attacked and damaged on a regular basis before it was finally laid waste in 1541. The 1794 *Traveller's Guide to Ireland* described how *"At Downpatrick ... are the ruins of an old cathedral, said to have been built by St. Patrick"*. In fact, at that time, efforts were already well under way to replace the ruined building with a grand Cathedral. The Dean of the Cathedral, William Annesley and William Hill, later the first Marquess of Downshire, combined energies and finances to establish a substantial restoration fund whose donors included King George III. Almost a century later the *County Down Guide and Directory* of 1886 described the restored Cathedral thus:

"The Cathedral of Down occupies a part of the site of the abbey founded by St. Patrick in the 5th century. It stands at the head of English Street on one of the hills included in the ancient municipality, and is partly surrounded by trees, which form a curtain to the main walls and heighten the picturesque effect of the tower as seen from the North-western approach to the town".

The *"building of majestic proportions"* is actually more of a new build incorporating certain retained features from previous versions than a completed restoration project. Published in 1846, *The Parliamentary Gazetteer of Ireland* put it like this:

"The present cathedral, though usually called a restoration of the previous pile, and though incorporating some part of that structure is really a new edifice, and is one of the most imposing modern specimens of the pointed style of architecture in the province".

So if pointed architecture is your thing, then you'll almost certainly enjoy your visit. Guided tour will encompass the main landmarks including the reputed graves of the three saints.

The second venue to visit is the Saint Patrick Centre Heritage Museum which perhaps a little misleadingly welcomes you to *"the Home of Saint Patrick"*. Whatever your theological standpoint, the Centre offers fascinating exhibitions of the life and travels of the man himself. Don't miss the 20-minute 5-screen

IMAX Cinema presentation or the state-of-the-art multimedia exhibition. With family tickets at under £15 (2018 prices) this is a tourist attraction that offers excellent value for money.

For me though, the essential place to visit is that mound we mentioned right at the start of the chapter. The *Mound of Down* is a tranquil hillock, overgrown and left (mostly) to nature, a drumlin island in the Quoile Marshes. It is a deceptively large enclosure, covering an area roughly the size of four football pitches and has been occupied by various groups, possibly since the Iron Age. The elliptical-shaped earthwork has been the subject of several excavations, most recently in 2012. These digs confirmed earlier views that the mound had been created, at least in part, as a *rath*, possibly around the time of Saint Patrick's presence locally, perhaps a little earlier. The main work had taken place around the time of John de Courcy, but the motte was abandoned, unfinished, possibly because de Courcy moved on to Carrickfergus where he found a more suitable site. In an intriguing twist, the publishers of the report into the 2012 dig, whilst concurring with previously-held views that this was primarily an Anglo-Norman motte, stated clearly that the possibility this has also been the site of an ancient Irish inauguration mound *"cannot be as easily dismissed as the other alternative explanations"*.[147] Aerial photography reveals the mound to be enclosed by an egg-shaped ditch which adds weight to the view held by some that this is indeed an ancient druid or other pagan site and a centre for ritual worship.

It is perhaps a shame that modern steps have been cut into the side of this rather unusual and compelling mound. Having said that, they make access to the summit somewhat easier, especially when the ground underfoot is boggy, and the view of Downpatrick and beyond is well worth the effort.

* * *

The Downpatrick area has been home to a few other superstitions over the years. Here's just one of them, related by William Home in his interesting and totally weird 1826 *Every Day Book*[148]. Home tells how

> *"At Stoole, near Downpatrick, in the north of Ireland, there is a ceremony commencing at twelve o'clock at night on every Midsummer-eve.—Its sacred*

147 *Data Structure Report: Geophysical Survey and Excavation at the Mound of Down, County Down 2012*, author Philip Macdonald

148 You can get a free digitized copy from Google books.

mount is consecrated to St. Patrick: the plain contains three wells, to which the most and there are heaps of stones, around some of which appear great numbers of people running with as much speed as possible; around others, crowds of worshippers kneel with bare legs and feet as an indispensable part of the penance. The men, without coats, with handkerchiefs on their heads instead of hats, having gone seven times round each heap, kiss the ground, cross themselves, and proceed to the hill ; here they ascend on their bare knees, by a path so steep and rugged that it would be difficult to walk up: many hold their hands clasped at the back of their necks, and several carry large stones on their heads. Having repeated this ceremony seven times, they go to what is called St. Patrick's chair, which are two great flat stones fixed upright in the hill; here they cross and bless themselves as they step in between these stones, and while repeating prayers, an old man, seated for the purpose, turns them round on their feet three times, for which he is paid; the devotee then goes to conclude his penance at a pile of stones named the altar. While this busy scene of superstition is continued by the multitude, the wells, and streams issuing from them, are thronged by crowds of halt, maimed, and blind, pressing to wash away their infirmities with water consecrated by their patron saint; and as powerful is the impression of its efficacy on their minds, that many of those who go to be healed, and who are not totally blind, or altogether crippled, really believe for a time that they are by means of its miraculous virtues perfectly restored. These effects of a heated imagination are received as unquestionable miracles, and are propagated with abundant exaggeration".

It's something of a muddled legend where participants move from Downpatrick to the scene of St. Patrick's Chair many miles away as if it were just a short walk away, but it gives you a flavour of the kinds of superstitious rituals that were once commonplace.

* * *

Wherever a town or city has its own museum you will usually find it to be a source of invaluable local knowledge often given freely. The Down County Museum in Downpatrick is no exception. Based in a former gaol-house, the museum tells the story of the building, its former uses and its connection with the system of transportation to Australia[149].

---

149 The museum offers half-or full-day tours of the former gaol that include a lunch and drinks for around £12 per person.

The site was carefully chosen – midway between courthouse and cathedral, supposedly the sites of earthly and heavenly justice. From planning to completion took seven years. The three-storey structure opened to new inmates in 1796. Prior to that, two buildings, neither of which still stand, served as temporary jails, to be used as and when required. You see, in those days, imprisonment was rarely used as a punishment. When found guilty, most were fined, flogged[150] or sentenced to death. Jail-houses were mainly places for pre-trial detention, as holding stations for prisoners awaiting transportation, or for locking up those with major debts (in this case, as much for their own protection).

Nineteenth century prisons were squalid affairs. A Royal Navy surgeon, Thomas Reid, visited Downpatrick in 1822 and included his observations in a book *Travels in Ireland*[151]:

"About ten we arrived in Downpatrick, after breakfast visited the gaol, which is almost as bad as it is possible for a building of that sort to be. The construction renders classification, inspection and employment utterly impractical. Females of all descriptions, tried and untried, innocent and guilty, debtors and murderers, are all thrown together in one corrupting mass, and kept in a cell not near large enough. Sick or well there they must remain both night and day. There were twenty one thus confined when I saw it, one of whom had been sick for four months; it would not have surprised me had they all been sick. Over this cell is a place where a school is kept; it contained several spinning wheels, which is the only kind of industry in the prison.

The smell from some of the felon's cells was intolerably offensive. The prison is insecure; and so wretchedly constructed, that, although room is much wanting, there is one yard of which no use is made; it is covered with weeds and long grass. A school has also been established for the males; and this, was well as that for females, has been productive of great good, notwithstanding the disadvantages that operated against them. As hope is held out that "another prison will shortly be built or the old one enlarged", to point out any more defects would be unnecessary. I will merely take the liberty to offer my unbiased

---

150 Or given some other form of corporal punishment.

151 Read or download the entire book here:
    https://archive.org/details/travelsinirelan00reidgoog

149

and disinterested opinion, that no enlargement or alteration can convert the present one into what a prison should be; the experience of making it even more tolerable would go a considerable way towards the building of one on a commodious plan, in which the morals of the persons confined would not be deteriorated as at present".

Prisoners regular dietary requirements were *met* by the following ration allocations:

"Each person is allowed nine ounces of oatmeal, which, boiled with water, forms the article "stirabout", and half a pint of new milk, for breakfast; four pounds of potatoes and half a pint of new milk for dinner, with half an ounce of salt".

A new prison was built at a cost of £60,000 and opened less than ten years later which operated for seventy years. It was largely demolished in the 1930's with just the gatehouse and outer prison walls remaining. The gatehouse, outside which public hangings were a regular feature, is the main entrance to Down High School. The prison walls were lowered but retained, apparently to protect the school from the advances of the Quoile fog – not to keep the pupils in.

The earliest recorded jail in Downpatrick was a town centre building known as *Castle Dorras*. This was another of John de Courcy's grand residences, from the twelfth century. The castle stood at the foot of English Street near to the junction with Church Street, serving as a gatehouse to the town overlooking a landing place for boats. No trace of it exists, with the Down Recorder newspaper offices standing in the equivalent spot. This building was once the town's post office and was known as De Courcy Place. The 1886 *County Down Guide* mentioned how, *"while the foundations were being sunk, an underground passage was discovered".* Unfortunately before it could be fully explored it was *"industriously filled with rubbish by a road contractor".* At that time, just *"a fragment of one of the watch-towers"* remained standing in a private garden. Sadly, even this has gone.

Legend has it that Castle Dorras was the final resting place of Redmond O'Hanlon – or at least his severed head! Who was Redmond O'Hanlon and why did he come to such an end?

Conservative party politicians have long been known as *tories*. The term is derived from an Irish word *tóraidhe* which one dictionary defines as meaning an *outlaw* or *robber*, while another source says it represents a *pursuer*. To dig a little deeper we need to look into seventeenth century Ireland. At that time, *tories* were very different – fighters siding with the Irish Confederates and vigorous opposers to Cromwell's invading English Parliamentarians. Redmond O'Hanlon was one such *tory* – his exploits earning him the nicknames *Irish Robin Hood* or *Irish Rob Roy*.

Since many of Redmond's activities took place away from County Down, I will leave it to you to find out more about the man who was given the title *"Count"* in recognition of his services to the French Army. It was in County Down though, where he lost his life, so this part of the story will be told here.

Whether you view O'Hanlon as a murdering robber or brave hero, for a long time the authorities in England and Dublin had a price on his head. There are two differing accounts of the Count's death. His foster brother Art MacCall O'Hanlon admitted shooting him dead, but claimed the event took place after a quarrel near Eight Mile Bridge[152] in the Mourne Mountains. Other accounts confirm the same identity for the killer but that Redmond's murder was cold-blooded as he lay sleeping. Art was pardoned for his crime and received a cash reward. Redmond's head was removed and exhibited on a spike outside Castle Dorras in Downpatrick.

The town of Downpatrick has revealed some of its secrets to us, and a few darker moments. Now we are going to Kilkeel where we'll start with another one before things brighten up.

Further Reading:

A.M. Wilson, St. Patrick's Town: History of Downpatrick and the Barony of Lecale, Isabella Press (1995)

J.F. Rankin, Down Cathedral, Ulster Historical Foundation (1997)

---

152 Now known as *Hilltown*.

T is for Tullaghmurry Lass, Trough & the Teck Emeralds

Coastal communities invariably have long associations with fishing and, as we have seen, it is a dangerous way to earn a living. Kilkeel has,for some time, been the busiest fishing harbour in County Down. The 1886 *Directory* had this to say on the subject:

"Deep sea fishing is carried on to a considerable extent by the inhabitants of the villages along the Down coast. Ardglass is the chief point of interest in connection with this industry. In the herring fishing season as many as 500 luggers discharge there ... Kilkeel ranks next to Ardglass. It is not uncommon to see a fishing fleet of 300 sail there in summer".

The guide book also revealed Kilkeel to *"have a good safe harbour"* and its own fleet of *"30 sail and 35 row boats engaged in fishing"*. Nowadays the harbour is home to a permanent fleet of around 100 boats, yet fishing is comparatively new in Kilkeel. Thomas Bradshaw, writing an account of Kilkeel for his *General Directory* of 1820 made no mention of fishing in this *"handsome village"*, instead noting *"in the summer season, the shore might be made the resort of bathers and invalids, from the fine sandy beach which here presents itself to the eye"*. Bradshaw compiled a detailed alphabetical list of Kilkeel residents and their occupations. There were grocers, bakers, linen merchants, farmers and quite a few nailers, whilst Moses Hill, listed as the lone mariner was the nearest Kilkeel had to a fisherman.

Kilkeel's growth as a fishing port is directly linked to the development of modern harbour facilities. Prior to the second half of the nineteenth century, the townland of Kilkeel was focussed around a small square with almost all buildings radiating off here within a hundred yards or so. With a market house, church, school, meeting place for Presbyterians and a small hotel, Kilkeel was little more than a seaside village, albeit strangely configured a short way inland. By the beginning of the twentieth century, with a harbour established and two stone piers breaking the water to provide a safe haven, homes and commercial buildings were springing up between the square and the harbour. Nowadays, most of the population of Kilkeel live nearer to the sea than the historic village centre. This expansion and the conversion of fertile agricultural land into residential areas and industrial complexes has led to the town of Kilkeel as you see it today being an amalgamation of five older townlands or villages – Magheramurphy, Dunnaman, Drumcro, Derryoge and the thirteenth century village of Kilkeel itself.

Fishing is a dangerous occupation, and with more than half of Northern Ireland's entire fleet based in Kilkeel, tragedies are an unfortunate inevitability. *Tullaghmurry Lass*, a thirty-foot wooden-hulled trawler left Kilkeel in total darkness shortly before 4 o'clock on the morning of 14th February 2002. The vessel's skipper for the day was Edward Michael Greene, a man with twelve years experience as a Deck Officer. With Michael, as he preferred, were his father and eight-year-old son, both also called Michael, on their way for a day's fishing trip. Winds were light, the sea was calm, and, as day broke, visibility was good – ideal conditions to be at sea.

When contact with the Greene's was lost, family members ashore became increasingly concerned for their welfare, and by the following morning an air and sea search for the missing vessel commenced. It soon became apparent that the three were unlikely to be found alive. Small items of floating debris were spotted among patches of diesel fuel and one piece – a broom handle, provided incontrovertible evidence that some terrible catastrophe had occurred.

The search for survivors soon turned into a seabed search for wreckage. It was five weeks before what was left of the *Tullaghmurry Lass* was found at the bottom of the Irish Sea seven miles offshore.

Rumours quickly spread that the fishing trawler had been the innocent victim of a collision. The prawn fishing beds favoured by Kilkeel's crews are busy waters, regularly used by much larger ships and stories of submarines in this area were not unheard of either.

Despite, often treacherous wintry storms, local crews joined naval and Irish Fisheries Protection ships in sonar searches of the seabed. On 22nd March, the *Ken Vickers* located wreckage at a depth of 23 fathoms and the following day sent down a team of divers who confirmed this was indeed the remains of *Tullaghmurry Lass*.

All three bodies were recovered in mid-April.

The official investigation found that an explosion had taken place, with the cause being the LPG used to power the onboard stove. A hole had been ripped in the hull, causing the trawler to sink in a matter of moments – giving those onboard no possibility of escape.

A memorial to all those from Kilkeel who lost their lives at sea was erected in the harbour shortly afterwards. It is located outside the Nautilus Centre, which itself is an important place to visit in order to understand more about Kilkeel's fishing heritage. The Mourne Maritime Visitor Centre occupies the entire first floor of the Nautilus building and tells the story of Kilkeel as a fishing port and harbour. Here, you can step on board a full-size replica boat and take the wheel without leaving land. One of the most interesting features is an exhibition of photographs and other artefacts from 20 local fishing families.

Also inside the Nautilus Centre is the Mourne Seafood Cookery School. With prices starting at £50, participants can take part in a cooking masterclass before sitting down to enjoy the products of their labours. There are less costly ways to eat out in Kilkeel, but the novelty of consuming restaurant-class seafood, cooked with your own hands is perhaps worthy of the additional premium.

The harbour and Nautilus Centre form a logical starting point for a tour around this historically and commercially important town, points not lost on local officials who have produced an excellent heritage trail[153]. I will focus on just a couple of stopping-off points. One is a hotel and the second is a water trough. Both are connected to the same family.

The Kilmorey Arms hotel dates from the 1840's and, as you might expect, features a coat of arms above the main entrance. This is the coat of arms of the Earldom of Kilmorey, a title presently held by the sixth Earl, Sir Richard Needham, who chooses to be known simply by his first name. The first Earl, Francis, represented Newry, and therefore Kilkeel, in British Parliament until his death in 1832 when his eldest son, another Francis succeeded him as second earl. It was this Francis who invested heavily in the development of Kilkeel as a trading harbour, recognising its strategic importance for the transportation of coal, potatoes and granite as well as for bringing in fish.

When it was built, the town square looked very different. How you see it today is the result of extensive alterations made a couple of decades ago. The Market House and Court House that once stood adjacent to the hotel are long gone and Kilmorey Square, or the Upper Square as it is known by many locally, is a wide

---

153 Download it here: http://www.visitkilkeel.com/history-heritage/

lane extending along Knockchree Avenue. In the middle of the avenue opposite the hotel entrance stands a small stone water trough, which was originally positioned at the junction of Bridge Street and Harbour Road. These days the tough is much more likely to be filled with flowers than water, but was donated to the town, for the benefit of thirsty livestock and horses by Lady Kilmorey, Ellen Needham.

Born Ellen Constance Baldock in London in 1858, Nellie as she became known, married the third Earl of Kilmorey in Westminster in 1881 before settling at Mourne Park, the Kilmorey seat near Kilkeel. It was her adulterous relationship with a German Prince – Francis of Teck, brother of Queen Mary, that got her in the headlines during the German's lifetime, but when he died as a heirless bachelor in 1910 and bequeathed family emeralds to his mistress, Mary was incensed. After much legal wrangling, a deal was struck and the emeralds remained with the Royal Family. Queen Mary, Queen Elizabeth II and Princess Diana[154] have all worn them. For her part in the deal, Nellie received £10,000 – a princely sum in anyone's money at that time.

Ellen's legacy to the town of Kilkeel is the aforementioned water trough. It is inscribed

BE KIND AND MERCIFUL TO ALL ANIMALS

METROPOLITAN CATTLE TROUGH ASSOCIATION

There are some that claim the trough was donated by Lady Banbury, yet with no evidence that she ever visited Kilkeel, and several sources identifying local girl Nellie, I'll stick with Ellen as the benefactor.

Evidence of a former industry not far from Kilkeel can be found by taking a westwards walk down a narrow lane off the Ballyardle Road about a mile out of town. The three-storey building and associated water wheel was once known as Ballymagart Mill. This was a corn mill with a longer two-storey flax mill nearby. Power came from the aptly-named White Water River running alongside the mills.

---

154 Diana's other connection with Kilkeel is a rather sorry one. The 545 granite blocks that make up the memorial fountain installed in London in 2004 were all crafted at S McConnell and Sons in the town.

Prior to flax and corn being milled here, Ballymagart had County Down's first and largest paper mill[155]. Now, most people probably think of wood as being the main raw material in paper manufacturing, but this is not necessarily the case. In fact, cellulose is what is needed to produce paper, and cotton is almost 100% cellulose. A relatively recent trend in most parts is the concept of "cash for clothes" where unwanted items of apparel are traded in for recycling or reselling, often overseas. In the seventeenth century, old damaged clothes could be traded for a few pennies with the fabric being shredded, pulped and the cellulose used to produce paper. This is the likely origin of the phrase "*from rags to riches*". By the early nineteenth century, the practice of manufacturing paper in this way led to the creation, possibly in America, of this popular rhyme:

Rags make paper,

Paper makes money,

Money makes banks,

Banks make loans,

Loans make beggars,

Beggars make Rags.

At Ballymagart, the mills turned out paper from rags until at least 1829. After that, flax and corn were the only products. The 24-foot diameter water wheel was only put in after paper manufacturing ceased. In fact, analysts believe the entire complex as can be seen today dates from this period and that the original paper mill stood on the same spot.

Rags also came to Ballymagart as a by-product of Kilkeel's once-flourishing brown linen industry. Paper production was a lengthy process – it was incredibly hard work for those involved, many of them children. Phase one involved cutting or tearing rags into tiny strips and then soaking batches in water until fermentation began. Then the second phase involved three or more cycles of beating and rinsing until the pulp took on a porridge-like consistency. This slimy substance was then spread out thinly on wire racks and dried out to form large sheets of paper.

Acquiring linen rags was costly and until it was discovered that wood pulp was

---

155 A second mill at Kilbroney near Rostrevor also produced paper in the early nineteenth century.

an effective substitute, many other materials were tested. These included nettles, straw and potatoes. Over on the other side of the Atlantic, one mill owner even imported Egyptian mummies by the shipload to reuse the 300 yards of linen bandages wrapped around each corpse.

* * *

Patrick Murphy was reputedly born at *Cassy Water* near to Kilkeel. Now, if you were called Patrick Murphy and lived in Ireland you'd possibly use a nickname. This particular chap was known to all as *"Giant Murphy"* for a very good reason.

He was tall.

Very tall.

At the age of twenty-one Patrick stood an inch taller than eight feet high. By the time of his death, from smallpox, in France just five years later, he had added another eight, possibly even nine inches to his height according to some reports.

However, it seems that much of what is retold about Giant Murphy is something of a tall story. He was measured by the highly regarded German Physician Rudolf Virchow at the age of 24 and found to be a mere 7 feet 3 and a half inches tall.

Patrick was the subject of many stories, possibly all of which have little or no basis in fact, but I'll share them with you all the same. On one occasion, whilst playing football, he settled a dispute between two other players by lifting both off the ground completely and banging their heads together. Another time, when being bothered by the unwanted attention of a stranger, Patrick picked him up and hurled him straight over a dry-stone wall into a neighbouring field. Possibly, my favourite, and one that some claim inspired C.S. Lewis to include a prominent gas lamp in Narnia, was that Patrick was so tall that he could light his pipe directly from the village gas lamps in Rostrevor. He spent time travelling with a circus troupe after reluctantly agreeing to appear in front of an audience whilst spending time in Liverpool. It was as a circus showman that he ended his days.

Murphy's exceptional height was attributed to an abnormality in his pituitary gland function. Unusually, he did not grow disproportionately. At the age of sixteen he was weighed at twenty one stone, with a waist measurement of 52 inches – relatively normal for a young man of such stature.

Patrick was an ordinary fellow who just happened to be unusually tall, he never really relished attention and apparently avoided the limelight as much as possible. And with our County Down Giant we will leave Kilkeel and its environment and take a tour around a museum with many more stories to tell.

Further Reading:

A.F. Young & D. Quail, Old Kilkeel and Annalong, Stenlake (2004)

An Old-Timer Talking: Reminiscences and Stories narrated by Hugh Marks of Kilkeel to W.J. Fitzpatrick was first published in 1963 by the Mourne Observer Press. With their consent, the entire book is now free to read online at http://www.lennonwylie.co.uk/HughMarks1.htm

U is for Uniquely Urban

Holywood (yes, pronounced *Hol-ee-wuud*, just like it's cousin overseas, but never, ever spell this one with the extra "l"), is officially classified as a medium town. Believe me, if you've never been, when you first arrive, you wont feel like you are in a town at all. There's something about Holywood that just makes it feel … *different*.

As we've travelled along the Northern Irish coast we've encountered towns and villages of all descriptions, but with two largely shared characteristics. Firstly, most have real *age* – often going back one two or even three millennia. Secondly, for many of them the Plantation of Ulster was a defining time, transforming the future, sometimes even wiping away the past. With regard to Holywood, neither age or the usurping of land by foreign invaders has particularly *shaped* the modern town.

Don't get me wrong, Holywood is an old settlement. Monks were living here in the seventh century and Holywood is well-documented as an emerging port in the seventeenth century. And, it does share the same primary reason for its emergence in the nineteenth century with other coastal communities such as Portstewart, Bangor and Portrush – *tourism*.

The metamorphosis of Holywood into a seaside resort came about largely because several wealthy Belfast industrialists, with plenty of money to burn and little desire to spend their spare time in a town[156] that was cramped, dirty and, well, just too close to work for comfort, chose to build themselves mansion houses overlooking Belfast Lough there.

The result of these property investments became known as *"High Holywood"* and was described nicely in the 1886 *County Down Guide*

> *"Then there is 'High Holywood', so called for the reason that the town has succeeded in climbing the magnificent hill which rises immediately behind it. Nowhere in the country have the facilities for producing real terraces been taken advantage of to a like extent. All the way up the hill, from many street openings, are villa residences, unpretentious as to architecture, that invite most temptingly*

---

156 Belfast remained a town until Queen Victoria granted it city status in 1888.

owing to the lavish floral and arboral adornments in their grounds".

So, although Holywood is a commuter-town like Coleraine, an ancient port like Kilkeel, a monastic site like Downpatrick and a resort like its neighbour Bangor, it is probably the influx of wealth that has made Holywood a uniquely urban area on this stretch of North Down that has been given the appropriate nickname of *"Gold Coast"*.

As a comparatively *young* town, Holywood goes to great lengths to celebrate its heritage – even if some of its treasures aren't quite as old as the authorities like to make out. Take the famous maypole in the centre of the town. Nobody can argue with the claim that a maypole has been here since the seventeenth century. The evidence is clear – a maypole is shown on Thomas Raven's maps[157] dating from 1625 or thereabouts. However, the maypole that is the town's focal point and the centre of festivities on the first Monday in May every year is less than 25 years old. The reason for the discrepancy is that maypoles are made from wood and this only, the only surviving maypole in Ireland[158] is no exception.

What can be said then is that the custom of dancing around a maypole is one that continues to this day in Holywood and has likely gone on for at least 400 years. Given that it dates from the early Plantation years and that the 1611 Commissioners report described Holywood as *"80 newe houses all inhabited with Scotyshmen and Englishmen"* we can presume it was the English who introduced this pagan ritual, as the Presbyterian Scots traditionally refrained from any involvement with events of pagan origin. One of the earliest poles apparently came from the wreck of a Dutch ship, most likely when the crew, out of gratitude to the local people who rescued them recycled the ship's mast. This explains the unusual addition of two horizontal cross bars about half way up the 55-foot pole. Then there was the Harrison family of Holywood House who paid for the pole to be replaced on at least two occasions, before the local council

157 Raven's maps can be viewed in the North Down Museum in Bangor. He received his commission to draw them up from Scotsman Sir James Hamilton who had been granted a large estate including Holywood by King James as part of the Plantation of Ulster.

158 There have been several others in the past. Downpatrick and Kilmore in County Down both had one, as did Maghera in County Derry and Belfast used to have one on the High Street in the nineteenth century. Over the border, the City of Dublin at one time had three maypoles. Some, including the pole at Maghera were deliberately cut down following the troubles of 1798.

took over responsibility, particularly after the pole came crashing down during a storm in 1943, narrowly missing several startled folk onboard a passing bus.

The maypole stands on the town's main crossroads, as does the Maypole Inn, more commonly known as Ned's Bar or Carty's to those who frequent it. Licensed to serve alcohol for more than 150 years, but situated in a building dating from the seventeenth century, the bar has only been owned by three families. Ned Carty moved across from the Star & Garter Hotel in the 1960's, taking over from Mick O'Kane who had owned the bar since 1908. Brian Carty, Ned's son is the present proprietor of a lively bar that has served Sean Bean and Rory McIlroy amongst others. This unassuming character, where international celebrity and local sporting hero alike can stroll into a town-centre bar for a drink alongside regular customers was described way back in 1910. The compilers of that years *Belfast and Ulster Towns Directory* said this

"In no town in Ireland are the relations between all creeds and classes so amicable as in Holywood. All work together for the good of the town, and under the present happy condition of affairs there is no reason why the prosperity of the place should not go on, and thus render Holywood an ideal residential locality for the wealthy and well-to-do, as for the humble and honest working man".

The language may not be politically-correct by modern-day standards, but the point is clear. Throughout the worst years of The Troubles, Holywood, two-thirds Protestant and a quarter Catholic largely avoided violent acts and to this day the town has an atmosphere of tranquillity – an anonymous poet put it like this in 1822:

Close by the water's farther side,

There sits in clean and modest pride,

The cheerful little Holywood.

Not so little any more, of course. When that simple verse was written, Holywood had a population of around 1,200 whereas now well over 12,000 live in the seaside town.

The *cheerful little* town was already on its way up at the time of Samuel Lewis's 1837 *Topographical Dictionary*. Lewis wrote:

"The village, which is delightfully situated on the eastern shore of Carrickfergus

bay, and on the road from Belfast to Bangor, previously to 1800 contained only about 30 dwellings, chiefly poor cabins; but from its proximity to Belfast, and its fine sandy beach, it has since been greatly extended, and is now become a favourite place of resort for sea-bathing. It contains at present 225 houses, mostly well built; bathing-lodges have been erected for the accommodation of visiters, a new road has been made along the shore, and a daily mail has been established. There are several good lodging-houses in the village and its environs; and from the increasing number of visiters, several houses in detached situations, and chiefly in the Elizabethan style of architecture, are now in progress of erection on the Cultra estate, by Thomas Ward, Esq., after designs by Millar. These houses are sheltered with thriving plantations, and beautifully situated on a gentle eminence commanding a richly diversified and extensive prospect of Carrickfergus bay, the Black mountain, Cave hill, the Carnmoney mountains, and the town and castle of Carrickfergus, terminating with the basaltic columns of Black Head".

Writing in 1913, Mary Lowry, who never used more words than was absolutely necessary, summed things up nicely when she simply called Holywood *"a pleasant place of residence"*.

While words like *amazing* and *fabulous* have become commonplace and undervalued in modern society, the word *pleasant* is used much less frequently, and whereas it once signified a place, person or experience of high quality, it is now more usually associated with mediocrity, most definitely not the sentiment Lowry was attempting to convey. Like settlements, vocabulary changes over time.

One nineteenth century Belfast man with family connections to Holywood, William Hugh Patterson published *A Glossary of Words in Use in the Counties of Antrim and Down*. This carefully-compiled reference work included many of the words and phrases used in towns such as Holywood as a direct result of the influx of Scots in the seventeenth century. Some of them, such as *angle-berries* and *fitty forra coo* you are unlikely to come across. The former describing warts hanging from a horse's mouth with the latter being a cow without calf that has gone without milk for an extended period. Others, such as *feth and troth*, a statement of honesty (faith and truth) are still in everyday use. It's an interesting and entertaining read[159] and may help you to understand why you should steer

---

159 Available freely from
   http://www.archive.org/stream/glossarywordsin01coucgoog#page/n143/mode/1up

clear of *hallions* (idle, worthless fellows), how you can assist someone complaining of a *skelf* (splinter of wood) or to make sense of requests like *"wud ya hog me a wheen o'sticks"*[160]?

Patterson's nephew was Robert Lloyd Praeger who was born and raised in Holywood. He trained as an engineer, worked as a librarian, but is remembered for his enormous contributions to the field of botany. Given that his interest in nature had bloomed through childhood and that as an 11-year-old he was already a member of the influential Belfast Field Naturalist's Club, his life-long obsession with the great outdoors came as no surprise to those that knew him. At the age of two, Roberts parents presented him with a sister – Sophia, and shortly afterwards, a new family home, Woodburn House, on Croft Road in Holywood, replaced a smaller house on The Crescent. A blue plaque marks the pairs childhood home from 1868, as does another outside Ballystewart House, number 5 the Crescent a short distance away. Neighbours on Croft Road included a former senior surgeon in the military, Dr John Milford Barnett and Charles McElester, a Presbyterian minister. Both children attended McElester's day school at his church. Sophia, as she grew up, took on her middle name of Rosamund and went from pupil to teacher at the same day school.

Rosamund Praeger is remembered as a writer and illustrator of children's literature, and for her sketches that appeared in her brother's botanical writings but primarily for her work as a sculptor. She used bronze, stone, terracotta and marble, but her preference was to work with plaster.

After many years working from several different studios in Belfast, Rosamund returned home in 1914 and opened a studio on Hibernia Street in Holywood. She continued to display her work at this studio - St Brigid's until 1952, a couple of years before her death.

Many of Robert's books are still in print, and, of those that aren't most can be found digitised online – often with illustrations provided by Rosamund. One of his books, published in 1900 – the *Official Guide to County Down and the Mourne Mountains* finds him saying this about the town of his birth in a section headed

County Down Tourist District

---

160 Whereas the noun *hog* is a pig, as a verb, to *hog* is to cut, whilst a *wheen* is used to refer to a large number of objects, in this case most likely sticks for firewood.

"Holywood is prettily-situated on a well-wooded slope rising from the shore of (Belfast) Lough. The hills behind the town attain a height of 659 feet, and afford charming views of the Lough and the Antrim mountains to the northward, and of County Down and the Mourne Mountains to the southward. Holywood is an important residential place with a population in 1891 of 3,389, and is to all intents a suburb of Belfast".

Praeger also explained how the town got its name, enabling us to clear up the misapprehension that Holywood is a misspelling of Hollywood – it has nothing to do with the holly tree. Robert wrote:

"A church was founded here by Saint Laiseran, son of Nasca, in the 7th century; and an adjoining ancient tumulus, or sepulchral mound, was called after him Ard-mic-Nasca, the mound of the son of Nasca. This tumulus may still be seen in the garden of Moat House, the residence of Miss Reade, adjoining Millbrook Street. The place is mentioned under the name of Ard-mic-Nasca in several of the ancient books. The surrounding townland, which was named Ballyderry – the town of the wood – was referred to by the early English invaders as Sanctus Boscus, the Holy Wood, which name the town still bears".

The *Moat House* referred to, is possibly the one built in 1862, which is instantly recognisable as the design of Gothic Revival style architect W J Barre who we have come across already. This grand design was converted into eight luxurious apartments in the 1930's, but is 400 yards from the site of the seventh century priory. As for the *ancient tumulus*, Praeger likely was referring to the Holywood Motte, an Anglo-Norman mound a little way south of the priory site. Records show that Holywood did have a Millbrook Street at the start of the twentieth century, but I have been unable to find it recorded on any maps leading me to conclude that Brook Street, which runs in an east-west direction and has the mound immediately to the north of it is the most likely candidate. A short row of old terraced cottages do indeed have the Motte in their gardens.

The Motte has been excavated recently confirming it to date from the late twelfth century. Records found in the *Calendar of Documents Relating To Ireland 1171 – 1307* of King John's journey between Carrickfergus and Dublin in 1210 indicate that he passed through Holywood, staying overnight in the Bailey built atop the mound. His onward journey to Dundonald took him along Victoria Road and Croft Road, which explains why it was once known as King John's Highway. Claims that the site is indeed an ancient tumulus continue to be made although no archaeological evidence has yet been discovered to give the suggestion any firm foundation.

As you tour the heritage sites of Holywood, don't miss the chance to take note of *Johnny the Jig*. There are two ways this can be done[161]. Holywood's *Johnny* is on the High Street in front of a children's playground, while his twin is in the North Down Museum along the road in Bangor. The High Street sculpture has a simple inscription below it which reads

"Johnny the Jig"

by

Rosamund Praeger

(1867 – 1954)

of Holywood

Sculptress, illustrator, writer

who loved children.

In 1953, shortly before she died, Rosamund was moved to present this bronze work of an innocent-looking boy sitting on a rock playing the accordion when she heard of the recent tragic death of a local lad – Fergus Morton, who was killed in a road traffic accident whilst engaged in *"bob-a-job"* duties as a boy scout.

Rosamund lived at *Rock Cottage* on the Ballygrainey Road for her final years and was joined there by Robert, by then a widower himself. Nowadays, Holywood has grown to largely consume the villages of *Craigavad* where Rock Cottage is found and *Cultra,* home to the Ulster Folk and Transport Museum.

Robert Praeger described Cultra as a pleasant seaside suburb, indicating that it was already being swallowed up by Holywood, noting its *"scattered villas overlooking the Lough, with much boating during the season"*[162]. Praeger also provided a brief insight into the geology of this part of the North Down Coast:

---

161 A third *Johnny the Jig* – this time a restaurant, further along the High Street, underwent a recent transformation and is now called Betty's.

162 The Cultra Sailing Club was established in 1893 by Sir Robert Kennedy, local landowner and an enthusiastic sailor himself. The club amalgamated with the Ulster Canoe Club and is now known as the Royal North of Ireland Yacht Club.

"Cultra is especially interesting to the geologist, as in its vicinity occurs one of the few exposures of Permian rocks in Ireland. The geology of the coast as one walks from Holywood, is remarkably varied … A couple of hundred yards west of Cultra Pier, a fault brings up the Lower Carboniferous shale with characteristic fossils, such as Modiola Macadami (whilst) further east, opposite Rosavo, a small patch of yellow dolomite … contains characteristic Permian fossils".

Praeger also described how the local Permian dolomite, although in limited supply, proved to be a popular building stone, establishing it as the stone used in Holywood's *"old church"* as well as for the castle at Carrickfergus. The stone had a further use, in medicine.

Some of the dolomite was shipped to Glasgow where it was ground and processed to extract *Sulphate of Magnesia* – or as it is more commonly known in medicine – Epsom Salts. Thanks to Ferdinand J.S. Gorgas and his 1901 book on Dental Medicine we can be clear of the many and varied benefits (apparently!) of this treatment:

"Sulphate of magnesia is administered as a saline purgative in acute inflammatory and febrile affections, to depress the arterial tension, and also to relieve the kidneys when they are hyperaemic; hence it is a valuable remedy in renal and cardiac dropsy, constipation of lead colic, acute dysentery, dyspepsia with constipation, etc., etc."

Further, Gorgas recommended the use of the sulphate in dentistry "to *reduce the arterial tension in acute inflammations of the dental organs, such as acute pulpitis".*

Several years earlier, Andrew Ure's *Dictionary of Chemistry* had warned on the dangers of over-prescribing this medicine describing cases where examinations of corpses revealed over four pounds of undigested Sulphate of Magnesia lodged in the colons of the unfortunate patients.

Returning to Holywood, Robert Praeger also provides us with a rather succinct description of Craigavad or *Creig an Bháda – the rock of the boat*, written many years before he lived there with his sister. He called the village simply *"distinctly picturesque"* before going on to inform readers of a souterrain, his *"Cave Glen"*, which he established was an artificial cave with a main chamber 16 feet by 5 feet and about 6 feet high with two additional passages and chambers. Other than recording it to be *"half-a-mile from the station"* Praeger, who recorded several visits and studies conducted here in his other works, gives little to go with in determining exactly where this *Cave Glen* could be located.

There has not been a railway station at Craigavad since 1961. Half a mile west of the former station site is Cultra Manor, formerly the estate and ancestral home of the Kennedy family who came here from Ayrshire around 1688. The Manor House itself was only built in 1902, making it one of the last grand mansion houses to be built in the area. It has a splendid appearance, albeit somewhat angular comprising mainly basalt with contrasting sandstone lintels and decorative features.

In the 1960's the Kennedy family gave up their 135-acre estate and manor house, after which the building and site were converted into a pair of museums, now combined as the Ulster Folk and Transport Museum[163].

Since we are talking about two museums in one, and you really could spend an entire day (or longer) in each, we'll look at both parts separately.

When H. G. Wells novella *The Time Machine* was first published in 1895 it caused a sensation and instantly popularised a concept that has been imitated repeatedly ever since, that of time travel. It seems highly unlikely that any of us will ever see a device such as the one used by Wells' *Time Traveller*, but should we wish to visit Northern Ireland as it was in Edwardian times then the Folk Museum in Cultra is the place to go.

Established by an Act of Parliament in 1958 (the Ulster Folk Museum Act), the principle behind the museums creation was to preserve as much as possible of the traditional rural way of life that was already being usurped by industrialisation at the start of the twentieth century – before it possibly disappeared altogether. Introducing the bill to parliament, the finance minister T.M. O'Neill had this to say:

"This is a small and, perhaps, to some hon. Members an unexciting Measure. I trust, however, that as a result it will not be the occasion for the generation of any heat or passion. Folk museums are essentially the children of Northern Europe. This type of institution first manifested itself in Scandinavia, since when both Holland and Great Britain have followed suit. I personally would like to

---

163 A second grand country house – Dalchoolin – was included in the estate adopted by the new museum. These were the days before conservation was given priority over demolition, so the building was bulldozed to make way for a car park.

think that Her Majesty the Queen, who was so impressed by the museum in Oslo, should before too long have the opportunity of visiting a museum here which would show in similar manner our interest in the lives of our forbears".

Estyn Evans[164], one of the driving forces behind the idea (he'd consistently promoted the idea since 1946, along with two of his students, Alan Gailey and George Thompson – both of whom would later take up senior positions at the museum) wrote this on the matter before his death in 1989:

"The Folk Museum is intended to be an instrument of education and research as well as a demonstration of traditional crafts and values".

It was an ambitious target, requiring the acquisition and movement of many buildings from all parts of Ulster. Brick-by-brick cottages, shops, farm buildings, even a church and a fully functioning water-powered spade mill, were taken down, transported and carefully re-assembled on the Cultra Kennedy estate.

The spade mill came from Coalisland in County Tyrone where it is known to have passed through at least five generations of the Patterson family[165] before the final owners, J Stephenson & Company, agreed to it being dismantled and relocated to the new Folk Museum. The mill is actually two buildings, as will as the mill house which has the giant water wheel and its associated mechanics, the second structure which was originally the spade finishing shops now also serves as an exhibition space telling the history of spade making in Northern Ireland.

You might not think of spade production as being particularly important, and you'll have to visit the museum to get the full story but suffice it to say that at one time, spades were the tool of preference in farming. Partly this was due to economics – most were too poor to be able to afford a plough (and horse), but most simply did not have enough land to wield a plough in even if they had the finances to pay for such an extravagance. More than 170 different varieties were known to be manufactured throughout the island of Ireland by highly-skilled

---

164 An academic at Queen's University, initially appointed to lecture in Geography in 1928.

165 Many spade mills throughout Northern Ireland were in their care. The National Trust now operate William George Patterson's fully-working eighteenth century water mill at Templepatrick in County Antrim.

craftsmen[166]. What spade an agricultural labourer used was determined as much by local custom as by the requirements of the task and the ground conditions – cutting into a turf bog, for example, required an entirely different spade shape to one designed to work in heavy clay.

If moving the mill, brick by brick and stone by stone was a challenge, dismantling, transporting and reassembling the two giant external wheels that drive the cast-iron internal wheel which in turn trips the massive iron hammer, must have been a mammoth undertaking.

Evans was always keen to recognise the delicate nature of Northern Ireland's heritage – a land largely shaped and moulded by the unwelcome intrusion of Englishmen. His view was that the museum must represent and preserve elements of the industrial, social, cultural and personal past, without favouring either the loyalist or Unionist side. Perhaps, sensitive to these issues, the museum site includes examples of both Catholic and Protestant church buildings.

Originally the church of St John the Baptist in Drumcree, County Armagh, and dating from 1793, when the Catholic church was repositioned at Cultra in 1990, a nineteenth century pipe organ from a Church of Ireland building in Dromore, County Down was installed inside. This particular Catholic church was apparently selected due to its design mirroring that of contemporary Presbyterian churches in the province of Ulster. This was the second church to be relocated to the museum. Earlier, in 1976, the late eighteenth century Church of Ireland building from Carnacally, Kilmore in County Down had been moved. Inside are the original box pews as well as the more recent benches typically found even now in most churches of this type.

Most structures, but not all, are original buildings that have been relocated. An example of a replica, though you wouldn't be able to tell with the naked eye, is the Parochial hall. This is an exact copy of St. Patrick's Hall in Portaferry, which as a listed structure still stands there. Nearby is another replica, this time of the Parochial house in Newtownards. This time, though, the original structure, was in a poor condition, but was painstakingly, measured and photographed so that an exact likeness could be created. The Newtownards building was demolished

---

166 Shapes range from wedge-shaped to straight, square to tapered, with the unifying feature that distinguishes Irish spades from their English cousins is the long straight, always wooden, shaft.

in 1994.

The Folk Museum also has a police station, courthouse, school, print shop, cottages, terraced houses, a flax mill, blacksmiths forge, a pub, a weaver's house and many more other buildings. Inside or near to several of them people dressed in traditional costumes demonstrate artisan crafts such as basket-making and carpentry.

As I said, you can easily spend a couple of days (ideally dry ones, as you will spend much of your time outdoors) touring the Folk Museum, but this is just half of the story.

The *Transport Museum*, formerly the *Belfast Transport Museum* until it merged with the Folk Museum in 1967 is *"one of Europe's largest and most comprehensive transport collections"*[167] and tells the ongoing stories of travel on land, water and in the air.

The *Irish Railway Collection* has more than 40 locomotives, carriages, wagons and associated railway buildings as well as thousands of artefacts and assorted items of railway paraphernalia. Amongst the steam locomotives, look out for *"No 30"*, first operating in 1901 on the Belfast and County Down Railway, whose line passed through Cultra – this is the only surviving engine from a route and railway company who,arguably opened up towns like Bangor, Donaghadee and Holywood to the emerging market for seaside trips and holidays.

Should you wish to take a break in this area of the museum, the tea room is actually a wooden structure formerly based on a platform at Belfast's York Road Station. Near to it is a newspaper kiosk from Portadown.

Before the advent of the railways, mentioning the prospect of a ride in a carriage, would have produced a rather different mental picture. The *Taken for a Ride* gallery has some fine examples, with horses (albeit they life-size models), from the nineteenth century. These carriages were symbols of wealth and status – for most, travel, other than in connection with work and the need to be sustained, just didn't happen. And, when it did, it was on foot.

The museum has a landau carriage built at Robson's Belfast Royal Victoria Horse and Carriage Bazaar. This was used on occasions of state, including to convey the High Sheriff of County Antrim to and from the quarterly County Assizes.

---

167 https://www.nmni.com/our-museums/ulster-folk-and-transport-museum/Home.aspx

Alongside the landau is a Brougham carriage. This was the Mini Cooper of its day – a small, compact, lightweight, relatively affordable, but also stylish method for conveying two comfortably, and four at a tight squeeze. A novel feature of the Brougham was the method for passengers to attract the attention of the driver. A pull-cord within the carriage connected with a hook attached to his belt, giving him little excuse for ignoring the demand for attention.

If the Brougham was the equivalent of a Mini Cooper, then the Phaeton was the E-Type Jaguar. This was a sporty model in every sense, and was designed for its owner to take the reins and drive himself. The Transport Museum has a fine example of a Mail Phaeton made by Peters & Sons of London. The name *Mail* comes not from the carriage's use in conveying post. It didn't. What it did have was the same spring suspension used in mail carriages, so that weighty items of luggage could be carried behind the driver and his valet.

The *Wheels of Business* exhibition area has a real rarity – a tramcar from the Giant's Causeway Tramway, the world's first hydro-electric powered rail system which operated between Portrush and the Giant's Causeway until 1949. A section of the line between the World Heritage Site and Bushmills, two miles away, formerly operated by the Giant's Causeway, Portrush and Bush Valley Railway & Tramway Company Ltd but now running as the Giant's Causeway and Bushmills Railway has been open to the public since 2002. The Wheels of Business section is diverse to say the least, with exhibits ranging from a horse-drawn delivery van belonging to the Inglis Bakery of Belfast, long before it was swallowed up by the Rank Organisation to become a distributor of *Mother's Pride* bread, through to an *Austin A125 Sheerline* van used by the Belfast Telegraph to deliver it's newspapers to Londonderry, apparently covering more than 50,000 miles between the two cities every year. With a four-litre engine, the Austin Longbridge factory in Birmingham, England produced around 11,000 Sheerline vans between 1947 and 1954, with most of the vans ending up on the roads as ambulances for the newly-formed National Health Service.

For those whose interest is in the pioneers of aviation, the *Flight Experience* exhibition space has a real treat. You'll recall the exploits of Harry Ferguson from earlier chapters. His flights from and over both Counties Derry and Down attracted phenomenal interest from the public, if not the press, as this report from the *Belfast News-letter* in August 1910 exemplifies:

"Yesterday evening (8th August) Mr Harry Ferguson flew a distance of almost

three miles over the Newcastle foreshore, in the presence of a large number of people. He rose near Dundrum Bar, and flew at heights varying from 50 to 100 feet, and alighted safely on a strip of sand near Blackrock. The crowds along the beach cheered lustily as the aviator passed".

This was less than seven years after the Wright Brothers first powered flight, and just nine months after Ferguson had become the first man to take to the skies of Northern Ireland (or the entire island of Ireland for that matter) when he completed a flight over Hillsborough, County Down in December 1909.

Ferguson built five different versions of his monoplane before being persuaded to abandon flight on safety grounds. The museum has a full-size replica, built in the 1970's of his final design that incorporates Ferguson's original pilot's seat.

By the way, that *News-Letter* article from 1910 concluded with this sentence *"Mr Ferguson has now fulfilled his contract with the Sports Committee, and is to be congratulated on a very successful flight"*. The *contract* referred to an agreement made by Ferguson to the Newcastle Sports Committee to attempt to win the £100 prize offered for the first person to complete a powered flight of at least two miles over Newcastle Strand.

The County Down village of Crossgar is five miles west of Killyleagh and roughly the same distance north of Downpatrick. It is the birthplace of James Martin whose invention has saved thousands of aviation lives since 1946. The *Martin-Baker Ejection Seat* was produced by Martin, partly in response to a specific request from the Air Ministry, but as much driven by his own desire for a reliable method of evacuating failed aircraft in the wake of his business partners death in a plane crash in 1942. An example of Martin's Ejection Seats is an important exhibit, and a further reminder of the importance of Northern Ireland in the development of aviation.

As powered flight expanded, the military in particular were keen to have an aeroplane with as short a take-off and landing space requirement as possible. Helicopters did not require runways but had a limited range and were restricted in speed and weapons capacity. In 1957, the Belfast firm of Short Brothers came up with the SC1 – the world's first VTOL (Vertical Take-Off and Landing) aircraft. It was a research plane, never intended for commercial production, but it played a crucial role in the future development of VTOL planes, most notably the *Harrier*. The five-engined second prototype (four to get the plane airborne and back to earth safely and a fifth to fly with) is the centrepiece of the *Flight*

Experience exhibition.

The Transport Museum also has a fascinating collection of road vehicles including several DeLorean cars made at the American company premises in Dunmurry on the outskirts of Belfast. The most recognisable of these is the gull-wing DMC-12 which many will remember from the *Back to the Future* movie trilogy. Before the company went bankrupt in 1982, just over 9,000 models were produced – a fifth of them in a single month[168]. It is estimated that around two-thirds of the iconic car with its distinctive paint-less stainless steel bodywork are still roadworthy.

Finally, the museum also commemorates the White Star Line and its Olympic class trio of liners, Britannic, launched in 1914, Olympic from 1911, and, of course Titanic, which sailed on a single unfinished voyage in 1912. The *Titanica* exhibition may not be anywhere near as large as the world-famous Titanic Belfast centre, but it offers a fascinating insight into the lives (and deaths) of many of the people involved with the catastrophic events of April 1912. From design to build to launch and the ultimate disaster, the exhibition will inform and pull at the heartstrings in equal measure.

And there we must leave this fascinating museum and the Holywood area. We've spent much of the last few chapters in County Down so a spot of fresh air in County Derry will probably do no harm.

Further Reading:

J. McConnell Auld, Holywood Then and Now, Con Auld (2002)

T.M. Owen (Ed.), From Corrib to Cultra, Institute of Irish Studies (2001)

---

168 All but 12 of them were left-hand drive. Just one car was produced with right-hand drive AND automatic transmission. The model in the museum is a left-hand drive vehicle.

V is for Victorian Values

Samuel Lewis wrote this in his 1837 *Topographical Dictionary of Ireland*:

"The air here is serene and pure, the scenery grand and picturesque, the country well cultivated, planted, and embellished with elegant mansions".

Lewis acknowledged *"the exertions of the proprietors, John Cromie and Henry O'Hara"* who have *"raised this place, in the space of a few years, from a group of fishermen's huts to a delightful and well frequented summer residence".*

Where is this *delightful* source of *pure* air which, almost 100 years later was still being lauded, albeit by the Ulster Tourist Development Association (UTDA) for the curative properties of its *"salubrious air simply laden with the ozone of the Atlantic Ocean"*?

Portstewart.

Before we look at how Portstewart has grown to become one of Northern Ireland's most attractive resorts, let's consider that early description in a little more detail, particularly the notion that prior to Cromie and O'Hara it was little more than *"a group of fishermen's huts"*.

Bronze Age pottery was found in the dunes near Portstewart in the latter part of the nineteenth century. Now, we know that dune systems are dynamic – they grow, move and die, so a few pieces of broken pot on their own is not sufficient proof of a human population. When you put together finds from the various excavations carried out between 1879 and 1948, the many flints, stone tools, bones and shells point very strongly to the opinion that people were here at least 1,000 years before the time of Christ.

The village was known as *Port na Binne Uaine*[169] until John Cromie came along with the new name of Portstewart in 1794. So, why did he give it the suffix *-stewart* and not *-cromie*? The reason is that Cromie was acknowledging an earlier leaseholder of the land, a Lieutenant Stewart, who apparently sold on his

---

169 A name still used by many locally. A nearby island and townland is also called *Benoney* which derives from *Binne Uaine* as does *Benone* – the name given to the long sandy beach beyond Portstewart to the west.

title rights to Cromie's father, Stephen.

William Adams, in *Dalriada*, published by the *Coleraine Chronicle* newspaper in 1906 wrote this on the subject:

"Portstewart as a village did not exist until the year 1790 when a gentleman named Lieutenant Stewart from Donegal, who owned some land in the locality, got four sod houses built on the site now occupied by the residence of Mr. Jack James A. Lyle. He brought four fishermen from Inishowen in Donegal, which is only eight or nine miles across the bay and put them in these cottages and bought them a boat and lines to enable them to follow their business of fishing. After the death of Mr. Stewart, the property passed to a Mr. Stafford, a friend who lived in Portrush, and after him to Mr. Cromie".

Acquiring land from someone is hardly reason to name a village after them you'd think? And you'd be right. There was a different reason for honouring the Stewart name – Cromie's maternal ancestors were Stewarts – he'd bought the land from family!

The Cromie/O'Hara relationship was anything but a *happy family*. The two men feuded constantly from their Portstewart homes of Cromore House and O'Hara's castellated three-storey tower house, known simply as O'Hara's Castle or the Rock. In one oft-told story, Cromie's labourers needed to make use of a right of way belonging to O'Hara in order to shift sand from the beach to their building locations. Every night O'Hara's men would cut a trench to prevent access and every morning Cromie's men would promptly fill it in again. Tittle-tattle like this went on for years but it took its toll on Henry O'Hara who died from a heart attack in 1844 after discussing another dispute with his solicitor in Coleraine.

O'Hara's *"grim and gaunt castle"*[170] was bought by the Cromie family after his death and greatly altered. In turn, it was sold on to an order of Dominican Sisters in 1917 who also carried out restorative work as well as further additions including a chapel in 1935. Nowadays, this prominent whitewashed feature of Portstewart's coastline is Dominican College, a Catholic Grammar School with almost 700 students, including many from the Portstewart Protestant community.

Cromore House underwent several similar periods of metamorphosis and expansion, as well as many years of neglect before conversion into student

---

170 Ulster Tourist Development Association, 1935

accommodation and then a residential care home. There are much grander houses to write about, so the connected stories of a couple of its former occupants will occupy the next couple of paragraphs, but prepare yourself, it is not pleasant reading.

Born in 1854, Robert Acheson Cromie Montagu was the fourth, and youngest child of Lord Robert Montagu and his wife Ellen Mary Cromie, making him the great grandson of John Cromie by my reckoning. At the age of fifteen he was serving as a midshipman aboard *HMS Liverpool* on its tour of the *Pacific*[171]. It was the start of a lengthy naval service that saw Robert rise through the ranks to Lieutenant-Commander before returning to live at Cromore House. The official line on this was that duties concerning the management of the extensive family estate required Montagu to remain home, but the story in common circulation was that years of constant seasickness finally got the better of him.

Montagu married Annie, the daughter of Scotsman Gilbert McMicking in 1880. Exactly nine months later she gave him their first son, followed by five more boys in the space of just under six years. Annie was *"a famous beauty (and) noted lawn tennis player"*[172] as well as being known widely for her skilled management of horses, but it was her mismanagement of her first-born daughter for which she is remembered.

Mary Helen Montagu, the couples seventh child and first daughter, was born in February 1889[173]. Her death at the age of three in February 1892 led to newspaper coverage around the globe and questions being asked in parliament.

After darkness had fallen on Saturday 13th February, a doctor was hurriedly summoned to attend Cromore House. There was nothing he could do. Little Mary had passed away. An inquest, which, unusually also took place in the same house a couple of days later, heard Annie admit that in disciplining the child, she had secured Mary's hands to a ring on the wall in an upstairs room and then locked the girl in – for three hours.

---

171 Before his seventeenth birthday, Montagu had sailed to Brazil, Australia, New Zealand, Tasmania, Japan, Hawaii, Chile and South Africa – not bad for a youngster who complained of seasickness throughout his entire naval career.

172 According to several newspapers and magazines including the *Australian Town and Country Journal*.

173 According to most sources, although some put the event six months earlier.

How the poor child came to be asphyxiated to the point of death, the inquest could not determine, but the jury found that the mother should stand trial for the felony.

Remarkably, even to the point of the matter being raised in parliament, Montagu was granted bail and subsequently fled Northern Ireland for a while before returning to stand trial.

Sectarian divisions (the Montagu family were Catholic in a largely Protestant area) added to the complexities of the legal process. Legal counsel for Annie argued that a fair trial would be impossible in County Londonderry where local people, including many of the household staff at Cromore were outraged by the child's demise.

In the end, Annie Montagu, five months pregnant with the couple's ninth child[174], stood trial in Dublin, was found guilty of manslaughter, and, during her year in Grangegorman Prison (also in Dublin), gave birth to a baby girl – who, some say distastefully, was given the name Mary.

The trial itself attracted the attention of the world's press. Australia's *Western Mail* carried an interview with the dead girl's father who supported his wife's *"spirit of discipline"*, and, with the vocal assistance of his local Catholic priest, vigorously accused the legal system of bias against her on religious grounds. In Wales, the *Cardiff Times* made specific reference to the accusation that Mrs Montagu was a serial offender with its headline *CRUELTY TO CHILDREN*. Not only was Annie accused of the manslaughter of her only daughter, but charges of ill treatment of three sons, Austin, Walter and Gilbert[175], were also pursued. The *Washington Post* carried graphic accounts of alleged abuse. A former governess testified that *"Walter Montagu, a son, four years old, had upon one occasion been tied to a tree in the park and left there from early morning until sundown"* whilst a former member of the household staff reported *"she had once seen Mrs. Montagu dragging another son, Austin, along a corridor by the heels, his*

---

174 An eighth, Alexander, was born in 1890.

175 Walter went on to become a Jesuit priest and died from wounds received on the Western Front in 1918. Younger brother Alexander died on board HMS Bulwark which exploded off the Lincolnshire coast in 1914. Austin lived and worked in London, married and started a family relatively late in life (aged 48), whilst Gilbert married twice, firstly in 1918, and again in 1932 following the death of his first wife, before dying himself in 1944 at the age of 57.

head trailing and bumping on the floor".

In today's world it would be considered extraordinary that a jury would plea for mercy after finding the defendant guilty in such a case, but this is exactly what happened. Furthermore, the prosecution chose to serve a *nolle prosequi* notice for the other three charges, effectively dismissing them.

Annie was released from prison at the end of her sentence and promptly spent the next two years touring Europe with her presumably forgiving husband. They had no more children together and she ended her days in California, passing away in 1916.

Was Cromore House typical of an aristocratic home in Victorian Northern Ireland? I cannot say. Similarly, it is impossible to discern whether children in "poorer" homes endured similar abuses. The tragic death of Mary Montagu serves, however, as a stark reminder of events in the past as well as sadly, many more in contemporary history.

* * *

Regardless of what you or I may think about the Cromie's or the O'Hara's, were it not for the long-term investment in Portstewart by both families, it would never have become a nineteenth century seaside resort, that by 1935 was being described in one publication as *"deservedly one of the most popular and progressive seaside resorts in Ulster, as it caters exceptionally well for the holiday-maker"*[176]. Holidays for the masses were a relatively new concept in the 1930's. Before the 1871 Bank Holidays Act, the principle of time off (with or without pay) was rarely found in practice. Most worked six and a half days every week, including 25th December. After 1871, all could look forward to at least four days annual leave. Railway lines connected major centres of population with the coast and entrepreneurs came up with a wide range of methods for extracting what little money families had with their for their day trip to the seaside.

The 1910 *Belfast and Ulster Towns Directory* simply described Portstewart as *"64 ½ miles from Belfast by rail. A watering place. Has productive fisheries. Population – 685"*. The same guide listed no fewer than five hotels in the village, a clear indication that in the late Victorian period preceding this time, Portstewart was drawing more than just armies of day-trippers.

Many arrived in Portstewart by train. The railway station being located away

---

176 Ulster Tourist Development Association.

from the seafront, a connecting tramway service began operating in 1882. This continued, albeit with a series of economic hurdles to navigate along the way until the 1920's.

In common with most of the rest of Northern Ireland's coastal resorts, Portstewart could not compete with seaside towns offering a variety of health benefits from the consumption or bathing in mineral, spring or spa waters. John MacPherson's 1871 guide to *The Mineral Waters of the British Islands* had just this to say on the subject:

> *"But if Ireland is poor in mineral waters, it can vie with any portion of Great Britain, in its sea-bathing places all round its coasts … If you want the fresh air from the north, you have Portrush and Port Stewart".*

Modern Portstewart tries to cater for all values, not just those of the affluent, as perhaps it was guilty of in the Victorian period. The promenade has recently seen a £1.5 million upgrade, now giving the resort a beautifully sculpted walkway from the town's hub to the two-mile long beach that continues to draw in thousands of visitors from all walks of life. That very Victorian concept of sea-bathing for health, has largely been replaced with recreational facilities. The natural inlet of *Port-na-happle* still draws plenty of sea bathers as does the *Herring Pond*, a deep-water pool, bounded on two sides by artificial sea walls. This retains water from the high tides and offers sheltered bathing at a slightly higher temperature than the open sea. Until the 1980's when it was removed on health and safety grounds, the rock pool also featured a diving board. For those with very young children, an outdoor paddling pool is a very popular summer draw.

A relatively new feature on Portstewart's Crescent has been the installation of a water feature comprising 33 fountains that produce jets rising up to 15 feet, all synchronised to music and with a coloured light display after dark – be prepared to see children (of all ages) getting soaked to the skin, so bring plenty of towels. You have been warned!

Portstewart is a great base for those interested in walking holidays. Whether you want a simple walk along the Strand and back through the dunes, or you can manage a more energetic 6.5 mile trek to Portrush (with a variety of public transport options for your return) or you want a real challenge of over 10 miles to Castlerock, the Walk Northern Ireland website is sure to have something for you[177].

All of the above walks leave you with the risk of getting caught out by the weather especially given Northern Ireland's well-earned reputation for being able to produce all four seasons in a single day. With any rural or semi-rural walk, always prepare yourself and your party for every climate possibility. Abandoning a countryside or coastal walk midway is not good.

In Derry City, there is one great walk that is easy to stop and start should the weather turn. Let's head there now and find out more.

Further Reading:

H. Kane, Portstewart: Ebb and Flow, Self-Published (1994)

J.R.L. Currie, The Portstewart Tramway, Oakwood (1968)

---

177 Strands and dunes:
   http://www.walkni.com/walks/385/portstewart-strand-sand-dune-estuary-trail/
   Portrush:
   http://www.walkni.com/walks/152/port-path/
   Castlerock:
   http://www.walkni.com/ulsterway/sections/castlerock-to-portstewart/adjoining-quality-walks/

W is for What's in a Name?

Richard George Salmon King wrote this in the 1930's:

"VISITORS to Ulster should not fail to spend a portion of their itinerary in the ancient and historic City of Londonderry, the Walls of which, erected in 1617, and still in perfect preservation, are surmounted by the ordnance which enabled its heroic defenders to repel the assaults of the enemy during the ever memorable Siege of 1688 and 1689, of which the golden pens of Macaulay, Reid, Witherow, and Lecky have left undying records".

King, at the time was Dean of Derry, based at St. Columb's Cathedral, and, as I'm sure you could tell, was a staunch Unionist. The above extract from a piece in a tourist publication, was headed

LONDONDERRY

"THE MAIDEN CITY"

Further evidence of King's political persuasion.

Throughout this book I've tried carefully to balance out my use of the words Derry and Londonderry, so as not to imply any particular personal preference. You see, this is a very thorny issue that symbolises much of the ongoing differences between those in support of the Union and those with Nationalist leanings.

The earliest known settlement here was a monastery founded on the hill of *Daire* (sometimes *Doire*) reputedly by Colmcille in the sixth century. It's easy to muddle some of these names up, and it would take ages to explain, so, suffice it to say, that *Colmcille* and *Columcille* who we met in Downpatrick earlier, were contemporaries but probably different men and Colmcille who is also often known as *Columba* is the man whose name was taken (and shortened by a letter) for the Church of Ireland Cathedral.

The word *Daire*, which means an *oak grove* is where the name of Derry originates. It is the prefix *London-* that causes so much contention. An English garrison had been established in Derry during the reign of Queen Elizabeth, but constantly under attack. A second, more substantive garrison was created in

1600 and saw many battles during the Nine Years War. In turn, the O'Neills, O'Donnells and O'Dohertys all fought unsuccessfully to retake the settlement from its English landlords (although Cahir O'Doherty successfully overwhelmed the English in 1608, but chose to burn the town to the ground rather than attempt to maintain a stronghold on the small town).

James I, then *planted* his supporters throughout much of Ulster, including Derry, which received many protestant colonists, mostly associated with the livery companies from the City of London. The town received a Royal Charter, became a city and added London- to its name. A move still disputed to this day. As recently as 1984, Derry City Council went to the High Court in London in the latest attempt to reverse the imposition of almost 400 years earlier. After lengthy consultations, the *"final"* decision (for now, at least) was that the official name of Londonderry could only be changed by order of the reigning Monarch. So an uneasy stand-off continues, with road-signs and maps showing both names, while Catholics invariably only ever speak of Derry and Protestants refusing to call City or County anything other than Londonderry.

A consortium of *"six and twenty honest and discreet citizens of London"* representing the *planted* London businesses was established in 1613, under the rather long-winded title of *The Society of the Governor and Assistants, London, of the New Plantation in Ulster, within the Realm of Ireland*. Little wonder it was quite quickly abridged to *The Honorable The Irish Society*. A contract agreed earlier included a stipulation that as well as *"sixty houses built in Derry … with convenient fortifications … should be built and perfected by the 1ˢᵗ of November 1611"*[178]. The men of the Society taking rather more note of *fortifications* than *convenient* approved and got funding for a project that took almost seven years to complete – the creation of a walled city.

Captain Nicholas Pynnar, as the appointed inspector of fortifications throughout the whole island of Ireland reported on the condition of the new walls in March 1619. He wrote:

> *"The Cittie of London Derry is now compassed about with a verie strong wall, excellentlie made and neatlie wrought, beinge all of good lyme and stone".*

---

178 As reproduced in *A concise view of the origin, constitution, and proceedings of the Honorable Society of the Governor and Assistants of London of the New Plantation in Ulster : within the realm of Ireland, commonly called the Irish Society*(1842).

A poem published in a 1794 retrospective collection of papers put it this way:

"Derry whose proud and stately walls disdain,

By any foreign en'my to be ta'en,

Betwixt surrounding hills which it command,

On an ascending brow does snugly stand".

Derry's walls are the sole remaining completely intact city walls in the whole of Ireland, and are widely acknowledged to be amongst the best in Europe. The walls of Toledo, in Spain are, at least in part, much older and dominate two sides of the city. In France, the walls of Carcassonne have earned it World Heritage Site status but it is an amalgamation of many walls rather than a single structure. The walls of Londonderry arguably eclipse all of its competitors as these are the only truly complete (bar one minor planned breach) walls that completely surround a city AND were constructed as a single entity.

What we call them and how we think about them again raises the same issues. Catholics will argue that Derry belongs to the Irish and had no need for walls to keep the Irish out of their own lands and see them as symbolic of the ongoing struggle against the English. Protestants revere the walls of their *"maiden city"*, called thus because every attackers attempts to breach them failed.

The mile-long walls of the city can be walked at any time of day or night, free of charge. There are seven gates in and out of the old city. The four original gates being Bishop's Gate, Ferryquay Gate, Butcher Gate and Shipquay Gate. A further three gates were added later, namely - Magazine Gate, Castle Gate and New Gate.

On busy days in the summer months, the narrowest (12-feet wide) sections of the wall can get pretty busy, especially during special events, so you may prefer to time your visit for a quieter period, particularly if you have mobility needs or young children with you. Planning ahead can give a further benefit as there are many different guided tours available, including full-costumed *living history* tours that include music and dancing as well as entertaining story-telling.

A few points to pause along the way include:

Roaring Meg – a large cannon (one of several), on the Double Bastion section of the West Wall. This is inscribed *"Fishmongers London 1642"*, a clear reference to both its origin and age, having been shipped to the City by *The Honorable The*

Irish Society following a lengthy siege in 1641. The cannon gets its name from its reputation for its booming noise being more terrifying to the enemy than the 18lb cannonballs it fired. The cannon is sometimes repositioned, so if you don't see it here, try looking in the Memorial Hall Garden nearby.

St. Columb's Cathedral – built in 1633 on the site of a former place of worship, bears this inscription plate on its foundation stone:

IF STONES COVLD SPEAKE

THEN LONDONS PRAYSE

SHOVLD SOVND WHO

BVILT THIS CHVRCH AND

CITTIE FROM THE GROVND

The inscription is attributed to Sir John Vaughan, Governor of the City at the time. With leadership support from his son, Henry, Sir John had a troop several hundred men permanently garrisoned in the city. One of Sir John's final acts before his death in 1643 was to oversee the cities resistance to the Irish Rebellion of 1641.

The Apprentice Boys Memorial Hall was first built in 1877 and dedicated to the memory of the thirteen young male apprentices who closed and locked the cities gates in the final days of 1688. The hall, on Society Street has been somewhat extended over the years, and does open to the public from time to time, usually to coincide with commemorative events. Each year on the first Saturday in December, the gates are closed and on the second Saturday in August, the Relief of Derry is marked by a march of the Apprentice Boys at the end of a week-long Maiden City Festival. The bright red flags you'll see flying at these times represent the crimson emblem hung from the walls during the siege, and a flag subsequently hoisted at the Cathedral during both events.

You may well see an effigy being paraded or even burned. This is not Guy Fawkes, but Robert Lundy, former Governor of Londonderry who has been reviled in this way ever since his apparent act of treachery at the head of a group of men[179]. Lundy declared the defence of Derry was futile and urged

---

179 Amongst other things. I use the word *apparently*, since some contemporary analysts now doubt the accuracy of at least some of the records from the period in question. The website www.thetrialoflundy.com has much more on this subject.

fellow Protestants to abandon their resistance. To many this was the talk of a traitor, while others simply acknowledge Lundy as a realist.

Memories of the siege still stir up emotions and re-open deep wounds. As long ago as 1794, a poet named only as *"Alfred"* urged:

> *"O ye descendants of those gallant Spirits,*
>
> *Who fought and bled round DERRY's sacred walls,*
>
> *Impress their great example on your hearts,*
>
> *And nobly emulate their fame and virtues".*

I cannot ask Alfred why he capitalized the *"S"* in *"Spirits"*, but this along with his use of the word *sacred* reminds me that all too often in the bloodiest of disputes, those on both sides go out to fight, often to the death, in the belief that God is with them.

The **Guildhall** is not the original building erected for the purpose. The first Guildhall was put up inside the Walled City not long after the walls themselves in an area known as *the Diamond*. When a fire destroyed the building in the nineteenth century[180], members of *The Honorable The Irish Society* chose to turn the site into a city square and build a new Guildhall just outside the walls, beside the river. Work was completed and the new hall, then called Victoria Hall opened in July 1890. It survived for just 18 years until fire struck once again. This time wrecking most of the building or putting it beyond repair, leaving just the clock tower free from major damage. It was the scene of two separate bombings in 1972, leaving yet more damage – this time costing over £1.5 million to rectify. Partisan politics apart, the building has to be one of the grandest you'll see in Northern Ireland. With stained-glass windows, oak panels, decorative marble and ornate plaster ceilings it is a visual feast – and it's free to get in!

The **Diamond** is the heart of the walled city and is accessed by leaving the wall at any one of the four original gates and walking inwards. In many of the world's cities you'll find roads laid out in a geometric pattern, and aligned to points of the compass. Derry's four original gates and their roads face North-East, South-

---

180 Few tears were shed at the loss of the structure. Commenting somewhat prophetically as it turned out in 1862, the *Dublin Builder* wrote *"a regret must also be expressed that the vista should be impeded by the ugly Town-hall that stands midway in 'the Diamond' – a building we shall be glad to see soon replaced elsewhere by a better"*.

East, South-West and North-West, so that the four corners of the Diamond itself point North, South, East and West.

Take care approaching the central square as you will have to cross a main road. The main feature within the Diamond is the cities War Memorial. This was originally planned in February 1919, but, in common with so many other places, the collection of public subscriptions to fund the project was laborious and the subject of ongoing dissent. Officials pondered over the location and design. Many favoured locally quarried granite and/or a quiet position away from the busy city centre. What they got, courtesy of the work of the March brothers, was a forty-foot high Portland Stone column flanked by two stone pedestals. The latter support a life-size bronze soldier and sailor, representing the army and navy[181], while the centrepiece, also cast in bronze is a pagan icon – the Roman goddess Victory holding a laurel wreath in her outstretched arm. The names of Derry's war dead are inscribed on the sides[182]. It was June 1927 before the memorial was finally unveiled. Vernon March also sculpted miniature versions of all three figures. These can be seen within St. Columb's Cathedral[183].

Brooke Park is a short walk north of the City Walls. Here is a statue known locally as the *"Black Man"* that once stood in the Diamond but was relocated in 1927 to make room for the new war memorial. The subject of the seven-foot bronze work was not a *black man* at all – the nickname comes from the use of black paint and years of grime – but Sir Robert Alexander Ferguson, one-time member of parliament for Londonderry. In 2016, the statue underwent specialist restoration, including the removal of all the paint and is now a gleaming bronze once again.

The park itself is known to many as *"The People's Park"* and is a great place to get away from the hustle and bustle of Derry City life (for example to take a

---

181 The Royal Air Force was not founded until 1918. Prior to that, military aviators served in either the Royal Flying Corps (army) or the Royal Naval Air Service.

182 Not everyone went to war. Many of those associated with the International Bible Student's Association (later Jehovah's Witnesses), Quakers and Methodists chose to refuse to accept their call-up papers, often enduring persecution and/or imprisonment for taking their stand.

183 An almost-identical cenotaph in Cape Town, South Africa was also the work of Vernon March, and was completed in 1924, three years before Londonderry's.

picnic or tea break part way round a tour of the walls). To many of the folk of Derry it is known fondly as the *Green Lung*. Brooke Park is really two parks in one. The northern end as formerly the site of Gwyn's Institute, a boy's orphanage established by the trustees of linen merchant John Gwyn's estate. Gwyn died in 1829, leaving no heirs and £40,000 specifically so that:

> *"as many male children of the poor or lowest class of society resident in and belonging to the city of Londonderry and the precincts around the same, as hereafter described, as the said funds will feed, clothe, and educate, orphans or such children as have lost one of their parents always to be preferred"*[184].

A site was acquired and the orphanage opened its doors in 1840. The grounds were laid out in a style fashionable at the time, incorporating formal gardens as well as functional areas including an orchard and kitchen garden for the boys to take care of. Many of these features and the interconnecting pathways have been retained in the modern park. The orphanage itself was demolished in 1986. Renovations of the park in 2015 led to the discovery of a lead time capsule that had been placed in the orphanage's foundation stone shortly before 1840. Amidst great excitement, the badly corroded capsule was carefully opened to reveal that it contained several coins from the period and copies of John Gwyn's legal papers including his will. A similar time capsule was discovered in 2010 during renovations of the Guildhall. This time, the contents were known in advance thanks to an article printed in the *Londonderry Sentinel* in August 1887 when the glass jar was sealed and deposited:

> *"The contents of the jar were copies of the latest numbers of the local papers, copy of the London Times, a statement concerning the hall, with the names of Irish Society and of the corporation; the new coinage of the realm, including sovereign, half-sovereign, crown piece, double florin, half-crown six pence, three-penny piece, penny and halfpenny".*

When Elizabeth Brooke, sister of James, died in 1897, the trustees of his estate moved to purchase Gwyn's Institute and some adjoining land in order to satisfy that condition made out in 1865. A quarter of the estate had to be retained to cover annual maintenance costs, still leaving a considerable fund from which to establish the park.

---

184 You can read more at:
    www.derrystrabane.com/Subsites/Brooke-Park-Regeneration/Welcome

Completed and opened to the public in 1901, within two years, the park had its first royal visitors. King Edward VII and his wife Queen Alexandra toured the park on 28th July 1903 and planted trees, at least one of which is still standing[185]. Right up until the 1970's the park was well kept and saw several extended periods of investment in new planting.

During the worst years of the Troubles, the park was occupied by the British Army who removed trees and shrubbery, deeming them to be a threat to security, and the Gwyn building was firebombed and left as a burnt-out shell until 1986.

It has only been in the last decade that a concerted effort has been made to return this remarkable green space to its Victorian splendour – see it for yourself, but allow yourself plenty of time to benefit from the breath of fresh air that is Derry's *Green Lung*.

Butcher Gate would have been your most likely entry/exit point for travelling between the walls and Brook Park. This was one of the wall's four original gates and was the location that came closest to being breached during the 1689 siege. So much damage was done to the gate and its wooden doors that it was almost completely rebuilt later. The name comes from the street that connects it to the Diamond – Butcher Street, the former base for the cities butchers, which (in very new buildings) is now home to a hotel, bank, job centre, bar and upmarket apartments.

Coward's Bastion is the most northerly corner of the city walls, and is so-named according to the 1837 *Ordnance Survey of the County of Londonderry "for it was observable that such* (cowards) *resorted there, it lyeing most out of danger"*. The same text described it as a *demmy* bastion, indicating that fortifications here are less strong than elsewhere – hardly the ideal choice for a coward to lurk behind? Think again. Shortly before the folk of the Ordnance Survey completed their tour of Londonderry, much of the original Coward's Bastion had been removed – it was originally a much higher and thicker section of wall, and likely the last place that attackers would attempt to breach.

The **Tower Museum** is immediately apparent just inside the walls at this northern point. Unlike many others in Northern Ireland, this one charges a small

185 Other royal visitors to Brook Park have included King George VI (1945), Mary, the Princess Royal (1952) who also planted trees, using the same silver trowel as King Edward VII, and the newly-crowned Queen Elizabeth II toured Brooke Park in 1953.

entrance fee, but this more than pays for itself when you ascend (by lift) to Londonderry's only open-air viewing area overlooking the entire walled city and River Foyle. But, don't miss out on the excellent exhibitions within the museum, so allow a good amount of time[186] to see everything.

Ferryquay Gate, another of the original access points, is, unsurprisingly the one nearest to the River Foyle. Its appearance belies the fact that in December 1688 this was the most difficult for the Apprentice Boys to close since it had a heavy drawbridge to haul up rather than just a pair of wooden gates to shut. The original gate, drawbridge and tower that stood here were replaced in the middle of the nineteenth century. The *Dublin Builder* described the new structure in June 1866:

> *"The new gate will have a main and two side arches. The first will be 17 feet high by 18 feet wide; the latter will have 5 feet of span and 10 feet of height. Both fronts will be finished in finely wrought freestone, with rusticated ashlar quoins. The keystones of the arch will be carved into memoheads, and the structure will be surmounted by a handsome parapet, with freestone balustrading".*

The *memoheads* feature on the outer arch George Walker, one-time Governor, and James Gordon[187], Presbyterian minister at the time of the siege on the inner arch.

This gate is also the start point for one of the many guided tours that are available. This one, operated by Derry City Tours, operates throughout the year, several times each day, and for a small fee you get an interesting commentary on the main features – and a hot drink at the end!

Should you be here on the first weekend in December, Ferryquay Gate is the

---

186 The museum recommends at least 90 minutes, but I reckon you might need up to half a day to get the most out of your visit – especially if the day is bright and clear as you might spend an hour or more in the viewing space alone.

187 You can find out more on the man described as *"eloper and libertine ... the creator of a sort of Gretna Green ... state spy ... and the possessor of second sight"* by reading J.M. Bulloch's 1911 work *The Strange Adventures of The Reverend James Gordon, Sensualist, Spy, Strategist (?) and Soothsayer* which has been digitised by The National Library of Scotland and is available freely at http://digital.nls.uk/histories-of-scottish-families/archive/95615095

place to be at midnight on Friday. Since this was the first of the gates to be closed in 1688, it is here that commemorations commence every year. A single cannon is fired initially, followed by three further explosions – the 1 + 3 being symbolic of the 13 Apprentice Boys who rushed around the walls closing the gates. There are no gates to close as part of the ceremony, so present-day apprentices walk around and "touch" each gate instead.

The **Siege Heroes Mound** is not easy to miss. Within the grounds of St. Columb's Cathedral is a grassy knoll topped by a stone obelisk surrounded by iron railings. Many come here to pay their respects to either the thirteen Apprentice Boys or the estimated 8,000 who died (almost all from starvation and/or disease) during the three-month siege. What most do not realise is that this is not a burial mound at all. An advertisement placed in the *Derry Journal* on 15th May 1861 helps to unravel the confusion:

"At a meeting of the General Committee of the Apprentice Boys of Derry held on the 14th May, 1861 it was unanimously resolved:- that we have observed, with extreme regret, the heartless conduct of the parties engaged in carrying out the changes in the Cathedral, ruthlessly exposing the remains of the illustrious dead interred within its walls, before, during and after the eventful siege of 1688-9 ; and we are surprised to find that no proper effort has been made by the Cathedral Dignitaries to have them decently re-interred in their original resting places".

At that time, the Cathedral was undergoing major renovations, during which time some human bones had been unearthed, with the suggestion made that these were the remains of some of those who died in the siege, and possibly even the bones of the legendary Apprentice Boys themselves. As a result of the Apprentice Boys intervention, two decisions were taken. Firstly, the bones were collected together and re-interred in a vault within the Cathedral. Secondly, the excavated earth, which possibly contains further bone fragments (no-one knows for sure) was formed into a raised mound and dedicated with the placement of the stone obelisk that stands there today.

Where the majority of the dead were buried is pretty much unknown and fiercely debated with many different theories offered. Some say that it is impossible to dig up a spade full of earth from any point within the walls without turning up human bones. Another suggests mass graves exist outside the walls, possibly in the vicinity of Bishop's Gate or a little further to the east of

190

the city near the Sally Port beneath Church Bastion. The latter seems to be a plausible option. Removing bodies through a main gate whilst under siege would be risky, whereas using the small opening known as a Sally Port (for sallying forth to collect water, or for armed men to make sallies against the attackers) which was well defended being overlooked by a pair of high watchtowers would be a much safer strategy.

As with most tales of old, there is likely to be some basis in fact, but with a lot of exaggeration, embellishment or just plain fiction added over the intervening centuries.

One dictionary defines a legend as *"a traditional story sometimes popularly regarded as historical but not authenticated"*. There is no doubting the authenticity of most accounts of the 1689 siege. The same cannot be said of our next destination.

Further Reading:

G. Douglas, Derriana: A Collection of Papers Relative to the Siege of Derry, and Illustrative of the Revolution of 1688, G. Douglas (1794) is worth battling with the old-style spellings to read online at:
https://archive.org/details/derrianaacollec00douggoog

C.D. Milligan, The Walls of Derry, Ulster Society (1996) - although it is a reprint of two earlier publications, with a foreword by David Trimble and will likely cost you £20 - £50, this is the most comprehensive study of Derry's Walls I have found.

X is for eXodus: An X-rated horror story

The Castle Ward area on the southern tip of the Strangford Straits is home to one of those unexplained mysteries that just won't go away.

Audley's Castle is a mile to the north-east of Strangford and is the remains of a three-storey tower house once owned John Audley in the sixteenth century. It commands impressive views over Strangford Lough, but is a largely unremarkable structure, there being hundreds, possibly thousands of similar towers built within enclosed *bawns*. The castle was built as much as a hundred years before Audley took ownership of it. Who built it in the first place is not known. What we do know is that the Audley family had been around these parts since the late thirteenth century, and that the castle was sold by Robert Audley to Bernard Ward for £351 in November 1641.

The castle is a great place to visit, as much for its views as the structure itself. Admission to the castle and grounds is free, but it has become a very popular attraction in recent times, since being used to film scenes for both *Game of Thrones* and *Dracula Untold*.

Mount Panther House has one of those names that you'd associate with works of fantasy like those just mentioned, but it is a real mansion, sadly in a very rundown condition on the edge of Dundrum. It was to here that a Cornish widow, Mary Pendarves moved following her marriage to Patrick Delaney, the Dean of Down in 1743. Mary Delaney's involvement in our mystery stems from one of her works of art dated from 1762.

At that time, Mary, who travelled extensively and mixed in all the social circles, produced a piece of art capturing the Castle Ward hilltop temple[188] and surrounding estate. It is a fairly ordinary work of art, but is important to the telling of this particular tale as it also shows Audley's Castle with a small village settlement alongside – this is, or perhaps I ought to write *was* Audley's Town.

When the Ordnance Survey maps of County Down were first published around

---

188 Built as a summer house in 1750 for Lady Anne Ward, and later extended to be used as the home of the head gardener who tended the walled garden (built in 1830) nearby.

1835, Audley's Town was shown clearly. By the time of the second edition in 1863 it had disappeared – replaced by over 100 acres of new woodland. What was it, what became of it, and where did its population go, are all questions requiring answers.

As well as painting, Mary Delaney was a prolific writer, especially of letters. On one occasion, discussing the Castle Ward estate in an exchange with her sister Anne, Mary wrote of Lord and Lady Ward *"If they do not do too much they can't spoil the place, for it hath every advantage from nature that can be desired"*.

It transpired that building a village on a hilltop, may just have constituted doing *too much* for a subsequent owner of the estate.

Edward Southwell Ward, the third Viscount Bangor had inherited the Castle Ward estate on the death of his uncle Nicholas, who died unmarried, of unsound mind and heirless in 1827. A year earlier, Edward had married Harriet Margaret Maxwell, the fourth child of Reverend Henry Maxwell and Lady Anne Butler, Baron and Baroness Farnham respectively.

When Edward died eleven years into his marriage with Harriet, she was left a widow and four years later married again – this time to Major Andrew Savage Nugent of Portaferry House, who, with his wife retaining her title of Lady Bangor, was therefore entitled to manage and alter the entire Castle Ward estate, which after years of neglect in the hands of the much-troubled second Viscount, was more than ready for some serious investment.

Don't worry if you're not keeping up with all this – we've reached the protagonists of our story. It seems that Harriet grew exceedingly troubled by the view of her estate, with the scar of Audleystown on a hilltop causing her to seek a remedy. Planting trees to screen the village from view was not an option – the trees would take too long to reach maturity, and may not grow tall enough anyway. Building an alternative home with a different perspective was an expensive, yet affordable possibility but this did not solve the problem completely – the village was still an eyesore whilst out and about.

No, the only complete solution was to remove the village – completely.

How do you get rid of almost 200 villagers, from what was for them an idyllic countryside setting overlooking the lough? Yes, times had been particularly hard in the Great Famine years, but rural communities had lived hand-to-mouth, largely from their own produce (potatoes mostly) for generations, so Harriet, with the help of her husband's inherited coffers had to come up with an *offer* too good to refuse.

For the next part of the story we have to travel outside the territory covered by this book briefly – about 70 miles west to County Tyrone and the *Ulster American Folk Park*. This is the place to be if you want to learn about the history of emigration to America over three centuries. In the first nine months of 1848, for example, the Port of New York accepted 72,896 migrants from Ireland – more than from every other land combined[189]. More than two million people ultimately left Ireland to brave the 3,000-mile Atlantic crossing in search of a new life in the New World. It is an enormous number, but, to put it in perspective, one million stayed and died in Ireland in a handful of years during the Great Famine.

Within the Folk Park's extensive archives is a document from the Castle Ward Estate from the year 1852 establishing that all 25 families living in Audleystown (just over 200 men, women and children) left on the 28th October on a ship named *Rose*, bound for America. The document – a rent book, further reveals that the families did not leave voluntarily, neither were more than a third of them in rent arrears. The biggest debtors only owed three shillings.

If cross the Atlantic is what the villagers actually did, then they could not have selected a much worse departure date. Crossings could take several weeks and at that time of year the ocean was at its most unforgiving.

But it is a big *if*. The ship *"Rose"* was not known for carrying passengers to North America, being one of many regularly travelling between Ireland and South America to bring back cargoes of guano and no records exist of it ever landing and offloading passengers at any of the east coast ports.

The most likely scenario is that while Major Nugent was away serving in the army during the Crimean War, Lady Bangor made the most of her husband's absence to make a few adjustments around the Castle Ward estate. One such adjustment involved the forced eviction and exodus of the Audleystown villagers

---

189 Figures for the other lands (1st January - 30th September 1848):
Germany 40731, England 17223, Scotland 4974, France 2007, Holland 1374, Switzerland 1243, Norway 4206, Wales 899, West Indies 335, Spain 225, Italy 241, Sweden 113, Poland 53, Denmark 33, Portugal 35, South America 21, Russia 11, Mexico 7, Belgium 4, China 1

followed almost immediately by the demolition of every home and farm building. The *offer too good to refuse* turned out to be no offer at all.

Eyewitnesses from the period passed on stories of stone from the village being used to build boundary walls elsewhere on the estate, while others remembered baking batch upon batch of bread to feed the forced migrants on their long and perilous voyage.

The Biblical Exodus account is backed up by archaeological evidence of all three key components – a place of departure; a journey (in this case the Red Sea crossing) and an arrival settlement. This Northern Irish exodus has ample evidence to verify the first two components, but nothing at all for the third.

Evictions of entire villages were not uncommon at that time. All 300 inhabitants of the village of Ballinlass in County Galway were turfed out at the height of the Great Famine so that their landowner[190] could increase the amount of grazing land for her livestock. Charles William Vane, the third Marquess of Londonderry voiced his concerns on the matter in the House of Lords in March 1846. Saying that he was "deeply grieved", the Marquess described how the seventy six families[191] "*had not only been turned out of their houses*" but also "*mercilessly driven from the ditches to which they had been taken themselves for shelter*". Who drove them from the ditches? Soldiers and Police officers, apparently enforcing the landowners right to evict her tenants. The British governments response?

Silence.

Some unscrupulous landlords even exploited an amendment to British law designed to bring relief to those hardest hit by the potato blight. The Irish Poor Law Extension Act came into force in June 1847. The main component of the new regulations "*An Act to make further Provision for the Relief of the destitute Poor in Ireland*", was, in spirit, an act designed to pass control directly to landlords who, in theory, at least, knew their land and tenants and how best to support these afflicted people. In practice, many landowners saw this change as simply dumping responsibility on them for providing for the needs of those who

---

190 Marcella Gerrad had a 15,000 acre estate and allegedly evicted up to 4,000 tenants over a three-year period in a similar fashion.

191 Other accounts say 61 families, 270 people in all, but the numbers are far less important than the deed.

the Poor Laws were designed to protect. The inevitable response from some, but by no means all, was to make this financial *burden* go away – for good.

To be fair, many landlords acted compassionately and gave generously of their time, finances and other resources. Others simply exploited the situation and used the new law to evict tenants and increase their own income. Finlay Dun summarised things neatly in his 1881 book *Landlords and Tenants in Ireland*. He identified George Bingham, Lord Lucan as one of them:

> *"Lord Lucan has 60,570 acres in Mayo, part of it around Castlebar, where his substantial old house stands; part of it at Cloona Castle, near Ballinrobe. From several parishes extensive evictions were made from 1846 to 1850; Lord Lucan, in his terse, incisive style, asserted that "he would not breed paupers to pay priests".*

Malnourished and homeless, many died from a combination of starvation and exposure in the open air. Inevitably, crime increased. This case from Downpatrick (reported in the *Tyrawley Herald*) not far from Audleystown shows how desperate the situation had become:

MURDER AT DOWNPATRICK

We are informed that a brutal murder was perpetrated a few days ago at a place called Castletown, close to Downpatrick, within about four miles of Ballycastle in this county. The victim was a poor old widow, named Mary Hegarty, 75 years of age. The poor woman had a small bag of meal in the house, and this circumstance being known to a boy, named James, who lived in the same locality, he determined to avail himself of the absence of her family and to rob her of the meal. He accordingly went to the widow's house, and either to effect his purpose, or to prevent discovery, he inflicted six or seven desperate wounds on her head with a loy which he found in the house. He then seized on the bag of meal, and just as he was leaving the house with his bloody booty another boy, belonging to the village, happened to be passing by, and seeing the old woman weltering in her gore, he, at once, thought that all was not right and immediately pursued the murderer and robber. Having overtaken him he took the bag of meal from him and, of course, identified him.

What became of the Audleystown villagers has never been established. You'd think that if they made it to North America, there would be at least one account documented of their ordeal and subsequent rebirth *in the land of the brave, home of the free*. There are none. This leads to the inevitable conclusion that not one of them survived.

Shipwrecks and sinkings were an all-too-common event, so accidental deaths are a real possibility. The alternative is that foul play took place. The histories of transporting convicts to Australia and the movement of people to fuel the trade in slaves are littered with tales of ships whose captains, having been paid to carry passengers (willingly or otherwise), promptly dumped them at the first opportunity. Sometimes this might be an uninhabited island, but all too often the unfortunate passengers were simply herded overboard to their deaths.

What we do know is that the *Rose* was not wrecked on that voyage – if indeed it ever sailed to America. Records show that it continued on the South American Guano run for many more years afterwards. It is possible, of course that the villagers never boarded her, or any other vessel for that matter.

No-one knows for certain what really happened. A few footings of the village's stone cottages can just be made out overgrown with moss, ivy, bracken and fallen tree branches if you look carefully. The National Trust, in whose care the entire estate now belongs, have plans to carry out excavations at some point in the future. Perhaps it will throw up new possibilities. Maybe some kind of epidemic struck the entire village and a mass grave will be found? Could there perhaps be some other outcome that is more palatable than the horror story presumed by most to be the reason for the extinction of Audleystown?

We may never know.

Further Reading:

F. Dun, Landlords and Tenants in Ireland, Longman (1881) which is available online at https://archive.org/details/landlordstenant00dunf

H. Dixon, An Introduction to Ulster Architecture, Ulster Architectural Heritage Society (1975)

Y is for a Yew Tree at the Head of the Strand

Time and again throughout this guide I've had to use words and phrases like allegedly, reputedly, legend has it, and so on to describe events and stories enshrined in Northern Irish history as facts when, some or all of them may well be nothing more than tales of fiction.

Don't get me wrong – I'm not telling you what to believe. I'm just being careful to present material to you carefully and accurately.

With that in mind, lets spend some time exploring the *"frontier town"*[192] and latterly *city*[193] that is Newry.

Newry is as far south as you can get on the Northern Irish coast but is well worth the trip. Described in 1910 as *"a thriving market town"* by 1935 it was promoted as *"one of the most progressive and up-to-date towns in Ulster"*. Do these comments mean that Newry is a modern *"new"* town?

Far from it!

Look at what Samuel Lewis had to say about Newry in 1837. He called it

> *"a sea-port, borough, market, and post town, and a parish ... containing 24,557 inhabitants, of which number 13,134 are in the town"*.

And then he said this

> *"It was a place of some importance from a very remote period"*.

How remote?

According to *The Annals of the Four Masters*, compiled in the seventeenth century, St. Patrick planted a yew tree at a monastery here – which means Newry was *likely* occupied by monks from at least the fifth century[194]. This

---

192 Also the title of an excellent book on the history of Newry by Tony Canavan, a former curator of the town/city museum.

193 Newry and Lisburn were both awarded city status by Queen Elizabeth II in 2002.

194 Scholars disagree about the dates of Patrick's life, the general opinion is that he died anywhere between 40 years and 10 years before the beginning of the sixth century.

cannot be established as a fact without any hard evidence. A Cistercian Abbey was indeed founded here, but not until 1153 and it did have a Latin name – *Viride Lignum* – which translates as the *green tree*. Yews are evergreen conifers, remember.

When Henry VIII began his purge and ultimate dissolution of all Catholic monasteries in England, Wales and Ireland in 1536, there were just three monks residing at Newry with the accounts from the period showing a total income of just £30 – per year! For twelve years (from 1538 – 1550), the monks craftily worked around the new prohibitions by rebranding the abbey as a place of learning. Eventually the Abbot had to surrender the building and land to the authorities, namely Sir Nicholas Bagenal, who reused much of the stone work for a building of his own and eventually the whole site was cleared as the *"new"* town of Newry expanded at the start of the nineteenth century. Bagenal's castle did not appear on the first Ordnance Survey map of the town, indicating that it had gone before 1835 at least.

Much of this was largely forgotten until 1996 when a long-standing bakery – *McCanns* invited archaeologists to take a look at some stone feature work on the walls of their building prior to the bakery closing down. What they discovered was that the bake house had been built over and around a much older structure – and when much older survey maps were consulted and some building plans in London's National Archives, it turned out it could only be one structure, Bagenal's castle.

Fast Forward to 2004, and with the help of a substantial grant from the Heritage Lottery fund, the entire former bakery and adjoining warehouse underwent a major transformation to become the new home for the Newry and Mourne Museum. The museum houses a permanent gallery describing Newry's very long history as well as having frequently-changing special exhibitions.

Many pieces of jewellery have been found in this area pointing at there being a Bronze Age settlement here based around what was possibly one of Ireland's very first factories – producing metal clasps. Three of these are displayed at the Ulster Museum in Belfast.

Exactly what went on and where is the subject of much speculation with little firm foundation, so we'll focus our investigation on more recent developments.

Newry already had a market, customs house and a watermill at the time of the

Dissolution of the Monasteries and Arthur Bagenal, son and heir of Sir Nicholas is known to have been granted rights to markets and an annual fair by James I in 1613.

These rights were summed up well by Thomas Bradshaw in his 1820 *General Directory*:

"The patent grants to Arthur Bagnal, Esq. His heirs and assigns, the town of Newry, with all the demesne lands of the dissolved monastery — the manor, lordship and castle of Greencastle—the lordship, country or territory of Mourne, with two islands in the main sea —the manor of Carlingford,with the monastery and its appurtenances, and the lands of Cooley—the ferry between Carlingford and Killowen—the customs of anchorage, and certain customs of goods and merchandize imported into or exported from Carlingford — the territory of Omeath, and all wrecks of sea, happening upon these properties.

It grants a market at Newry, to be held every Thursday, with tolls, customs and commodities:also a custom or toll of six gallons from every butt of wine called sack, and three and a half gallons from every hogshead of wine sold in Newry; three gallons from every barrel of ale, and 4d. out of every barrel of salt—and the assize of bread and wine in the town of Newry.

It grants to the patentee, to hold, by his senes-chal, a court at Newry, to determine causes of debt, trespass, &c. when the sum shall not exceed £ 66 13s. 4d. and also all the profits and fines appertaining to the said court.— It grants all fines and amercements which shall be imposed, assessed, ad- judged and decreed at any assizes or sessions to beheld in the county, upon any of the inhabitants of the manor.

It permits a court to be held at Greencastle, to hold pleas of actions, not exceeding forty pounds sterling; and a court at Carlingford for actions not exceeding £ 10.

It grants also a court baron to be held from three weeks to three weeks, to hold pleas of debt, tress-pass, &c. not exceeding £ 40. Likewise a court-leet twice a year, in Newry and Mourne— together with all the profits, fines, &c, arising out of the same.

The patent further grants two fairs to be held at Newry yearly, each for three days; and at Greencastle a weekly market on Friday, and one fair in the year, with courts of pipowder—together with all the tolls and customs belonging to the same;requiring from the patentee 6s. 8d. yearly for the privilege of holding these markets and fairs, and of appointing the clerks of the markets".

A few terms used here perhaps need further expansion. A *pipowder* (more usually written as *piepowder* or *pie poudre*) court was a temporary tribunal established during markets and fairs to settle disputes arising from trade. The right to a *court-leet* effectively devolved certain legal powers, including court processes to the landowner. The role of the *senes-chal* (more correctly *seneschal*) was to act as a steward for the landowner and carry out the day to day legal tasks on his behalf.

By the middle of the eighteenth century Newry, with its new canal dug and fully effective took on a very different aspect. The canal diverted so much water that the Glenn Bog dried up, creating a large new area of fertile ground and its route through the town saw new buildings spring up along either side. These by-products of the canal, dug, not for Newry, but to help the owners of the Tyrone coalfields to transport coal more speedily to Dublin and beyond, proved to be a watershed in the history of Newry.

George Tyner's 1794 *Traveller's Guide Through Ireland* nicely summed up Newry at the end of the eighteenth century like this:

"(Newry) suffered much in the rebellion of 1641, and in 1680 was set on fire by the Duke of Berwick, in his retreat from Duke Schomberg and the English army, who on their approach, found it in flames; a few houses and two or three castles were all that escaped the conflagration. It has increased considerably of late years, both in trade and population, owing in a great measure to the Canal lately made through it, between Carlingford bay and Lough Neagh. The town stands in hollow ground about a mile from the head of Carlingford bay, on both sides a brook of its own name, and is increasing and improving very fast".

Tyner concluded his short description of Newry with

"It belongs to Mr Needham".

So, we really ought to find out a little more about him.

Again, we'll let Thomas Bradshaw, through the pages of his 1820 directory fill in the details:

"The manors of Newry, Mourne and Carlingford,having been enjoyed by the Bagnal family, for upwards of a century, were latterly shared by two proprietors,

201

Robert Nedham and Edward Bayly, in whom they vested by the will of their father-in-law, Nicholas Bagnal. In 1715, they were divided. The Down and Armagh estates fell to Nedham, and the Louth to Bayly. Edward Bayly was great-grandfather to the present proprietor, the Earl of Uxbridge. The next, Robert Nedham, on his decease, left two sons. George, the elder, sold part of the estate to enable him to discharge certain debts with which it was encumbered; having, for this purpose, procured an act of Parliament. William not having married, nor having any near male relations, left the estate by will to the predecessor of the present proprietor, Francis Needham, Viscount Kilmorey. His lordship's income, arising from the Newry and Mourne estates, amounts at present to about £15,000".

Newry was most definitely on the up as you might say at that time, but not without tribulation. Bradshaw added this comment:

"The old custom-house, a very good building, is situated on the river, opposite to what was formerly the lowest lock of the canal. It has latterly been occupied as a fever hospital. The present custom-house stands on the Merchants'-quay, and is a plain building. Lately, extensive and well-built stores have been erected in the adjoining yard".

Busy custom-houses are a clear indicator of good trading conditions – but a *fever hospital?*

Dr J. Morrison, physician at the *Newry Dispensary and Fever Hospital* submitted an annual report for the year 1837 in which it was noted that 507 cases treated in the previous twelve months were of typhoid fever. To put this in perspective, some comparisons are helpful. In the same twelve-month period, 176 patients were treated for influenza and 21 for bronchitis.

Typhoid fever reached epidemic proportions throughout most of County Down in the years between 1815 and 1820. Writing in 1820, Dr William Harty noted in his *Historic Sketch of the Causes, Progress, Extent and Mortality of the Contagious Fever epidemic in Ireland during the Years 1817, 1818, and 1819*:

"a more general epidemic never, perhaps, existed in any country of equal dimensions and population; or according to every account, whether public or private, it would appear that not only every city, town, and village was visited by the disease, but that even very few of the isolated cabins of the poor escaped".

Downpatrick was the first place to report outbreaks in October 1816. In Newry, according to the *First Report from the Select Committee on the State of Disease and Condition of the Labouring Poor in Ireland*, by 1817 it was a *"very formidable epidemic"*. The fever hospital mentioned by Bradshaw opened its doors on 12th July 1817 and admitted almost 1500 patients in its first six months. In the worst eighteen month period 57 people from the Newry population died from either the typhoid fever or a related condition. Interestingly, if you were wealthy, you were far more likely to pick up the infection, but also much more likely to survive it. If one member of a poorer household – often with several generations of the same family living in just a couple of small rooms – picked up typhoid, the inevitable consequence was that the whole family went down with the disease. By 1825, demand for treatment exceeded capacity in the old market house building and the hospital expanded into a neighbouring grain store.

But, to put the figures into perspective, out of a population of approaching 18,000 in and around Newry, less than 1% died as a result of typhoid in that time. Nevertheless, the prospect of contracting and succumbing to the fever was enough to put fear into the hearts of most.

Similarly, many feared the possibility of drowning at that time. Bradshaw noted this, observing *"the many afflicting instances of death occasioned by drowning, which had of late years occurred in Newry"*. In 1814, a Humane Society, specifically charged with *"the recovery of persons apparently dead"* was formed in the town. Quite what Thomas Bradshaw was suggesting here requires a closer look before you start wondering if the impossible was being performed two hundred years ago, without getting the attention of the world and being replicated everywhere ever since.

In 1815 the very first issue of the *Newry Magazine* (also known as the *Literary and Political Register*) was published. Tucked away at the bottom of page 20 we find the answer:

> *"The Humane Society have purchased an excellent resuscitative apparatus, and have appointed a number of receiving houses in convenient situations. They have also published cards of instruction for restoring suspended animation"*.

So, no miracle cures, but certainly a forward-thinking strategy in its day for giving unfortunate victims the best possible chance of making a recovery from immersion in the waters.

The next page of the same journal described another recent Newry innovation -

the deliberate immersion in salt water – for medicinal purposes:

"Two years ago, doctor Johnston, one of the physicians of the town, constructed cold and tepid salt water baths at Newry. He had frequently found it necessary to send his patients to Dublin, for the sole purpose of using the tepid bath; and being convinced of its great utility, both by the good effects experienced from it by his patients, and by the favourable testimony of many eminent medical practitioners, he determined on preparing baths at his own house, trusting that they would afford comfort and advantage to the public, as well as profit to himself".

The journal reported that Johnston had yet to make any financial gain from his *"most perfect construction"* with a daily capacity of *"twenty to twenty four persons"*, each paying 15 pennies for a cold bath or almost three times the price for a soak in tepid salt water. Thanks to the same magazine article I can give you an illustration of what the customer could expect for their money:

"Including furniture they (the baths) cost £412 (and) consist of two tepid baths, a cold bath, a shower bath and a reception room. The tepid baths are heated by steam. To each, a neat dressing-room is attached, with a fire-place, and every suitable article of furniture".

The system operated on tidal flow – 130 feet of pipeline carrying the incoming sea water into a reservoir from where it would be pumped up as required. It was a costly business, consuming up to a ton of coal to heat the water every ten days.

There must have been a market for tepid baths, because by 1823 in neighbouring Warrenpoint, *"one of the most salubrious and agreeable places in the Empire"*, Warm Baths *"for the Gentry, nobility and Public"* were being advertised as opening on 1st July. The advertisement posted in newspapers including the Newry Commercial Telegraph (who were also responsible for the description of Warrenpoint just now, added

"They are to be established at the house lately occupied by Mr. Hawthorne, in Best Row. It is intended that comfortable sleeping apartments, with well aired bed, attendants, a Coffee Room, and Dublin and Newry newspapers will be provided, also a confectioner's shop for public convenience and accommodation".

Although the concept struggled financially, Newry and/or Warrenpoint continued to be served by tepid salt baths for many years – with several changes of ownership along the way. By the start of the twentieth century, all had gone, with Warrenpoint providing the only land-based saltwater dips – at the public baths opened in 1908. These are sadly, also long gone.

For those who don't know Warrenpoint personally, the name likely rakes up memories of the terrible events of 27th August 1979, in which 18 soldiers were killed by an IRA ambush and, in the subsequent retaliatory gunfire from the army, an English tourist watching events unfold from, what he thought was a safe distance was also shot dead.

Like Newry, Warrenpoint has uncertain origins. Even the name, attributed by most to being derived from the Waring family who were resident here from at least the second half of the eighteenth century, is disputed. Samuel Lewis, in his *Topographical Dictionary* supposed *"the site of the present town was originally a rabbit warren"*, yet there was no basis for the theory. He went on to say that, as of 1780, Warrenpoint *"consisted only of two houses, with a few huts for the occasional residence of the fishermen for the oyster season"*. By 1837, this had increased to 462 houses. William Waring definitely owned land in and around Donaghcloney in 1658, and documents show that his name was sometimes spelled as Warring, even Warren – but this was many miles north of Warrenpoint and other sources have a settlement in the same place at that time labelled as *Rinn Mhic Giolla Ruaidh* which broadly translates as McIlroy's Point.

Perhaps we should just stick with the colloquialism favoured by many who live there and just call it *the point*?

Newry's modern Irish name is *An tIúr* which means the *Yew Tree* and is in turn shortened from *Iúr Cinn Trá* which gives rather more detail as the *"yew tree at the head of the strand"* adding further weight to the claims of a past link to Saint Patrick. As a general rule of thumb, perhaps all we can say is that a place name in Northern Ireland doesn't necessarily give anything away about the place and its history. Take the modern blue-and-white signs on the approach roads to Newry, for example:

Fáilte go Cathair an Iúir

Which is translated into English as Welcome to Newry City. The word cathair though has become used to mean a city, when its original use was to describe a ring-fort or a battle-axe.

It is the *head of the strand* that we will focus on now, however. In Ireland, a *strand* is usually a stretch of coastline, typically in the form of a sandy beach – think of Benone Strand in County Derry or the West Strand (sometimes known as Millstrand) between Portrush and Portstewart in County Antrim, for example. Newry's strand is three miles of muddy riverbank as the Newry River drains SSE into Carlingford Lough just beyond Warrenpoint. Even the most imaginative of minds would not look at it and think *beach*. The river itself has two names. The old name, sometimes still seen on maps and used by many locally – *Clanrye*, is a corruption of *Glanrye* which derives from *Gleann Righe* meaning simply *valley of the river*. This particular river valley runs north-east of Newry as far as the rivers source, just a few miles away near Rathfriland. When it reached Newry, the rivers course had traditionally formed the boundary between two neighbouring counties – Down and Armagh. As Newry grew, in particular expanding beyond the river into Armagh to form what is now the suburb of Ballybot, so the need for an administrative centre to serve the needs of all who used the town from both counties grew with it.

A town hall was the obvious answer. But, where should it be placed. Building it on either side of the river would suggest favouring one county over the other. Architect William Batt, born in County Londonderry and resident of County Antrim, had no bias and came up with a novel, possibly unique solution to the dispute. He built the town hall in 1893 atop a three-arched bridge over the river straddling both counties. Five years later, the Down/Armagh border was altered so that all of Newry fell in a single county – Down. Don't mention it too loudly to those who live on the Armagh side of the river though.

Newry's diverse trading history is well illustrated with this list of street names:

Buttercrane Quay

Mill Street

Corn Market

Hide Terrace

Merchant's Quay

Kiln Street

Sugar Island

The Buttercrane Centre is now a busy retail complex, which presently attracts

206

shoppers from both Northern Ireland and the Irish Republic. Similarly, Merchant's Quay is now almost entirely modern retail and commercial office space. The *New York Times* called Newry, the European Union's *"Hottest Shopping Spot"* at the height of the banking/economic crisis of 2008.

Newry is also a very popular tourist destination. It is well located for touring the Mourne Mountains, the coastline of South Down, Armagh's beautiful Ring of Gullion AONB and for trips across the Irish border – even Dublin is only just over an hour away by car and not much longer if you fancy a train ride.

Then again, for many a holiday is often a long-awaited and much-needed opportunity to get away from the hustle and bustle of everyday life, so its appropriate that the final chapter of our tour explores a few of Down and Derry's hidden treasures.

Further Reading:

T. Canavan, Frontier Town: an Illustrated History of Newry, Blackstaff (1990)

A. Smyth, Newry: an Illustrated History and Companion, Cottage Publications (1996) is a much smaller book but includes many beautiful paintings by the late Colin Turner.

Z is for *Zzzz... Zzzz... Zzzz...*

An accepted treasure can lose its value pretty quickly. In my *Antrim Coast* guide I wrote about the sudden popularity of the *Dark Hedges* between Stranocum and Armoy in the wake of their featuring in the *Game of Thrones* television series. At one time you could walk this strange and beautiful avenue of beech trees and not see another person. Now, you may find it difficult to get a good view of the trees at all there are so many visitors including several daily coach parties. Some scientists warn that the rise in popularity is causing permanent, irreversible damage and that the *Dark Hedges* may not exist at all in a few more years.

With that in mind, here are a few quieter places on or near the coast, that, so far at least, seem to have avoided the mass tourist markets, and will hopefully continue to do so in the future.

Kilbroney Forest Park just outside Newry is possibly not the first place you'd think of for peace and tranquillity. A caravan and camping site, tennis courts, children's play park, cafe and visitors centre all smack of noise and activity, not calm and solitude, but you'd be surprised how easy it is to find the latter in a park that has plenty of the former.

The Cloghmore Stone is a granite boulder estimated to weigh around 40 tonnes, a legacy of the last ice age, deposited on a hilltop (also scraped flat by the retreating glacier) 10,000 years ago and a fantastic landmark to aim for if you are looking for a short but strenuous hike[195]. The views over Carlingford Lough towards the Ring of Gullion, and in another direction, of the Mourne Mountains make it well worth the effort. Don't expect to be on your own in high summer, but if you plan your trek for a bright day in any other season, you may well have the summit to yourself.

This is a good place to look across the Irish Sea in the direction of Scotland and remember that as recently as 14,000 years ago this part of Northern Ireland was connected to northern mainland Britain by a vast ice sheet with coastal sea levels around 450 feet lower than they are now. Climate change continues to melt ice and raise sea levels, posing an ever-increasing danger to coastal

---

195 http://www.walkni.com/walks/259/rostrevor-cLoughmore-stone/

communities – all the signs are that the rate of change continues to increase.

Kilkeel may not spring to mind as a place for a quiet life, but the tiny hamlet, or *clachan* as they're called in Scotland and Northern Ireland, of **Hanna's Close** a mile away in Aughnahoory is definitely worthy of a closer look[196]. Here you can see, or even stay in one of the seven restored cottages or the three newer additions and learn about how and why several members of the same family from the little Wigtownshire village of Sorbie ended up living here in the middle of the seventeenth century[197].

The Plantation of Ulster is full of stories of exploitation and abuse, but Hanna's Close is a reminder that many of the folk who came to Ireland in that period, did so, not to seek riches or power, but to escape persecution in their own land. You see, the Hanna's were part of the Scottish clan of Hannay who had been involved in a long feud with a rival clan – the Murrays, and several Hannay clan members took the bold decision to flee Scotland entirely for a new life in Ulster.

The layout of Hanna's Close gives visual clues as to the insecurity felt by those early settlers. The cottages are all really close together, with a single door, always facing inwards as if fearing intruders at any time. Amidst these fears and despite living with constant anxieties, the Hanna's flourished. Two wells dug nearby provided a safe and reliable water supply. The river flowing just a short walk away proved to have fish in abundance – and a resident otter family too.

Lots of people testify that a great way to relax is to take a brisk walk in the fresh air. The **Annalong Coastal Path**[198] has a little bit of everything on offer. The village has good car parking and/or can be reached using public transport. The path itself is tarmac and relatively level and dog-friendly too. Although walks that follow a circuit are often preferred over linear routes, this walk along the shore offers spectacular views in both directions so that turning round half-way is something to look forward to. It's probably easiest to start and end your walk in the village, where you might also like to visit the old cornmill which is now a fascinating museum telling not only the story of the corn mill which worked here for over 150 years, but also the long-standing granite industry in the area. As

---

196 http://www.walkni.com/walks/380/hanna-s-close-the-green-lane-walk/

197 https://www.mournecountrycottages.com/ has details.

198 http://www.walkni.com/walks/129/annalong-coastal-path/

you walk along the coastal path look out for large granite blocks, polished by years of wave energy – many of these have been washed along the seafront from Annalong harbour, having fallen from the quayside during loading.

Wildlife spotting is both relaxing and exhilarating. You may spot a common seal or two, and bottle-nosed dolphins, even minke whales have been seen along the shoreline, especially around the herring season. Look out for oystercatchers and the curved-billed curlew, Ireland's largest wader, in the air or on the ground in the shallows, searching out worms, shrimps, or even small crabs in the wet mud at low tide.

In a similar vein, the **Dundrum Coastal Path** starts in a village but quickly enters an area abundant with wildlife. So much so, that it is considered as part of the Murlough Nature Reserve. It's a popular place – winning a public vote for Northern Ireland's best nature reserve in 2018. Much of the land here is in the care of the National Trust who manage two excellent waymarked nature trails themselves[199].

The coastal path[200] begins and ends in a small car park just off the main Newcastle – Belfast road (A2) a hundred yards or so north of Dundrum Castle. Here the path follows the former railway line for just over a mile and a half. This is excellent cycling territory – so requires careful attention and consideration for other users, whether on foot or on two wheels. It is a grassy track that follows a raised embankment for part of the route so may not be fully accessible for all.

For birdwatchers the winter months are likely the best time to visit. This is when the mudflats are usually covered with an array of waders and other wildfowl. You may well spot curlew and oystercatchers again as well as rarer species such as redshank or even the black-tailed godwit.

At the northern end of the path, just beyond Ardilea Bridge you will find *Widow's Row* – the line of cottages built by public subscription following a tragedy at sea, mentioned earlier in this book.

From this point you can either turn round and return the way you came, or pick up or take a break at one of the three places offering refreshments nearby.

---

199 Find them at: https://www.nationaltrust.org.uk/murLough-national-nature-reserve

200 Here it is: http://www.cycleni.com/99/dundrum-coastal-path/

Due east of Portaferry is the tiny coastal clachan community of **Kearney**. To walk around this often wild and windswept little settlement of a dozen or so whitewashed cottages, you'd struggle to believe that less than 200 years ago, this was a thriving village with a population of over 150 people[201]. The National Trust carefully restored the cottages and take responsibility for the management of the area, but please remember that people live here in private homes – it isn't a working museum, so please respect the privacy of the villagers, but don't be put off from visiting this remarkable place.

Kearney was once the home of Mary Ann Donnan, of whom various accounts have been written. Most record her as owner and skipper of a large fishing boat, a *"she-cruiser"* crewed entirely by women, something that might not capture attention these days, but which was considered to be unique a century ago.

As with virtually every other coastal community along this stretch of County Down, tales of smuggling abound. Many ships have been wrecked on the perilous rocks here. In 1748, HMS Wolf, a 245-ton warship came to grief here in 1748 – *Wolf Rock* being named hereafter in remembrance of her complement of approximately 110 men who lost their lives when the ship was dashed to pieces in stormy seas on the last day of the year.

Some historians suggest that villagers in past times engaged in *wrecking* here – deliberately luring ships onto the rocks by the use of false lights and other unlawful practises. I could find no evidence to support this at Kearney, but there is no doubt that salvaging whatever could be brought ashore from wrecks happened in all parts.

As well as the wading birds, seal population and extensive rock pools to keep your attention, if you visit here in the late springtime, look out for splashes of bright yellow – not daffodils, but the rare yellow horned poppy. The name comes from the unusual shape of the seed pod that is exposed once the flower petals have dropped (around the end of June). As a general rule, it is best not to disturb the natural environment. With the yellow horned poppy, should you be tempted to break off a pod or two, be aware of these two facts. Firstly, they're a temperamental plant, thriving in quite specific conditions, unlikely to exist in your back garden. Secondly, and more importantly, the sap that is released when a stem breaks is poisonous – you have been warned.

---

201 http://www.walkni.com/walks/110/kearney/

Continuing north along the coast, we come to **Slan's Graveyard** on the edge of Cloughey. A short trail from the village was established recently[202], and while entrance to the graveyard is free, you might like to join one of the guided tours that are put on from time to time, where, for a small charge, you can learn all about the long history of this place.

Aerial surveys have revealed the graveyard to be at the middle of a large ancient settlement. Its exact age can only be estimated without proper archaeological investigation, but a large boulder on which a cross has been carved points to habitation here in early Christian times. The remains of a church are possibly a building identified in Papal tax records to date from the year 1306. And then there are the gravestones themselves. Centuries of coastal winds and rains have worn away many of the inscriptions, but you can still make out some, including some of slate with dates as far back as 1677.

Many of the graves that can be read serve to remind of the thousands who lost their lives in the waters near here. One gravestone reads:

Erected in memory of Joseph Erving

aged 16 years who was lost

in the Mally of Workington with the rest

of the unfortunate crew on Ringboy Point

the 24th of March 1810

But not every shipwreck ended with the loss of life. There is the remarkable account of the *Wild Deer,* which left Glasgow with a crew of 40 and 300 passengers, bound for New Zealand shortly after midnight on Saturday 13th January 1883. Within 24 hours, and with all passengers settled down in their beds for the night, the ship found itself the wrong side of the South Rock lightship and soon after got caught on the North Rock. Battered all night, the ship and the lives of those on it were probably saved when a mast broke and wedged against the rock providing some temporary stability. The following day, local lifeboat crews and other volunteers from the Cloughey area managed to bring every passenger and crew member safely ashore.

The trail to Slan's Graveyard is just a third of a mile. Midway between

---

202 http://www.walkni.com/walks/22692/slans-graveyard/

Donaghadee and Bangor, is **Orlock Point**, where undertaking a vigorous three-mile trail will yield many rewards[203].

Part of the trail follows the Orlock Coach Road, believed to have been dug, laid and carved in the early part of the nineteenth century for the benefit of those involved in the flourishing smuggling industry. Look out for a stone archway, where chisel marks are still evident.

The National Trust trail takes in much of this coastline that was considered of strategic importance during World War II. Evidence of this remains in the form of a lookout hut, which, according to Bill Clements, was one of only a handful of sites in Northern Ireland where women were employed in operational service. At the start of the war, a cable was laid across the entrance to Belfast Lough, between Blackhead on Islandmagee, and Orlock Point. The electronic cable, known as a Submarine Indicator Loop was designed to act as an early-warning system, detecting U-boats as they approached. From Orlock Point Command Post, a senior Royal Naval officer could also manage (electronically) the activation of a defensive minefield laid across the Lough. The discovery of underwater steel and wood structures nearby have also led some to speculate that the Royal Navy also used this position to refuel its own submarine fleet.

Nowadays, the single lookout point that remains (all other buildings having been demolished) acts as an excellent bird hide, and also gives spectacular views out to sea and the Copeland Islands.

Following the trail takes you to **Sandeel Bay**, where the old submarine cable can still be seen at low tide from time to time. The rock pools here are as good as you will find anywhere in Northern Ireland.

West of Bangor is **Crawfordsburn Country Park**, where an early twentieth century coastal battery – Grey Point Fort, has been carefully restored and opened as a military history museum. Just below it is a mile marker placed here by Harland and Wolff for measuring the speed of vessels undergoing sea trials.

A country park just a few miles from Belfast might not seem like the sort of place to get away from it all, but once you've left the main car park and the bustling visitor's centre area, you'll soon find that peace and solitude aren't too far away.

---

203 Get a map and guide at:
   www.nationaltrust.org.uk/strangford-Lough/trails/orlock-point-walk

The park sprawls over a large area and has several waymarked trails[204] to follow, each of which can be customised or merged depending on your available time and energy.

Our final port of call in County Down is **Victoria Park** in **Sydenham**. The park's next door neighbour is the George Best Belfast City Airport. Is there really an oasis of calm just round the corner from an airport that handles 2.5 million passengers every year? Most definitely.

Sydenham is officially part of East Belfast, although those who live here like to maintain a sense of independence and distinction from the large city, preferring it to be seen as more of a separate townland than a commuter suburb. It hasn't always been called Sydenham. Strandtown and Ballyminster are much older, and the name of Sydenham was only adopted in 1854 when Belfast architect and investor James Entwhistle[205] embarked on a major programme of house building and, either he or linen merchant William Ewing (who bought one of the first and grandest houses) introduced the name – a copy of the affluent London suburb, where the Crystal Palace had been the centrepiece of the 1851 *Great Exhibition* – in the belief that Strandtown did not convey the required sense of opulence. English artist and photographer Jacob Henry Connop's 1864 colour lithograph *a view of Sydenham, Belmont and Glanmachan* shows an aerial perspective of the fledgling town surrounded by open countryside.

The 1886 *County Down Directory* mentions Sydenham merely in the context of it's relationship to Strandtown:

> *"STRANDTOWN is a beautiful suburb, occupied most entirely by residences of business and professional men belonging to Belfast. It is a distance of less than two miles, Irish, from the Exchange, East by North, and less than a mile, English from the railway station at Sydenham".*

The author, George Henry Bassett went on to note:

> *"many of the houses ... are surrounded by parks, in which the highest effects of landscape gardening are produced".*

Victoria Park was first envisaged in 1854, when the Belfast Harbour

---

204 Download an extensive guide here:
www.walkni.com/walks/206/crawfordsburn-country-park-coastal-walk/

205 Some sources record his surname as *Entwisle*.

Commissioners agreed to put land to one side as a future park. An Act of Parliament, the Belfast Dock Act specifically authorised the commissioners to *"to set aside for the purpose of a public park to be called "Victoria Park" a portion of land not less than 50 acres"*. You might wonder why harbour officials were so keen on giving the public a park space. There's more to it, you see.

Prior to 1853, the *Queen's Pleasure Island* was a popular recreational facility for the people of East Belfast, Strandtown and Bangor. The problem was that Edward James Harland was an ambitious man and was about to establish what would become the world's biggest shipbuilding company with his new partner Gustav Wilhelm Wolff. Harland & Wolff needed more land and Queen's Island, as well as reclaimed land beside, was just what they wanted. The pleasure park would have to be sacrificed.

Not that there was any great rush to create the new park. The 50-acre site offered was boggy and difficult to drain. It was more than 50 years before Victoria Park finally opened to the public. When it did, there were some expressions of disappointment from those who remembered the old pleasure island. There were no animal enclosures, no diving board, and no glasshouses.

But the new park soon drew in the crowds. The boating lake was an instant success, and an outdoor swimming pool was added later. Sporting events were held here, with summer concerts and skating on the frozen lake in winter.

Nowadays, the birds that frequent the lake have warranted it earning the status of a site of Special Scientific Interest. Two different trails can be followed, or combined[206]. The shorter, broadly follows the water on an inner circuit, while the longer takes you around the outer edges of the lake.

If Victoria Park is distinctly urban, then our next destination is completely the opposite.

Gortmore Viewpoint is our first stopover in County Derry. We were close by in our chapter on Magilligan Point earlier. This time we are going to take a look at a strange work of sculpture and then embark on a bracing clifftop walk.

In Irish mythology, *Manannán Mac Lir* is a sea god who was both a guardian to the afterlife and was the owner of an invisibility cloak long before *Harry Potter*.

---

206 Download a guide here: http://www.walkni.com/walks/91/victoria-park/

The 9 foot high statue of the mythical sea god with outstretched arms aboard his boat *Scuabtuinne* was crafted by Dungannon artist John Sutton, whose works have also featured on Game of Thrones. It was installed in 2014 only to disappear a year later, provoking a full scale police search and rescue operation. The statue was found, badly damaged about 1,000 feet away, requiring Sutton to cast a replacement figure. Standing beside the sculpture on a clear day, panoramic views stretch all the way from the Donegal coast in the west to to Scotland in the east, taking in the islands of Jura and Islay on the way.

From here, a three-mile circuitous hike[207], which the producers of the Walk Northern Ireland website description of the trek as *"refreshing"* has to be something of an understatement, takes in waterfalls, dunes and Eagle Hill. Be prepared for some serious leg stretching, even though part of the walk follows the Bishop's Road.

You'll recall the importance of Magilligan Point in the Ordnance Survey's early work mapping Ireland. It's appropriate, therefore that we include a visit to **Ballymacran Bank** in this section of the book.

The *bank* itself is a sea wall made around 175 years ago as part of a major land reclamation scheme organised by The Honorable The Irish Society. Great swathes of richly fertile polder land were created by the sea walls and a complex system of drains and pumps, and the newly-levelled wall also provided an obvious route for the new railway line to follow.

Even in the height of summer, a walk along Ballymacran Bank[208] will bring a feeling of peace and calm, punctuated with exhilaration caused by looking across the Foyle towards Donegal or inland to Binevenagh or beyond Magilligan Point to the wild North Atlantic.

Better still, here is a place in the winter months where you can share this natural (almost) environment with great flocks of brent geese and Icelandic whooper swans.

Don't expect much in the way of facilities here – there are no toilets, cafes or

---

207 More on this at www.walkni.com/walks/2569/avish-to-eagles-hill/
   The walk can be combined with another nearby to make a 5-mile round trip if you are feeling particularly energetic.

208 www.walkni.com/walks/162/ballymacran-bank/

bars. You'll have to plan ahead and make a stop at somewhere like Limavady for these.

More of the same can be experienced by walking along **Ballykelly Bank** a couple of miles further south[209]. As you stroll along here, you'd find it hard to imagine that this was a busy air base and naval centre during the Second World War. Look inland and the concrete and metal structures you can see are what remains of RAF Ballykelly, from where countless shipping convoy escorts flew, and whose pilots were responsible for the sinking of at least a dozen U-boats. It was such a strategically important location that the German High Command ordered the commanders of all remaining submarines to report here to surrender.

Don't rush from the car park to the embankment. Take your time, and wait patiently (and quietly) by the river bank and you may well be rewarded by the appearance of one or more of the otters that live nearby. Train your nostrils rather than your eyes first. The dung of otters, known as *spraints*, give away their presence. Otter spraint can smell very pungent – almost as bad as rotten fish, but is a sure sign that these marvellously entertaining animals are in the vicinity.

These last two walks are linear, and whilst both of them give great satisfaction to the eyes and ears in either direction, sometimes a circular walk can feel more rewarding. Thankfully, an excellent opportunity for just such a thing is just around the corner. **Ballykelly Forest** was latterly known as Camman Wood until it became the first state-owned and managed forest in Northern Ireland in 1910. The takeover provoked a certain amount of controversy locally. Camman Wood had been predominantly populated with Ash trees for at least four centuries prior to this[210] and the new owners immediately planted several acres with Douglas Fir trees. Hurling sticks are traditionally made from Ash – now you see the problem.

---

209 http://www.walkni.com/walks/164/ballykelly-bank/

210 It is mentioned in *The Great Parchment Book* of 1639 as a *"parcel of land ... containing by estimation ten acres (Irish measure)"*.

As Camman Wood, this was a place of notoriety. Where highwaymen would use the shelter of the woods to lay in wait for passing travellers on the coach road between Derry and Coleraine. Food for thought as you plod through the forest[211].

We continue the woodland theme with our final two destinations. **Muff Glen Forest** is *the* place to go if you like your trees[212]. True, there is an awful lot of Larch around the park's 45 hectares, most of it planted in the 1960's, but if you look carefully you'll also find Hazel, Holly, Ash, Maple, Sycamore, Beech, Spruce, Poplar and Scot's Pine as you follow your way around the forest's marked trails.

And then again, in, on and beneath the trees you may well see red squirrels, jays, buzzards, even perhaps a heron or two. If the wildlife or the surprise encounter with a waterfall doesn't take your breath away, the walk itself may well do – it can be pretty steep in places.

Muff, or more correctly *The* Muff, is the former name of the nearby village of Eglinton. The original name, given by the founders – the Grocer's Company of London is based on the Irish phrase *an Magh* meaning "the plain". It was changed in August 1858 after many years of confusion since the neighbouring county of Donegal also had an identically-named village. The replacement name comes from the Lord Lieutenant of Ireland at the time, Archibald Montgomerie, a Scotsman, born in Sicily, and a member of the British aristocracy as the 13th Earl of Eglinton. The Earl's large estate in Ayrshire, centred on Eglinton Castle included large areas of woodland, possibly explaining why Muff Glen Forest retained its Irish roots rather than adopting the new name like the neighbouring village.

And with a final, hop, skip and a jump west we find ourselves in Londonderry and another ancient woodland. **Prehen Wood** is now in the care of the Woodland Trust so should not have to endure any more of the abuses that have reduced this once-sprawling forest to just 12 acres of ancient woodland. It is yet another example of native land taken over as part of the Plantation of Ulster – this time the Goldsmith's Company of London being the big business muscling in. Because the forested area has such ancient trees, the oft-held view is that it

---

211 www.walkni.com/walks/163/ballykelly-forest/

212 www.walkni.com/walks/276/muff-glen-forest-walk/

was planted at this time, by the planted settlers themselves, but the earliest map – produced by Sir Josias Bodley 10 years earlier, shows a massive forest already well-established.

Successive surveys and maps, even the Thomas Raven (who had been part of Bodley's team 13 years earlier) maps of 1622 show evidence of woodland being cleared partly to develop agricultural land and partly for housing. Yet, there was still almost 1,000 acres of woodland here at the end of the nineteenth century.

The man-made centrepiece of the estate, Prehen House, was built around 1740 by Derry architect Michael Priestley for the local member of parliament Andrew Knox and his recent bride, Honoria (nee Tomkins). The house has remained in the Knox family to this day, with one notable break.

The nineteenth century incumbent Colonel George Knox had married Rose Grimm from Switzerland. The eldest of their two daughters, Virginia, in turn married a German doctor, Ludwig von Scheffler, and their son Georg inherited the estate. George's full title was Baron George Carl Otto Louis von Scheffler Knox.

Baron.

George was given the title by the Kaiser in recognition of his loyal support and work as Adjutant to the Commander of the Cadet Corps Governor of the Royal Pages in the Prussian Army. When he inherited the Prehen estate on the death of his maternal grandmother in 1910, Georg became George and Knox was added too.

With the outbreak of war in 1914, the British Government didn't much like the idea of a former German military officer occupying a grand home in Northern Ireland, and attempted to severely restrict his movements and operations by placing the Baron in house arrest.

This didn't last long as he managed to escape and flee to Germany where he remained for the rest of his life (bar a brief return visit to Prehen in the 1950's).

With the house empty, after the war ended, the British Government took control of the entire estate.

During the Second World War, it was loaned out to the American military who converted the house (in somewhat shambolic fashion) into a large troop accommodation block with anti-aircraft stations (and matching holes in the roof!) in the loft space.

Outside, the Americans also removed substantial areas of wood and quarried a large site for stone to make a temporary quay for their naval vessels at Lisahalley on the Foyle.

The house was eventually reacquired by a Knox descendant when Julian Peck (whose mother was born Winifred Knox) took over the family home in 1972. Following Julian's death in 2001, a son, Colin decided to open up the restored house to the public.

Now, you can visit Prehen House as part of your tour of the ancient woodland nearby. Maybe just for a spot of afternoon tea, or a (pre-arranged) tour of the house, or even to stay overnight.

The Knox family of Prehen has thrown up several interesting characters over the years including Alfred Dillwyn Knox who worked at Bletchley Park on the project to break the Enigma code in World War II. In the First World War he had also been a leading member of the Room 40 team of codebreakers who famously decoded the Zimmermann Telegram – an event that brought America into the war[213]. He preferred to be known as *"Dilly"* and, in turn had a remarkable set of siblings. His older sister Winifred, was a prolific writer, as was his older brother Edmund, a satirist and one-time editor of *Punch* magazine. Younger brother Ronald somehow managed to fit in being a Roman Catholic priest alongside a job as a regular radio broadcaster for the BBC and a heavyweight literary career with works including a full Bible translation and a series of novels featuring detective Miles Bredon.

None of the above lived at Prehen, but one who did was Mary Anne Knox, daughter of Andrew and Honoria. How she came to be romantically involved with County Antrim man John MacNaghten is the subject of debate to this day, but it seems that MacNaghten had a long-term gambling problem and had been given support by his friend Andrew Knox. John and Mary Anne became acquainted to the point of declaring themselves to be married to one another – Mary Anne may only have been fifteen years old at the time. Andrew was enraged and barred his daughter from any further contact with MacNaghten. John, in turn, flew into a rage and when he found out that Mary Anne was being

---

213 The telegram proposed an alliance between Mexico and Germany, with the implication that the American states of Arizona, New Mexico and Texas faced possible subsequent invasion.

Departures

"Hello there, I haven't seen you for a while".

    "We've been away".

"Oh, where did you go"?

    "Where <u>didn't</u> we go"?

Ever had a conversation like that with someone?

It's been a bit like that with this journey through Down and Derry from A to Z.

Where didn't *we* go?

There's always someone who knows where you've been like the back of their own hand who will delight in expressing (with an air of incredulity):

"you mean you didn't find/go to/visit/see …."

If you are feeling disappointed that my tour through the alphabet made no mention of a particular favourite of yours then all I can do is apologise, and perhaps offer the following food for thought.

You may well have an A to Z street atlas in your possession. Have you looked at every detail? Have you been to every location? Even every page, let alone every grid square? We've been all over Northern Ireland – but not everywhere. Some places we've been to several times, and wouldn't want to miss out on returning next time we're in Northern Ireland, while others are still to be explored. It doesn't make the former any better than the latter – it's just how it's been.

One of the advantages of marketing books online is the data you collect about your purchasers. Don't worry, I don't receive any personal stuff about you whatsoever, but I do get a monthly breakdown of the geographical areas from which my readership is composed. From the data provided for my *Antrim Coast* guide, its clear to me that for some of you, Northern Ireland *is* home, whereas for others, it may well be your *former* home or *ancestral* home, whilst a third group could be summed up as those for whom Northern Ireland is a *holiday* home (existing or intended).

223

Whichever group you belong to, whether the book has stirred up memories, raised anticipation, or just fed your curiosity in some way, I hope that reading it has helped to make you feel *at* home in Northern Ireland.

As for all the places, people and stories that didn't make it into this guide or my companion book on the Antrim Coast – you may like to know that my next publication *The Hidden Coast of Northern Ireland From A to Z* is already in development.

Until we meet again, thank you and bye for now.

Go raibh maith agat agus slán go fóill!